Thomas Mann's Antifascist Radio Addresses, 1940–1945

Studies in German Literature, Linguistics, and Culture

Thomas Mann's Antifascist Radio Addresses, 1940–1945

Listen, Germany!

Edited by
Jeffrey L. High, Elaine Chen, and Hans Rudolf Vaget

Translated by
Jeffrey L. High and Elaine Chen

Rochester, New York

Editorial Matter © 2025 Jeffrey L. High, Elaine Chen and Hans Rudolf Vaget
Translation © 2025 Jeffrey L. High and Elaine Chen

All Rights Reserved. Except as permitted under current legislation, no part of this work may be photocopied, stored in a retrieval system, published, performed in public, adapted, broadcast, transmitted, recorded, or reproduced in any form or by any means, without the prior permission of the copyright owner.

First published 2025
by Camden House

Originally published as *Deutsche Hörer! 55 Radiosendungen nach Deutschland aus den Jahren 1940–1945* by Thomas Mann.
© S. Fischer Verlag GmbH, Frankfurt am Main 1987

Camden House is an imprint of Boydell & Brewer Inc.
668 Mt. Hope Avenue, Rochester, NY 14620, USA
and of Boydell & Brewer Limited
PO Box 9, Woodbridge, Suffolk IP12 3DF, UK
www.boydellandbrewer.com

Our Authorised Representative for product safety in the EU is Easy Access System Europe - Mustamäe tee 50, 10621 Tallinn, Estonia, *gpsr.requests@easproject.com*

ISBN-13: 978-1-64014-198-8

Library of Congress Cataloging-in-Publication Data
CIP data is available from the Library of Congress.

The publisher has no responsibility for the continued existence or accuracy of URLs for external or third-party internet websites referred to in this book, and does not guarantee that any content on such websites is, or will remain, accurate or appropriate

Contents

Acknowledgments — viii

Foreword: Thomas Mann's *Listen, Germany!*—Today an Appeal to the World — xi
   Frido Mann

Introduction: Thomas Mann's War on Fascism — xviii
   Hans Rudolf Vaget

Foreword to the Book Edition of 1943 — lv
   Thomas Mann

Translators' Note — lviii
   Jeffrey L. High and Elaine Chen

Illustrations — lx

The Addresses

1940
October — 1
November — 4
December — 6

1941
February — 10
March — 12
April — 15
May — 17
June — 19
July — 22
August — 24

August (Special Broadcast) ... 26
September ... 27
October ... 29
November ... 31
December 24 (Special Broadcast) ... 34
December ... 35

1942

January ... 37
February ... 39
March ... 42
April (Special Broadcast) ... 44
April ... 46
May ... 49
June ... 52
July ... 55
August ... 57
September 27 ... 61
October 15 (Address to Americans of German Descent) ... 64
October 24 ... 66
November 29 ... 68
December 27 ... 70

1943

January 15 ... 73
January 24 ... 75
February 23 ... 77
March 28 ... 79
April 25 ... 81
May 25 ... 84
June 27 ... 87
July 27 ... 89
August 29 ... 92
September 29 ... 94
October 30 ... 96

December 9 98
December 31 100

1944

January 30 103
February 28 105
March 28 107
May 1 110
May 29 111

1945

January 1 115
January 14 116
January 16 119
January 31 121
February 16 123
March 4 125
March 20 126
April 5 129
April 19 130
May 10 133
December 30 135

Index   140

Acknowledgments

Jeffrey L. High, Elaine Chen, and Hans Rudolf Vaget

THE PRESENT VOLUME, *Thomas Mann's Antifascist Radio Addresses, 1940–1945: Listen, Germany!*, began with the creation of a script for a dramatic reading of select German originals and new English translations of Mann's *Deutsche Hörer!* radio addresses, delivered at the November 2018 conference "German Art in SoCal—SoCal in German Art," which was organized by the German Studies students at California State University, Long Beach (CSULB). Just prior to the conference, in June 2018, the students had the pleasure of working at the grand opening of the newly acquired and renovated Thomas Mann House in Pacific Palisades, California, which included the formative experience of hearing Federal President Frank-Walter Steinmeier's defiant defense of democracy to an emotional audience, and where the students first met and recruited Frido Mann, Thomas Mann's grandson, to visit CSULB the next year. Five months later, the third and final day of the 2018 conference began with our second road trip to the Thomas Mann House, and closed with a dramatic reading of the first fifteen of our translations at the Villa Aurora—the former residence of Mann's fellow exiled author and neighbor, Lion Feuchtwanger. The reader was veteran actor and longtime friend of CSULB German Studies Eric Braeden, who bears a strong resemblance to Thomas Mann and is himself an emigrant from northern Germany who likewise settled in Pacific Palisades. Between his impassioned readings of the texts, Braeden frequently commented on the striking parallels between Mann's descriptions of Nazi leaders and tactics and those whose rise had then only begun to pose a credible threat to the democratic rule of the people and their republic in the United States. The riveting performance elicited a range of emotional responses, from solemn silence to laughter to tears, and closed with a thunderous ovation from the overflow audience.

In October 2019, Frido Mann made his first of four visits to CSULB (two via Zoom during the Covid period), during which he engaged students in discussions of the importance of dialogue and the threat of fascism to wobbling Western republics, in conjunction with the publication of his then forthcoming, now recent, book, *Democracy Will Win: Bekenntnisse eines Weltbürgers* (2021), which cites Thomas Mann's 1938 declaration of war on fascism in its title. The overwhelming response of the high school pupils, university students, and international scholars who attended these events encouraged our belief that the time had come for the first complete English edition of Mann's *Deutsche Hörer!* radio addresses, and we are thankful to the hundreds of students and scholars who participated in these events and inspired us to continue with this project. We believe that these addresses should be required reading for all who enjoy the benefits of the rule of the people and their law—as deeply flawed as such republics have been and still are—and for all who aspire to bring about a better state for everyone, beginning with the unfailing concern for the rights, hopes, and happiness of the most vulnerable individual.

The volume would not have been possible without the generous support of the Magic Mountain Foundation for the Promotion of Thomas Mann Research—Zauberberg-Stiftung zur Förderung der Thomas Mann Forschung—in Augsburg. We owe a debt of gratitude to the Department of Romance, German, and Russian Languages and Literatures and the College of Liberal Arts at CSULB for two Research and Scholarly Activity awards in support of Jeffrey L. High for the co-translation and co-editing of the book, as well as a book subvention for its publication. We are grateful to the Department of Germanic Languages and Literatures at Harvard University for their generous book subvention. We would also like to thank our lead Editorial Associate, Emily Wysocki (CSULB), for her indispensable collaboration as researcher, copy editor, and logistical manager of the project over the past three years. We also wish to express our most sincere thanks to Editorial Associates Trevor Teafatiller (Ohio State University) and Ashley Anderson (CSULB) for their many hours of work in the preparation of the manuscript, including comparisons of the original texts with the translations and researching illustrations and copyright terms; Courtney Yamagiwa (McGeorge School of Law) for her research, fact-checking, and translation support from the very outset; Luke Beller (Johns Hopkins University), Adam Davis (University of California, Davis), Jeff Jarzomb (University of Nebraska–Lincoln), Alexandra Petrus (University of Southern California), Rebecca Stewart-Gray (Oklahoma State University), and Xochitl San Vicente (CSULB), who contributed to the preparation of the final manuscript; Natalie Martz (University of Oxford) and Ashley Anderson for their excellent work in creating the index; Seán Allan (University of St. Andrews) for proofreading in particular Mann's use of terms regarding Great Britain; Friederike von Schwerin-High (Pomona College) for her thorough cross-checking of originals and translations; and Yancy Martinez for her striking realization of the cover concept.

We are forever grateful to Frido Mann for his years of support and friendship, and for the sense of historical urgency expressed in his moving foreword. The project has benefited immeasurably from our collaboration with Fischer Verlag, the publisher of the *Große kommentierte Frankfurter Ausgabe* (GKFA) of Thomas Mann's works, and from their kind permission to access the *Deutsche Hörer!* annotations of the forthcoming vol. 18 of GKFA, edited by Kai Sina and Hans Rudolf Vaget. Finally, we are deeply indebted to Jim Walker at Camden House for his by now predictably sage advice, patient support, and for his important contributions in comparing Thomas Mann's original radio addresses to our translations.

Foreword:
Thomas Mann's *Listen, Germany!*—Today an Appeal to the World

Frido Mann

I CONSIDER THE complete retranslation of Thomas Mann's fifty-eight *Deutsche Hörer!* radio addresses (1940 to 1945; fifty-nine if we include the "Address to Americans of German Descent")—undertaken by three experts in comparative literature from California State University, Long Beach, Smith College in Northampton, Massachusetts, and Harvard University in Cambridge, Massachusetts—to be a matter of particular urgency in our present international political and societal crisis. Perhaps the most important question regards what attention this translation will attract in the United States today: this plea, ultimately more humanistic than political, from a German author who had emigrated to the USA to his former countrymen who had stayed at home in the Nazi Reich.

Will the significance of the new translations be limited to fresh research projects by a few literary scholars, or perhaps to the interest of a handful of private Thomas Mann admirers? I do not think so. No doubt, the grave social and political wounds that the United States in particular has suffered in the course of recent decades, both in terms of foreign and domestic policy, cannot be compared in any way with the utter moral collapse that was the Nazi empire, which is the subject of Thomas Mann's speeches. But our nation—I was after all born in and am a citizen of the United States—which has fallen into a lamentable, strife-torn, and imperiled state, faces an extremely unsettled and precarious future. This future depends to an important degree on whether and to what extent the assaults of antidemocratic and increasingly racist forces—widely scattered yet effectively networked—will succeed in completely destroying the once great, yet substantially weakened, tradition of US-American democracy, or whether we can make common cause and succeed in holding these forces in check.

Who, then, in this disorientingly vast and heterogeneous country, will read this, on first glance, very case-specific warning from Thomas Mann with an eye toward its contemporary relevance after eighty years? Will it be primarily intellectuals, not just Thomas Mann admirers, but also generally interested minds who are critically concerned about our nation? Or will it perhaps be, against all expectations, people of very different social classes? For example, citizens "dependent" on social welfare, often with relatively little formal education, who in their isolation and loneliness "hunger and thirst for free speech," as Thomas Mann put it in the foreword to the first book edition of the first twenty-five addresses, citizens who seek a humanistic voice to uplift them; a voice that encourages them to take fate into their own hands and, in order to reclaim their dignity as human beings, to rebel with all due militance against the egoistic oligarchs "up there" who take everything for themselves and are largely to blame for the fate of everyone else?

Are there not possibly excerpts throughout these addresses that might speak to people, for example, who live in the marginalized and often deprived former coal mining and industrial regions of the Appalachians, Northeast, and upper Midwest? Or other less-fortunate minorities in the Deep South? Would not one of the earliest addresses published here serve as a possible entry point—for example, that of Christmas 1940, near the end of which Thomas Mann writes: "Germans, save yourselves! Save your souls by renouncing your oppressors, who think only of themselves and not of you; renounce your belief in them and your obedience to them! I live in the world from which you are cut off, even though you belong to it [...]"?

Like hardly any other, Thomas Mann directed his imploring and warning words in such agonized and poignant language, delivered his indictment with such incredulity at his own rage and powerlessness, and yet pleaded with his last hope to his imprisoned former fellow citizens that even today his words cannot fail to resonate with audiences on practically every continent. Away from the relative freedom and comfort enjoyed by many in the West, more truly and painfully, the darkness of real war, fear, terrorist bombings and arson, genocide and destruction, displacement and persecution, each comparable with practices of the Nazi regime, currently rage on. Whether it is Putin's full-scale assault on human life and dignity in Ukraine, or the journey by thousands of Middle Eastern refugees through rain and sludge to the sometimes deadly crossing of the Mediterranean and the misery of tent cities, or the labyrinth of perils that Central American refugees must surmount on the way through Mexico to the final hurdle of the American border; whether it is police violence toward African Americans or the poisoning of whole classes of school girls by henchmen of the Iranian state—to name only a few particularly outstanding examples—we still live in a world fraught with horrifying phenomena.

Those who encounter this English translation of Thomas Mann's appeal to reason, his call for the preservation of international law, and defense of the dignity of the human being will perhaps be able to experience something akin to what those Germans of eighty years ago felt. Listening to Mann's radio addresses was strictly forbidden, and those who fearfully tuned in to their *Volksempfänger*—radio receivers manufactured by the Nazis—could expect the harshest punishments for listening surreptitiously to the enemy broadcast between bomb-sirens. Like those who quietly heeded this call to resistance then, anyone able to receive it under increasingly similar conditions today might find strength and bravery in it. And is it not possible that today, in some terrorist state in Eurasia or Africa, some of the young members of the opposition, who have become desensitized to the constant bombardment of propagandistic lying that is state TV, or even those followers who have been slowly demoralized, depoliticized, will take note and find reason to pause and reflect? That in turn could inspire these people to search for other comparable texts, too, and furthermore to exchange ideas with like-minded individuals and join forces—whatever their sphere of influence may be.

Due to the dangers of accessing Thomas Mann's addresses, we do not know with any accuracy what influence they had on National Socialist Germany. What we do know from the testimony of eyewitnesses and condemnations of Thomas Mann in Nazi addresses, however, is that they got through to many in the Third Reich. Despite it all, the call for tenacious resistance against the criminals responsible for the suffering of millions of human beings and the measure of comfort and hope that call provided as a counterforce to the despair over Germany's descent into deep guilt left palpable traces, most notably in responses from listeners, including Hitler himself.

Eighty years after the victory over German fascism, I am convinced that much of what Thomas Mann wrote in his rousing addresses, which were intended exclusively for the German population of the day, will resonate with today's global readers. His appeals to risk blood and tears and rise up in the name of responsibility and freedom against the bluster of the "Führer" can still be applied in our world, a world rocked by hurt and defilement, desecrated by illegitimate rulers, be they secular or spiritual, a world that finds itself on the brink of the abyss, in which each reader can relate Mann's addresses to their own nation of origin—many of those nations, each destined for a 'place in the sun,' are now shrouded in night and horror, as Thomas Mann described Germany.

Today, it is only too easy to empathize with the insight, as Thomas Mann said in his time, that those in power delight in our all-too-great recklessness and blindness, and have every incentive to exploit the predictable weakness and apathy of democracy, which makes it all the easier for them to reduce us to dependence on monopolistic systems of exploitation and bring us under their control as mere vermin, collateral damage, and underlings—as subspecies destined for enslavement. With Thomas

Mann's model in mind, it appears all the more urgent to intervene at an early stage, in which we regain and strengthen our now wavering belief in ourselves, in order to fight back with all our might against temptation to surrender, against our own complacency, and stand resolutely against the lies and violence of oppressive systems of rule. Our global community demands freedom and strength in response to matters of life and death. To this end, I plead fervently that Thomas Mann's fifty-eight addresses to that Germany under the swastika not be read and marveled at today as historical museum pieces, but that they instead be understood as an urgent appeal to the world of the present. For this reason, I call for this new English translation to be made available to a broader international readership in digital form, for, I am convinced, almost everyone will find passages that are just as true today as they were then.

The recording and broadcast of these addresses was a laborious and complicated process, a fact I know not only secondhand but to some extent from my own experience. Thomas Mann was my grandfather, and from 1941, when I was one year old, until 1949, when I moved with my parents to Europe, I spent extensive time with my grandparents in Pacific Palisades, California. By the final year of the war I was old enough to be aware, even if indirectly, of my grandfather's exacting process of composing the addresses and preparing to record them. While for the first year, he had still sent the typewritten texts to London, where a member of the BBC staff who spoke German would then present them, from March 1941 onward, the author himself read each address aloud in the Recording Department at NBC in Los Angeles so that they could be recorded onto phonograph records. These recordings were first sent to New York and from there transmitted to London by telephone. Between 1938 and 1943, partially coinciding with the period of the radio addresses, Thomas Mann also undertook five antifascist lecture tours, which were directed toward the "other" side, the North American side. These mostly comprised months-long tours, during which he traveled, sometimes by night train, from city to city across the United States and Canada. Where the purpose of the radio addresses to Germany was to inspire resistance against Hitler, the lectures addressed to the American people were—in the spirit of President Roosevelt's fireside chats—an impassioned exhortation to the listeners to finally give up their majority isolationist position and join the war against the Nazi regime.

The outbursts of rage against Hitler that one can find in Thomas Mann's addresses to "German listeners," as well as in his diary entries, particularly during the two last years of the war, are consistent with my own earliest, still rather fuzzy memories of the atmosphere around the dinner table, where, in the general impatience about Hitler's frustratingly protracted demise, these topics came up again and again: already the invective "shit-for-brains" against Hitler in a diary entry from the end of

1941, or "stupid toad" (October 3, 1943), or the question, "When will they be crushed?" (December 22, 1943), ring familiar from my childhood. The expression of disgust and revulsion at the endless killing, and the despair over the continuous suffering that war produces, appear particularly frequently in my grandfather's diary around 1944, when he was working most intensely on his pact-with-the-devil novel *Doktor Faustus* (begun in 1943, published in 1947).

Probably my very first memory is that of my processing the assassination attempt on Hitler of July 20, 1944, and the commotion it unleashed in my grandparents' house the next morning. I stood, barely four years old, alone in my grandmother's bathroom and was just thinking about how only yesterday our most malevolent and most dangerous enemy in Germany was supposed to have been killed and how a great number had died and been injured in the struggle, though not the one who was supposed to have been eliminated, and how even this attempt to murder him was considered an admirable deed. I still felt the feverish tension and the roller coaster of emotions that had reigned in our house throughout the previous afternoon and evening. In my vague recollection, there were energetic discussions about it among my family members and constant phone calls, and there was a visitor, who appeared to be as excited as my grandparents. Nonetheless, as a small child, it all still remained hazy and beyond my grasp, an atmospheric memory, as it were. Moved by the words spoken the previous afternoon or evening, I commiserated with the disappointment over the failed assassination expressed by my grandparents, my parents, and those who visited. At the same time, I felt the unanimous, impatient, yet insistent conviction that it could not be much longer until the reign of terror in Germany came to an end.

It nevertheless did drag on, as Thomas Mann had predicted only three days before the assassination attempt. As though he had already at that time seen coming the tenacious and downright insane willingness of the Germans and even the child soldiers of the "Volkssturm" militia to fight on through the final days of the war, he felt that he could conclude, in his diary on July 17, 1944, as though looking back on a Nazi regime that was now in the past: "We should not forget, nor allow ourselves to be talked out of the reality, that National Socialism was an enthusiastic, pyrotechnic revolution, a German people's movement with a tremendous emotional investment of faith and zeal." Thomas Mann must therefore have understood how limited the impact of his years-long, strenuous, and exacting endeavor was. This did not, however, prevent him from persisting to his utmost until the bitter end of the war, regardless of how many or how few Germans he reached.

Both the writing of the fifty-eight addresses for *Deutsche Hörer!* and even more so the five lecture tours throughout the United States in the years 1938–1943 bear the mark of Thomas Mann's intimate political and humanistic attachment to, and above all his admiration and veneration for, the then incumbent president, Franklin D. Roosevelt. The lecture tours, in which Thomas Mann not only read his manuscripts aloud, but also, with the help of an interpreter, engaged in lengthy question-and-answer exchanges with his American listeners, gave the impression that for all of these lecture events, he stood at the side of Roosevelt with the entire weight of his character and celebrity, while the president, through enormous efforts and against formidable opposition, fought to stir America from its isolationist lethargy and enter into the war against Hitler. All the greater were the shock and loss for Thomas Mann when Roosevelt died on April 12, 1945, only a few weeks before the victory over Germany, which was largely thanks to him. It was also a loss for the majority of the US population. My mother was present at a memorial service for Roosevelt hosted by the San Francisco Symphony, in which my father played viola. My mother told me later that when the symphony performed the "Funeral March" from *Eroica*, loud sobbing could be heard throughout the darkened auditorium.

When one morning, several weeks later, back in Pacific Palisades, I was once again permitted to visit my grandfather before breakfast in his bedroom, where he still sat in a dressing gown at a little table and sipped his *Mokka* coffee before his morning ablutions, the topic of our early morning chatter settled on Roosevelt. My grandfather described nostalgically his honorable invitation several years before to a dinner at the White House with the president in his wheelchair, and he praised the energy that, despite Roosevelt's illness, had emanated from him, as well as his cleverness and particularly beautiful voice. Incidentally, my grandfather had always loved Roosevelt's "American laugh." And then he came to the most important topic: that of the president's sudden, deadly stroke. My grandfather demonstrated his impression of this event to me exceedingly vividly, sitting before me and rapidly letting his head fall so far forward that it touched the tabletop. This experience from my very early childhood of this touch of hero worship on the part of my grandfather had a lifelong impact on me.

One more thing seems important to me for contextualizing Thomas Mann's addresses to the Germans during the war. During my time in Pacific Palisades, in the summer months after the end of the war, there was often talk during mealtimes and evenings in the living room or on walks about the postwar chaos that reigned in Germany and about the general disintegration there in the form of the many suicides, executions, and arrests of war criminals, as well as about those who fled Germany early on out of cowardice. I cannot of course remember any specific phrases, but I could sense some things from those discussions, including the general mood that one can read in Thomas Mann's diary entries from April and May 1945 onward: not only the persistent dread, the disbelief, and the disgust, but also, more than that, the tones of compassion in the face of so much human deficiency, wretchedness, and lack of dignity.

Thomas Mann never harbored any trace of triumph, satisfaction, or even a thought of revenge, none of which would have been at all inappropriate after all those years of grueling struggle and impatient longing for the end of the Nazi terror. Only seldom do I read comments in his diary at once so stern, yet so filled with sadness, as the remark written on May 5, 1945, three days before the end of the war, that it would not be "possible to execute a million people without resorting to the methods of the Nazis. There are nonetheless about a million people who would deserve to be done away with."

Over a year later, after surviving serious cancer surgery and completing his novel *Doktor Faustus*, and as the sentencing approached at the end of the Nuremberg War Crimes Trials, Thomas Mann remarked, no doubt somewhat disgusted, exhausted, and resigned, yet at once noble in his self-restraint, prophetic and sovereign: "A few of them will be hanged. To what end?"

Introduction:
Thomas Mann's War on Fascism

Hans Rudolf Vaget

AT THE OUTBREAK of the Second World War in 1939, Thomas Mann (1875–1955) was the most famous living German author, having been awarded the Nobel Prize for Literature in 1929, largely on the strength of his novels *Buddenbrooks* (1901) and to a lesser degree *The Magic Mountain* (1924). Long before 1939, Mann's political views had changed sharply. During the First World War, he defended the German monarchy and rejected democracy, arguing that it was a form of government unsuited to the pursuit of "Kultur"—culture with a capital C. He poured all his fiercely anti-Western views and biases into a massive essay of 600 pages, tellingly titled *Reflections of a Nonpolitical Man* (1918). After Germany's defeat and the creation of a democratic republic in 1919, Mann came to embrace the political culture of the West and to support the fledgling Weimar Republic when parties on both the left and right of the political spectrum rejected and tried to undermine democratic rule. He voiced his new-found political beliefs in his essay "On the German Republic" (1922). With the rise of Adolf Hitler (1889–1945) to power in 1933, Thomas Mann and his family went into exile, first in Switzerland, and from 1938 in the United States. By that time, he had become an ever-more-vocal critic of National Socialism. Beginning in October 1940, one year after the outbreak of the war, and continuing beyond Germany's capitulation in May 1945 until December of that year, Mann wrote and delivered a series of monthly radio addresses to the German people that were broadcast to Germany and German-occupied Europe by the British Broadcasting Corporation. The resulting fifty-eight addresses form a remarkable body of antifascist, pro-democracy, political writing and represent Mann's most tangible contribution to the Allied war effort.

As the radio historian Conrad Pütter reminds us, during the Second World War, radio propaganda was ubiquitous. The war of the airwaves—the "Ätherkrieg"—supplemented and, in a fashion, dramatized the bloody war on the ground. It involved no fewer than seventy official and covert radio stations on the Allied side and some fifty on the German.[1] Their business was psychological warfare; its goal was to undermine the will to fight both on the military and civilian front.

It is difficult to gauge the effect or even the listenership of Mann's radio addresses: in Hitler's Germany, listening to them was a prosecutable offense, and sharing them was punishable by death. Although the addresses were published in German both during the war and just after it,[2] to this day, Mann's radio propaganda for the Allies, while by no means ignored by scholarship, remains controversial and underappreciated. Some of what he said in the addresses still feels raw, such as his reaction to the bombing of his hometown, the old Hanseatic city of Lübeck—including the Mann family home, known as the "Buddenbrookhaus" because Mann had used it as the setting of his first novel. His comment in the address of April 1942 sounds cold and stern: "However, when I think of Coventry, I have no objections to make against the tenet that everything must be paid for." In this case, what had to be paid for—avenged, one could say—was the bombing by the Luftwaffe of Coventry, London, as well as Rotterdam and other cities. Even more controversial is the continuation of his remark, suggesting that there probably were other people in Hamburg, Cologne, and Düsseldorf who "ha[d] no objection [to the bombing of those cities], and when they hear[d] the thunder of the Royal Air Force planes overhead, will wish them every success."

In the English-speaking world, despite twenty-five of them having been published in translation in 1943,[3] Mann's radio addresses are largely forgotten and, except to a few specialists, practically unknown. This is regrettable because they reveal a sharper and pricklier portrait of the political Mann than his essays in the 1942 volume *Order of the Day*. They also reveal a vastly more relevant portrait of Mann as a combatant in the war against Hitler than can be gained from the recent reconsideration of his early nationalist ruminations during the First World War, *Reflections of*

---

1   Conrad Pütter, "Rundfunk," in *Handbuch der deutschsprachigen Emigration 1933–1945*, eds. Claus-Dieter Krohn, Patrik von zur Mühlen, Gerhard Paul, and Lutz Winckler (Darmstadt: Wissenschaftliche Buchgesellschaft, 1998), 1087–103, 1087. Subsequent citations as Pütter, "Rundfunk."

2   Thomas Mann, *Deutsche Hörer! 25 Radiosendungen nach Deutschland* (Stockholm: Bermann-Fischer, 1942); *Deutsche Hörer! 55 Radiosendungen nach Deutschland* (Stockholm: Bermann-Fischer, Stockholm, 1945). The addresses are currently available in German as *Deutsche Hörer! Radiosendungen nach Deutschland aus den Jahren 1940–1945*, 6th Edition. (Frankfurt am Main: Fischer Taschenbuch Verlag, 2022).

3   Thomas Mann, *Listen, Germany! Twenty-five Radio Messages to the German People over BBC* (New York: Alfred A. Knopf, 1943).

a Nonpolitical Man.[4] The obvious reason for this gap in our knowledge is the fact that prior to the publication of the present edition, the interested public had no access to the complete series of Mann's texts in English.

There are, however, signs of a growing interest in the impact of Mann's fourteen-year presence in America, from 1938 to 1952, as evidenced by two excellent recent studies by Tobias Boes and Stanley Corngold. Boes paints a revealing portrait of Mann the exile, as the first citizen of the "World Republic of Letters" in which we now live, and in which his radio work during the Second World War functioned as "The Voice of Germany."[5] Corngold, focusing on Mann's years in Princeton, from 1938 to 1941, views the mature Mann's political writings very much as reflections of a *political* man. Reexamining the radio addresses, he judges them to be "by and large admirable in their sacred furor."[6]

Taken in its entirety, *Listen, Germany!* is a highly revealing political and personal document. The compilation of Mann's radio talks may be viewed as a condensation of his political thinking, cast in the most polemical mode that he was capable of striking. Even today, these radio talks convey a vivid sense of what it felt like to witness and comment on the events of the Second World War, and to help the Germans face the darkest chapter in their history.

Beyond that, the talks reveal various affinities to, and subtle resonances with, Mann's contemporaneous literary production. During the war, he completed his cycle of biblical novels, *Joseph and His Brothers* (1933–1943). Mann's sophisticated retelling of the biblical stories are a monumental tribute to the Jewish tradition and the Jewish people at a time when his home country aimed to destroy them. In *Joseph the Provider* (1943), the concluding part of the tetralogy, Joseph rises to the position of ruler over Egypt. He does so in the enlightened spirit of US president Franklin D. Roosevelt's (1882–1945) New Deal social policies, thereby providing a model of the ideal ruler that stands in sharp contrast to the fascist form of government. This novel, conceived and written entirely on American soil, may indeed be read, as Boes has written, "as an extended paean to American society

---

4   Thomas Mann, *Order of the Day: Essays and Speeches of Two Decades* (New York: Alfred A. Knopf, 1942). Subsequent citations as *Order of the Day*; Thomas Mann, *Reflections of a Nonpolitical Man*, trans. Walter D. Morris and others, introduction by Mark Lilla (New York: New York Review of Books, 2021). Subsequent citations as *Reflections*.

5   Tobias Boes, *Thomas Mann's War: Literature, Politics, and the World Republic of Letters* (Ithaca, NY: Cornell University Press, 2019), 166–70.

6   Stanley Corngold, *The Mind in Exile: Thomas Mann in Princeton* (Princeton, NJ: Princeton University Press, 2022), 136. See also Stanley Corngold, *Weimar in Princeton: Thomas Mann and the Kahler Circle* (New York: Bloomsbury Academic, 2022).

and especially to its president."[7] In his 1939 novel *Lotte in Weimar: The Beloved Returns*, Mann dons the mask of Goethe to unveil a poet more "knowing," more critical of Germany and the Germans, than the Olympian idol of Weimar that had been fashioned by the popular cult of Goethe during the German Empire after 1871. In the 1944 novella *The Tables of the Law*, written in the lighthearted spirit of Voltaire, Mann dons the mask of Moses (and Michelangelo) to mirror his own efforts on behalf of Germany in the efforts of the biblical lawgiver to whip his recalcitrant, eternally fallible, and seemingly hopeless people into a more God-pleasing shape. Finally, in the novel *Doctor Faustus* (1947), the crowning achievement of his American years, Mann undertook the melancholy task of uncovering the hidden concatenation of German music and German catastrophe, reminding us in eye-opening fashion that Germany entered a pact with the devil—and was going to hell—not despite its vaunted "Kultur," but rather because of it.

As a public intellectual, Thomas Mann did not act alone. Erika (1905–1969) and Klaus Mann (1906–1949), the eldest of his six children, cooperated with their father, albeit not always in perfect harmony, in their larger project of helping to liberate Germany from Nazism. They were indeed an "amazing family," as Harold Nicolson, the British diplomat and historian, dubbed them—amazingly talented and courageous.[8] Much of their appeal derived from the fact that they were, as Klaus Mann proudly pointed out, a "family against dictatorship."[9] As such, the Manns occupy a place of honor in the turbulent history of twentieth-century Germany.

At a time when democracy is experiencing ever more challenging stress tests all across the globe, including in the United States of America; at a time when authoritarianism is increasingly dressed up as the more efficient solution to today's social problems; the stances that Thomas Mann and his family took in their own time against the barbaric, antihumanist rule of a master demagogue shine a bright light as beacons of freedom and courage. Their example serves to remind us that much of what we are witnessing today was darkly foreshadowed in the tumultuous events of the twentieth century. It may also inspire us to recognize the lessons to be learned from their experience.

---

7   Boes, *Thomas Mann's War*, 195.
8   From a review by Harold Nicolson, "The Nazi Mentality Studied in Three New Works," *The Daily Telegraph*, April 14, 1939, 12. Among the books reviewed is Erika Mann, *School for Barbarians: Education under the Nazis*, introduction by Thomas Mann (New York: Modern Age Books, 1938).
9   Klaus Mann, "A Family against Dictatorship (1937)," in *Das Wunder von Madrid: Aufsätze, Reden, Kritiken, 1936–1938*, eds. Uwe Naumann and Michael Töteberg (Reinbek: Rowohlt, 1993), 260.

Mann as Defender of Democracy

We do not usually associate the author of *Buddenbrooks*, *Death in Venice* (1921), and *The Magic Mountain* with warfare. Indeed, Mann liked to think of himself as "a man of peace," firmly believing that peace was the indispensable condition for what he treasured above all: the creation of "culture, art, and thought."[10] War meant the opposite: a relapse into barbarism. Much had to happen, therefore, to turn an artist of his inner make-up into a fighter. But fight he did. When he saw forces inimical to the humanistic values of civil society threaten the peace that he craved as an artist, he joined the battle.

Mann's self-characterization as a man of peace first occurs in a landmark speech of 1922 that marked a turning point in his political thinking and profoundly shaped his career as a public intellectual both in his native Germany and in exile, first in Switzerland from 1933 to 1938, and subsequently in the United States, of which he became a citizen in 1944. In that speech, simply entitled "On the German Republic," he left behind the anti-Western and antidemocratic positions he had taken in his tortured wartime essays in defense of the German cause, notably "Thoughts in Time of War" (1914) and *Reflections of a Nonpolitical Man* (1918).[11]

"On the German Republic" was written in reaction to the assassination on June 24, 1922, of Walther Rathenau (1867–1922), the German Minister of Foreign Affairs, who was Jewish. The assassination was carried out by members of an antisemitic and antidemocratic organization; it represented, more than a year prior to Hitler's so-called Beer Hall Putsch on November 8, 1923, the most immediate threat to the Weimar Republic. In his speech, delivered in Berlin on October 13, 1922, Mann made public his conversion to republicanism and democracy and urged the youth of Germany to support and defend the republic. In response, friends and erstwhile ideological allies such as the composer Hans Pfitzner (1869–1949) and the poet and scholar Ernst Bertram (1884–1957), both admirers of his *Reflections of a Nonpolitical Man*, parted ways with Mann. They ended up supporting Hitler. In his Berlin speech, Mann made it clear that, notwithstanding his love of peace, he was "no pacifist." Indeed, his very speech in defense of the republic was itself a repudiation of pacifism in the face of evil. It may not have seemed so at the time, but his unexpected commitment to the new and fragile German republic foreshadowed the militant humanism that he came to advocate in response to fascism and dictatorship.

When in the elections for the Reichstag on September 14, 1930, the Nazi Party scored a dramatic breakthrough, Mann again stepped up. He returned to the same venue, the Berlin Philharmonie, where in 1922 he

---

10 Thomas Mann, "The German Republic," in *Order of the Day*, 8.

11 Thomas Mann, "Thoughts in Time of War," tr. Mark Lilla and Cosima Mattner, in *Reflections*, 491–506.

had presented his defense of the German republic, and delivered another landmark speech, "An Appeal to Reason."[12] It turned into a tumultuous affair as a handful of SA troublemakers in the audience kept heckling him. They were camouflaged in rented suits and had been dispatched by Joseph Goebbels (1897–1945), the future Nazi propaganda chief. Undeterred, Mann urged his compatriots not to be fooled by Hitler and to throw their support behind the Social Democratic Party.

Exile—An Alternative Route to Glory

A few days after Hitler took over the chancellorship on January 30, 1933, Thomas and Katia Mann (1883–1980) left Munich for a lecture tour to Holland, Belgium, and France. During a subsequent winter vacation in Arosa, Switzerland, friends in Munich warned them that their return to Germany, now in fact a dictatorship, would be dangerous and highly inadvisable. As we now know, but as he did not know then, Mann would have been arrested at the border and taken to the Dachau concentration camp.[13]

What finally tipped the balance against returning was the baseless accusation in a Munich paper on April 16, 1933, that Mann's recent lecture on Richard Wagner (1813–1883) constituted an unacceptable denigration of "our great German musical genius."[14] Pompously dressed up as "A Protest from Richard Wagner's Own City of Munich," this attack on Mann on ostensibly artistic grounds clearly came with some ominous political undertones. The protesters declared that he had "no right whatsoever" to critique the Master—famously one of Hitler's artistic idols—now "that the uprising of Germany as a nation" had been accomplished. Mann was painted as unfit to make any pronouncements on the creator of *The Mastersingers of Nuremberg* (1868) and *The Ring of the Nibelung* (1848–1874) because he had "the misfortune to forfeit his one-time national sentiments [...] exchanging them for cosmopolitan-democratic views"—a clear allusion to his departure from the camp of conservatism in 1922.

The lecture in question is "The Sorrows and Grandeur of Richard Wagner," a brilliant appreciation of the composer, which today is almost universally regarded as a landmark in Wagner Studies. Mann presented it first at the University of Munich on February 10, 1933, barely two weeks after Hitler came to power, and then again in Amsterdam, Brussels, and Paris. Though it was almost comically off the mark in portraying Mann's lecture as a denigration of Wagner, what the protest by the Munich

12 "An Appeal to Reason," *Order of the Day*, 46–68.
13 Hermann Kurzke, *Thomas Mann: Life as a Work of Art; A Biography*, trans. Leslie Wilson (Princeton, NJ: Princeton University Press, 2002), 364.
14 Anon., "A Protest from Richard Wagner's Own City of Munich," in *Thomas Mann: Pro and Contra Wagner*, tr. Allan Blunden, introduction by Erich Heller (Chicago: The University of Chicago Press, 1985), 149–51.

Wagnerians represented was a thinly veiled denunciation of Mann as a prominent supporter of the detested Weimar Republic and consequently as an egregious misfit in the new Germany. As it was revealed much later, the entire action was instigated, anonymously, by the ambitious music director of the Bavarian State Opera, Hans Knappertsbusch (1888–1965). His indignant "Protest" was endorsed by nearly forty of Munich's cultural luminaries, including the composers Hans Pfitzner and Richard Strauss (1864–1949). The glaring fact that six local Nazi officials also signed on turned the protest into a threat.[15] Mann sensed that this wicked attack would eventually lead to his "national excommunication."[16] The ensuing developments proved him correct. The decision not to return to Munich turned out to be a wise one: it was the beginning of exile.

During the next three years, living near Zürich, Switzerland, Mann maintained an uneasy, ill-advised silence about Germany's descent into fascist dictatorship. He did so chiefly upon the urgent request of his publisher Gottfried Bermann Fischer (1897–1995), who was struggling to maintain a presence in Germany and to sell books, most importantly those of Thomas Mann himself. As his diary reveals, Mann felt deeply conflicted about the awkwardness of this situation because the resulting discord in his own family—Erika and Klaus disapproved of his silence—weighed heavily on him.

Now in his second year of exile, he found it increasingly difficult to focus on the work at hand, *Joseph in Egypt* (1936), the third and most engrossing of the Joseph novels. He felt the need to send a clarifying and liberating signal to the world. In the aftermath of the so-called Night of the Long Knives, June 30, 1934, when Hitler cleansed his movement of some two hundred actual and perceived opponents, including Ernst Röhm (1887–1934), the servile leader of the SA, Mann considered writing a no-holds-barred open letter to *The Times* of London in which he would beseech the world, above all Great Britain, which was still of two minds about Hitler, to put an end to the shameful regime in Berlin. As his diary tells us, he wanted to write such a letter to "save his soul."[17] Fully aware of the responsibility of a politically conscious author, he felt keenly that it was incumbent upon him to change the world's perception of Germany

---

15 For a comprehensive treatment of the matter of the "Protest" against Mann's Wagner lecture, see Hans Rudolf Vaget, *"Wehvolles Erbe." Richard Wagner in Deutschland: Hitler, Knappertsbusch, Mann* (Frankfurt am Main: S. Fischer, 2017), 229–323.

16 Mann speaks of "national excommunication" in his outspoken "Reply to Hans Pfitzner," written in the summer of 1933. *Thomas Mann: Pro and Contra Wagner*, 154–67, 167. What he intended to be an open letter to be published in *Die Neue Rundschau*, was withheld for fear of reprisals. It finally appeared in 1974, nearly twenty years after Mann's death.

17 Entry of July 31, 1934, *Thomas Mann: Tagebücher, 1933–1934*, ed. Peter de Mendelssohn (Frankfurt am Main: Fischer, 1977), 488. Subsequent citations as *Tagebücher, 1933–1934*.

as a fascist dictatorship and help "re-introduce" the true Germany of culture and decency to the civilized nations.[18] Lofty thoughts, outsized ambitions. For five days in August of that year, he collected material and prepared to write a major political statement, perhaps on the scale of his *Reflections* of 1918.[19] He was still pondering a "Politikum" in April of 1935, a major "Memorandum to the German people," in which he would warn his compatriots of the fate that was in store for them if they continued to support the "enemy of mankind."[20] But once again, in deference to his desperate publisher, he continued to remain silent. Instead, he wrote a travelogue of his first visit to New York, in June of 1934, *Voyage with Don Quixote*, in which he studiously steered clear of any overt political commentary.

Thus, in January 1936, Mann felt greatly relieved when an article appeared in the *Neue Zürcher Zeitung* that presented him with the welcome opportunity to come clean about his attitude towards Nazi Germany. The author of that article, Eduard Korrodi (1885–1955), the paper's distinguished literary critic, argued that the writers who had fled Germany in 1933 were mostly Jewish and that Thomas Mann represented a quite different case, insinuating, wrongly, that he was keeping the door open for a possible arrangement with the Nazi regime.[21] Responding promptly a few days later, Mann explained to his well-meaning critic that the hatred of Jews in Nazi Germany extended beyond the Jews to all who, like himself, strove to represent the highest ideals of the German spirit; that National Socialism was undermining the foundations of Western civilization; that nothing good at all could come from present-day Germany; and that indeed he was part of the literature in exile. He concluded with an elegant flourish, quoting with a certain gusto a few stinging lines from his favorite poet, August von Platen (1796–1835), an émigré of a previous generation who wrote that it is wiser to bid goodbye to the fatherland when its servile population is venerating what is contemptible and evil.[22]

Having thus clarified his status as an émigré, Mann was formally expelled from the national community—the vaunted "Volksgemeinschaft"—though not until December 3, 1936.[23] The authorities did not immediately proceed

18 Ibid.
19 Ibid., August 5–11, 1934, 498.
20 Entry of April 19, 1935, *Thomas Mann: Tagebücher, 1935–1936*, ed. Peter de Mendelssohn (Frankfurt am Main: Fischer, 1978), 86. Subsequent citations as *Tagebücher, 1935–1936*.
21 Eduard Korrodi, "Deutsche Literatur im Emigrantenspiegel," *Neue Zürcher Zeitung*, January 26, 1936.
22 "An Eduard Korrodi," in *Thomas Mann: Gesammelte Werke in dreizehn Bänden* (Frankfurt am Main: S. Fischer, 1990), vol. XI, 788–93. Subsequent citations as *GW*.
23 Thomas Sprecher, "Deutscher, Tschechoslowake, Amerikaner. Zu Thomas Manns staatsbürgerlichen Verhältnissen," *Thomas Mann Jahrbuch* 19 (1996), 303–38, 319–20.

with the expulsion of so famous a personality as Thomas Mann, for the obvious reason that they feared bad international press during the run-up to the Berlin Olympics in August. When Mann's expulsion was finally decreed, he was branded a "Volksschädling"—a vermin in the body politic.[24]

The official expulsion triggered a rather pathetic gesture by the Dean of the University of Bonn, who felt compelled to follow suit and annul the honorary degree the university had bestowed upon the author of *Reflections of a Nonpolitical Man* in 1919. In response, Mann composed a scathing letter that was quickly published as a separate pamphlet and translated into several languages, thereby giving it the character of a manifesto addressed to Germany and, indeed, the world. That manifesto catapulted Thomas Mann into the position of foremost critic of Hitler and Nazi Germany.[25] Since it was not possible to make this inflammatory piece available to his German readers through the usual channels, so-called "Tarnschriften" were produced and distributed by various oppositional organizations in exile. These were "camouflaged publications, frequently disguised as street maps, tourist brochures, or other utilitarian examples of print culture, that were smuggled into Nazi Germany for propaganda purposes."[26]

Feeling liberated at last to speak his mind, Mann expresses his "abysmal disgust […] in the face of the inexpiable evil that is done daily in my country to bodies, souls, and minds, to right and truth, to men and mankind."[27] Writing in the final days of the year 1936, the year of the deceptively peaceful Nazi Olympics, Mann warns the world that the only meaning and purpose of National Socialism is to prepare the nation for war. Pouring contempt upon the debasers of German culture, he declares: "[The Nazis] have the incredible effrontery to confuse themselves with Germany! When, after all, perhaps the moment is not far off when it will be of supreme importance to the German people not to be confused with them."[28]

Today, Mann's letter to Bonn University is widely regarded as the crown jewel among Mann's political writings, and deservedly so. Its rhetorical brilliance matches the acumen of its historical insight. Clear-eyed and prescient, its author called out the German dictator, telling all the world that Hitler was preparing for war—a war that Germany must not win. Crucially for his role as an exile, he poured scorn upon the Nazis' claim to represent the German nation, rejecting it as false and fraudulent. And he predicted that one day soon Germany would be eager to renounce

---

24 Klaus Schröter, ed., *Thomas Mann im Urteil seiner Zeit: Dokumente 1891–1955* (Hamburg: Wegner, 1969), 280–81.
25 "An Exchange of Letters," in *Order of the Day*, 105–13.
26 Boes, *Thomas Mann's War*, 175.
27 "An Exchange of Letters," in *Order of the Day*, 108–09.
28 "An Exchange of Letters," in *Order of the Day*, 110.

Nazism, meaning after its defeat in the coming war. Most importantly, he signaled to the world that he intended to contest the Nazis' relentless propaganda equating Germany with Nazism, and that he was prepared to go to war against Hitler.

An early sign of that resolve was the statement that Mann made to the American press upon his arrival in New York, on February 21, 1938, at the start of his first transcontinental lecture tour. Proudly and succinctly, he stated: "Where I am, there is Germany."[29] Equally provocative was the title of the lecture that he had come to deliver: "The Coming Victory of Democracy." He predicted victory in a war that had not yet begun and that he hoped would come sooner rather than later. In his appearances from coast to coast, Mann attempted to move American public opinion away from its predominantly isolationist stance. Calling for a militant humanism, he attempted to impress upon his usually large audiences the necessity of going to war against Nazi Germany: "What is needed is a humanity strong in will and firm in the determination to preserve itself [...]. It must learn to walk in armour and to defend itself against its deadliest enemies [...] it must finally understand that a pacifism which admits it will not wage war under any circumstances will surely bring about war instead of banishing it."[30] Mann spoke in fifteen venues across the country before audiences totaling 43,000.[31]

To fully comprehend Mann's eagerness to join the battle against Nazi Germany, we must consult his diaries. They are indispensable for our understanding of both his overt politics and his personal motivations. The diaries show that, above and beyond the obvious political and moral reasons that spurred him on, he was perhaps even more motivated, if not driven, by his deeply characteristic ambition to achieve greatness. As a young man, he had aimed at greatness as a writer; now, as an exile, he strove for greatness as a historical figure.

Mann saw that, sadly, two of his artistic peers, Gerhart Hauptmann (1862–1946), the 1912 Nobel laureate and the reigning "king" of German literature, and Richard Strauss, Germany's most celebrated composer, had decided to compromise with the Nazi regime. Hauptmann, then seventy years old, flew the Nazi flag over his house in the hope of being left in peace.[32] Strauss, two years Hauptmann's junior, positioned himself to

---

29 "Mann Finds US Sole Peace Hope," *The New York Times*, February 22, 1938, 13.

30 "The Coming Victory of Democracy," in *Order of the Day*, 114–52, 147.

31 Hans Rudolf Vaget, *Thomas Mann, der Amerikaner: Leben und Werk im amerikanischen Exil, 1938–1952* (Frankfurt am Main: S. Fischer, 2011), 247.

32 Peter Sprengel, *Der Dichter stand auf hoher Küste: Gerhart Hauptmann im Dritten Reich* (Berlin: Propyläen, 2009), 28.

become the president of the Reich Music Chamber.[33] Both men helped to lend legitimacy to the regime's devious attempts to maintain the appearance of Germany as a land of high culture.

Looking at the example of Hauptmann, Mann reasoned that he himself was no more suited than his older colleague to bear the martyrdom of exile. What distinguished him from Hauptmann was his sense of honor, which allowed for no compromise with the contemptible ideology of National Socialism. Despite much petulance in his diaries about the hardships of exile, he in effect accepted his fate surprisingly early, in May of 1933. Going into exile was the only honorable option. What gave him comfort was the thought that the very decision to cut his ties to Germany bestowed upon him the aura of greatness and that "people like me will assume a kind of towering moral and cultural stature [...]."[34] In other words, Mann realized that not only was exile no barrier to greatness, it may even enhance his standing in the world.

The thought of compromising with the Nazis as Hauptmann had done and of returning to Germany did cross his mind, but only fleetingly and only during the first few months after his departure. Mann was the proud owner of a splendid villa in a leafy part of Munich where he had been living in great comfort. After a few months of a rather nomadic existence, it was only natural that he would miss living within his own four walls and to imagine what that would entail. It did not escape Goebbels's notice that, despite his well-known antifascist speeches prior to 1933, Thomas Mann had maintained a mysterious silence about the Nazi regime since choosing to live in Switzerland. To him—a fellow writer of sorts—it must have seemed as though the Nobel laureate of 1929 was leaving the door open, which apparently prompted him to go easy on the creator of *The Magic Mountain*, at least for the time being. This may explain why Thomas Mann's books were spared at the big book burning ceremony on May 10, 1933, in Berlin. In addition, there is an intriguing claim in the autobiography of Thomas Mann's younger brother, Viktor Mann (1890–1949), who was neither a writer nor an antifascist. According to Viktor, Goebbels personally spoke up for Thomas Mann and sent the same positive signal to Ernst Bertram, Mann's erstwhile friend and a Nazi sympathizer.[35]

---

33 See Bryan Gilliam, *The Life of Richard Strauss* (Cambridge: Cambridge University Press, 1999), 145–51; Tim Ashley, *Richard Strauss* (London: Phaidon Press, 1999), 160–66; Hans Rudolf Vaget, "Richard Strauss oder Zeitgenossenschaft ohne Brüderlichkeit," in *Seelenzauber: Thomas Mann und die Musik* (Frankfurt am Main: S. Fischer, 2006), 168–202.

34 Entry of January 31, 1935, *Tagebücher, 1935–1936*, 25. Also in *Thomas Mann Diaries, 1918–1939*, selection and foreword by Hermann Kesten, trans. Richard and Clara Winston (New York: Abrams, 1982), 233.

35 Viktor Mann, *Wir waren fünf: Bildnis der Familie Mann* (Konstanz: Südverlag, 1949), 468–69.

Mann was aware of the regime's interest in his return to Germany. It would have been a huge victory for the Nazis, on a par with the return of Marlene Dietrich (1901–1992), who was also on Goebbels's wish list. Their fame and celebrity status would have lent considerable credibility to his cultural policies. It is revealing to discover that as late as November 1933, the idea of returning was on Mann's mind as a possibility, albeit a very remote one. He would not conduct himself like Hauptmann and Strauss, he told himself: he could maintain a cold and distant isolation and join the "inner emigration."[36] Mann banished this idea for the same reason for which he had come to despise Hauptmann. It came down to a question of intellectual honor and self-respect. Under no condition was he prepared to serve as figurehead and advertisement for the Hitler regime.

When Mann arrived in the United States to settle in Princeton in September of 1938, he was a literary celebrity. His letter to Bonn University had appeared in *The Nation* in 1937 and was given additional exposure through a separate printing by his American publisher, Alfred A. Knopf (1892–1984).[37] Thus, during his first transcontinental lecture tour in the spring of 1938, and later that year, after a brief return to Zürich, when he emigrated to the United States to take up a lectureship at Princeton University, his literary stature was greatly enhanced by his fame as an opponent of the Hitler regime. During the first seven years of his American sojourn, until 1945, Mann was indeed almost universally viewed as the exceptional "good" German, as the man of "towering moral and cultural stature" that he had sensed in 1935 he would become. In Germany, such recognition would be granted to him only much later, and grudgingly at that.

Close readers of Mann's Bonn manifesto could hardly fail to see that it amounted to a veiled threat to declare war against Hitler and Nazi Germany. When the occasion arrived, in the wake of Germany's attack on Poland on September 1, 1939, Mann was ready and willing to act. He wrote a political essay, *This War*, in which he declared his solidarity with the country that was standing up to Hitler, and expressed his firm belief that Britain would prevail.[38]

This apparently attracted the interest of the higher-ups at the BBC. As his diary shows, Mann wrote *This War* on the prompting of his American translator, Helen T. Lowe-Porter (1876–1963), who was at the time living in Oxford, where her husband, Elias Lowe, was a lecturer in paleography at All Souls College. Early in October of 1939 she asked Mann

---

36 Entries of November 7 and 20, Thomas Mann, *Tagebücher, 1933–1934*, 243, 251.

37 Thomas Mann, *An Exchange of Letters*, trans. H. T. Lowe-Porter (New York: Alfred A. Knopf, 1937).

38 *This War*, trans. Eric Sutton (New York: Knopf, 1940). Also in *Order of the Day*, 186–227.

to write an article to be broadcast "by English radio" to Germany.[39] At first, Mann hesitated; the military situation did not seem to be ripe for commentary. One month later, realizing that Britain needed support, he started writing the essay, devoting five weeks to its completion. Since parts of the essay were indeed broadcast by the BBC, we may conclude that when she first sounded him out, Lowe-Porter was already acting at the behest of the BBC.[40] This leaves little doubt that indirect contacts between the BBC and Thomas Mann existed even before the corporation hired him as a regular contributor. It may well be that the BBC regarded *This War* as a test of his effectiveness.

The BBC had decided in October of 1938, as the threat of war was growing, to create a German Service, with the express purpose of countering the propaganda spread by the Reichs-Rundfunk-Gesellschaft, the Nazi radio service.[41] To that end they began recruiting exiled opponents of Hitler. Mann must have been on their radar early on despite the fact that he was only a recent convert to the British cause, having earlier been a vocal critic of Britain's ambivalent policy towards Nazi Germany. In a passionately argued essay that Knopf published as a little book in November of 1938, *This Peace*, he had severely castigated the misconceived policy of appeasement of Hitler by France and Britain at the Munich Conference that September.[42] To him, appeasement had led to the "rape" of Czechoslovakia, a country with a democratic form of government that he greatly admired.[43] Moreover, Czechoslovakia had generously granted citizenship to Katia and Thomas Mann in 1936 when they were in dire need of proper passports.[44] However, when Great Britain declared war in reaction to the German attack on Poland, Mann completely reversed his negative attitude towards Great Britain and rushed to their support. To his friend Kuno Fiedler (1895–1973) he confessed that he had written a "tremendously pro-British" piece and that he supported the Brits "whole-heartedly," adding that "all is forgiven and forgotten."

---

39 Entry of October 11, 1939, Thomas Mann, *Tagebücher, 1937–1939*, ed. Peter de Mendelssohn (Frankfurt am Main: Fischer, 1980), 486.

40 Letter to Heinrich Mann, dated March 3, 1940, in *Letters of Thomas Mann, 1889–1955*, selected and trans. by Richard and Clara Winston, introduction by Richard Winston (New York: Alfred A. Knopf, 1971), 326. Subsequent citations as *Letters of Thomas Mann*.

41 On January 1, 1939, the Reichs-Rundfunk-Gesellschaft was renamed the Großdeutsche Rundfunk.

42 *This Peace, together with the Address of November 9, 1938, in New York*, trans. H. T. Lowe-Porter (New York: Alfred A. Knopf, 1938); also in *Order of the Day*, 167–85.

43 *Order of the Day*, foreword, xiv.

44 See Sprecher, "Deutscher, Tschechoslowake, Amerikaner."

From the BBC's perspective, Mann's full-throated support of Britain in *This War* provided a reliable basis for cooperation. From Mann's perspective, Britain presented the only promising option to join the fight against Nazi-Germany because the United States, until the attack on Pearl Harbor more than two years later, continued to abide by its policy of non-intervention, cemented in the Neutrality Acts, which during the 1930s had been repeatedly reinforced by Congress from 1935 to 1939.

Enter Erika

At that stage, Mann's oldest daughter, the formidable Erika, came to play a crucial role in bringing about the arrangement that led to Mann's work for the BBC. Within the Mann family, she was the most eager to fight, and it was in large part due to the energetic and imaginative ways in which she conducted herself that the Manns truly deserved the label of "a family against dictatorship." As noted earlier, long before her father broke his silence, Erika and Klaus were active on the antifascist front. Erika was an actor, author, and was in demand as a lecturer. She soon realized, however, that to be effective and to go where the action was, she needed an American or a British passport. She proceeded to propose a marriage of convenience to Klaus's friend, Christopher Isherwood (1904–1986), the gay English writer. Isherwood declined but suggested that the poet W. H. Auden (1907–1973) might be willing. Auden was indeed "delighted" to be of help.[45] The two were duly married on June 15, 1935. Now equipped with a British passport, she was able to freely roam the world.

While Erika would go on to achieve fame as a war correspondent, she had already traveled widely as a lecturer. At a stop in Chicago in the spring of 1940, where her sister Elisabeth Mann (1918–2002) and her husband, the Italian antifascist historian Guiseppe Antonio Borgese (1882–1952), lived, Erika made the acquaintance of Duff Cooper (1890–1954), the distinguished British diplomat and historian. When Winston Churchill (1874–1965), the successor to Neville Chamberlain (1869–1940), became Prime Minister on May 10, 1940, he made Cooper his Minister of Information, which is to say, the counterpart of Nazi propaganda chief Joseph Goebbels. Erika lost no time in offering her assistance to Cooper, who apparently considered tasking her with the reform of the BBC's German Service.[46] Given her effectiveness as a public speaker, she must have seemed eminently qualified for such an undertaking. Thomas Mann closely followed Erika's activities in England, suspecting that Duff Cooper "was crazy about her, as so many are." Referring to the policy

---

45 See Irmela von der Lühe, *Erika Mann: Eine Lebensgeschichte* (Reinbek: Rowohlt Taschenbuch Verlag, 2009), 142–45.

46 Erika Mann, *Briefe und Antworten, Teil I: 1922–1950*, ed. Anna Zanco Prestel (Munich: Edition Spangenberg, 1984), 152–53.

of aiding Britain, known as the Lend-Lease Act, Mann proudly wrote to his confidante, the American journalist and philanthropist Agnes Meyer (1887–1970): "Send them destroyers. I am setting a good example and am sending them my daughter."[47]

Erika went to London where she witnessed the horrors of the "Blitz," which began on September 7, 1940. She denounced the bombing of civilians in nine radio addresses to the German people, which she delivered from August to October of that year.[48] In addressing German listeners as "Deutsche Hörer"—the same form of address her father would later use—she prepared the way for Thomas Mann to become a radio warrior. She also preceded him as a target of German propaganda. The official daily newspaper of the Nazi Party, the *Völkische Beobachter*, railed against Erika's radio addresses, calling her the "political whore of the House of Mann."[49] Thus when Mann began to broadcast his own addresses, German intelligence was ready to monitor and denounce everything that came over the airwaves from what was, to them, the already infamous "House of Mann."

Deeply steeped in the world of Wagner's music dramas as he was, Thomas Mann liked to view life through a Wagnerian lens. Observing Erika's fearlessness in the family's battle against fascism and in opposing his own silence during the early years of their exile, Mann liked to think of her as his very own "Wotanskind," referring to the epic Nibelungen cycle's troubled god, Wotan, and to his favorite daughter, Brünnhilde, his disobedient but loving child. Brünnhilde is also the heroic leader of the Valkyries, the spectacular warrior maidens of Germanic mythology who

---

47 *Letters of Thomas Mann*, 344. Agnes Meyer was of German extraction and was Mann's most ardent American supporter. In turn, he shared with her his most frank observations about himself and his work, including the radio addresses. For several years, Meyer was planning to write a book about Mann, hoping to increase the appreciation of her literary hero in her native country. As the co-owner and co-editor of the *Washington Post*, she was a well-connected Washington insider. The trouble was that—to Mann's silent chagrin—she and her husband Eugene Meyer (1875–1959), a former governor of the Federal Reserve during the Hoover administration, were Republicans and Roosevelt skeptics. Mann and Meyer's correspondence has been published as Thomas Mann/Agnes E. Meyer, *Briefwechsel 1937–1955*, ed. Hans Rudolf Vaget (Frankfurt am Main: S. Fischer, 1992). The volume contains a biographical essay on Agnes Meyer, 5–71. Subsequent citations as BrAM.

48 See Robert Galitz: "'A Family against Dictatorship.' Die Rundfunkstrategien der Familie Mann," in *Thomas Mann in Amerika*, eds. Ulrich Raulff and Ellen Strittmatter (Marbach: *Marbachermagazin* 163/164, 2018), 40–60, 47. Two of Erika's radio essays ("Eine Nacht in London"; "In Lissabon gestrandet") are reprinted in Erika Mann, *Blitze überm Ozean: Aufsätze, Reden, Reportagen*, eds. Irmela von der Lühe and Uwe Naumann (Reinbek: Rowohlt, 2000), 179–98.

49 Von der Lühe, *Erika Mann*, 250.

streak on horseback across the sky. In one of the most emotional and gripping moments of *The Ring of the Nibelung*, Wotan, as he comes to understand his daughter's motivation for opposing him, glorifies her as "du kühnes, herrliches Kind"—you valiant, glorious child. Erika Mann-Auden leading the charge in the war of the airwaves illustrates better than any other moment in her relationship with her father that resonant notion of her as a "Wotanskind."[50]

Mann at the Microphone

At first Erika proposed to the BBC a collaboration with her father: he would write an occasional column about the events of the war, and she would read it out in one of the programs of the German Service. We know from a letter to a BBC official that she had discussed this plan with her father before coming to London; in fact it was he, she says, who "originally suggested it."[51] Although there is no evidence in the diaries, it is quite plausible that in light of his positive experience with *This War*, Mann was interested in continuing to work with the BBC. He likely instructed his daughter to let this be known in London. To Mann, the BBC, with its considerable capabilities in the battle of the airwaves, offered the most effective outlet to turn his militant humanism into practical action.

Erika's idea of a father-daughter coproduction, however, found no favor with the higher-ups at the BBC. They felt that Mann's unique prestige could best be used if he were to be given his own spot on the program of the German Service. It was agreed that he should have five minutes of airtime each month. He was encouraged to submit philosophical reflections of a more general kind to complement his remarks on the course of the war. It was also suggested that he report on current events in the United States and thereby help fill the "information deficit" caused by continuing American neutrality.[52] As long as America was not involved, no war news as such could be expected; but information about political developments in the United States were still of interest to the BBC. By and large, Mann would follow these instructions.

---

50   The Wotan-Brünnhilde constellation became a running gag in the family. See Thomas Mann's letter of March 3, 1948, simply addressed to "Wotanskind." Thomas Mann, *Briefe 1948–1955 und Nachlese*, ed. Erika Mann (Frankfurt am Main: S. Fischer, 1965), 27.

51   J. F. Slattery, "Erika Mann und die BBC, 1940–1943," *Thomas Mann Jahrbuch* 12 (1999): 309–43, 313.

52   See J. F. Slattery's groundbreaking archival study, "Thomas Mann und die B.B.C. Die Bedingungen ihrer Zusammenarbeit," *Thomas Mann Jahrbuch* 5 (1992): 142–70, 157.

Unlike the work of other German exiles, Mann's addresses for the BBC were not censored. His reputation protected him from censorship.[53] In light of the resolutely pro-British stance he had taken in *This War*, control over Mann's talks seemed unnecessary. But as we shall see, his handlers in London occasionally saw fit to suggest a slight course correction or, at least, a change in tone. Mann's first address was broadcast in October of 1940. Apparently, his first few messages were telegraphed from Princeton to the New York studio of the BBC. From there, the messages were cabled to London and read on the air by Carl Brinitzer (1907–1974), a German-Jewish émigré and one of the regulars of the BBC's German Service, who would himself become a writer.[54] After the first four broadcasts, several important adjustments were made. Mann let it be known that he was unhappy about being restricted to five minutes and asked for more airtime. He was granted eight minutes. More importantly, for reasons of authenticity, he requested to be allowed to address his audience in his own voice.

This modus operandi was facilitated by Mann's move to Los Angeles, in March of 1941, where, at the sleek NBC Studios in Hollywood, at the corner of Sunset Boulevard and Vine Street (no longer in existence), he could record his talks more easily and transmit them more effectively. The resulting wax disks were sent by air mail to the BBC studio in New York; from there they were beamed by short-wave radio to London, where BBC technicians transferred the message back onto disks that then could be played in front of a microphone as frequently as they might like. Since German radio sets were not equipped for short wave, Mann's messages needed to be beamed to the continent on different frequencies, medium and long, to make sure that they could be received by the German "Volksempfänger," the popular radio set promoted by the Nazi regime, present in every household for the reception of its own propagandist messages.

As the extant recordings show, Mann was an effective speaker. He possessed a sonorous "radio voice" capable of almost theatrical modulation.[55] After all, reading from his works before an attentive and paying

---

53 Pütter, "Rundfunk," 1091.

54 See Carl Brinitzer, *Hier spricht London* (Hamburg: Hoffmann & Campe, 1969).

55 For a more detailed examination of Mann's radio performances, see Horst Heydeck, "Thomas Mann am Mikrophon," *Beiträge zur Geschichte des Rundfunks*, Jg. 5 (1971), Heft 3, 53–75; Martina Hoffschulte, *"Deutsche Hörer!" Thomas Manns Rundfunkreden (1940 bis 1945) im Werkkontext. Mit einem Anhang: Quellen und Materialien* (Münster: Telos, 2004), 253–56; Heike Weidenhaupt, *Gegenpropaganda aus dem Exil: Thomas Manns Radioansprachen für deutsche Hörer 1940 bis 1945* (Konstanz: Universitätsverlag Konstanz, 2001), 143–46.

audience had been part of his marketing strategy from early on. As we know from a letter he wrote to an admiring actress late in his life, he was in the habit of practicing enunciation to achieve clarity and the effect of easy listening.[56] Given his trademark virtuosic syntax, he knew that for maximum effect he simply had to read his messages himself.

Remarkably for that time, Mann possessed uncommon media savviness. This is evidenced, for example, by his brief radio address to the American people at the conclusion of his first short visit to New York in 1934.[57] Probably on the recommendation of his American publisher Knopf, Mann had used that occasion to express his hope that the United States would take a leading part in the material and spiritual reconstruction of a world in economic crisis and would help to create a "new Humanism" in the face of widespread political and moral degenerateness. He spoke in praise of the "magnificent invention" of radio communication and confessed that he was greatly attracted to the medium because of its magical power to reach people over great distances. But he was also quite aware of, and prescient about, the misuse of the radio for political ends, warning that a medium designed to overcome distances of all kinds could easily be used to promote separation, intolerance, and pernicious ideologies.

Precisely this, of course, was the practice on the Nazi side during the war. As might be expected, the German Ministry of Propaganda and Public Enlightenment was very much focused on the activities of the "enemy radio." When the war began it was decreed that listening to broadcasts from abroad was strictly *verboten*. Those who were caught merely listening to Allied broadcasts were sentenced to jail. But whoever "intentionally passed on news from foreign radio designed to undermine the fighting morale of the German people" could be punished by death.[58]

Among Mann's listeners, at least initially, was Joseph Goebbels himself. Reacting to Mann's address of August 1941, he dictated into his diary that it was "so feeble-minded ["blöd"] that it doesn't merit a response."[59] In reality, Goebbels knew very well that a response was needed, otherwise he would not have given orders to jam the BBC's German broadcasts. In

---

56 Letter to Annelies Schneidereyt, dated January 25, 1955, in *Die Briefe Thomas Manns: Regesten und Register*, eds. Hans Bürgin und Hans Otto Mayer, revised and supplemented by Gert Heine and Yvonne Schmidlin (Frankfurt am Main: S. Fischer, 1987), Vol. IV, 358 (55/30). Subsequent citations as *Regesten*.

57 "Rundfunkansprache an das amerikanische Publikum," *GW* XIII, 626–28.

58 See Sonja Valentin, *"Steine in Hitlers Fenster." Thomas Manns Radiosendungen Deutsche Hörer!, 1940–1945* (Göttingen: Wallstein, 2016), 302–03.

59 *Die Tagebücher von Joseph Goebbels, Teil II: Diktate*, ed. Elke Fröhlich on behalf of the Institut für Zeitgeschichte (Munich: Institut für Zeitgeschichte, 1996), 212. For a complete list of Goebbels's reactions to Thomas Mann, see Hoffschulte, *"Deutsche Hörer,"* 360–61.

addition, he instructed the German press to deal with Mann's broadcasts "polemically" and to take issue with the "daily flood of English lies."[60] Furthermore, a listening and monitoring service was created to summarize for internal use the propaganda coming from abroad. Those intelligence experts understood perfectly well what Thomas Mann was up to, namely "driving a wedge between the German people and the government, aiming to paralyze the collective will."[61]

In his foreword to the American edition of the first twenty-five radio addresses, published in December 1942 with a copyright date of 1943, Mann explained what attracted him to his radio work: "I believed that I should not miss the opportunity of making contact, however loose and precarious, with the German people [...] behind the back of the Nazi Government, which had deprived me of all means of exerting intellectual influence in Germany as soon as they had the power to do so."[62] His urge to seek revenge on the regime that had officially excommunicated him and to communicate, in principle, with the entire German people, not just with the old faithful readership that he used to be able to count on, is readily understandable.

Some old hands at the BBC, where objectivity and strict adherence to facts was the rule, felt uncomfortable with Mann's polemics, urging him to "be a little more objective." In regard to his address of November 29, 1942, for example, they admitted that, were it not from him, they should have never considered "putting [it] out."[63] On the questionable assumption that a more moderate tone "should probably get a larger audience for his talks," they instructed an administrator in their New York office, W. M. Newton, to tactfully ask Mann to curb his furor. Acknowledging the delicacy of the task, headquarters in London told Mr. Newton to remind Mann that although he enjoyed "a privileged position [...], we should be very grateful if he could be just slightly less abusive."[64] Mr. Newton passed along the BBC's concerns. He telegraphed to Mann that his November 29 talk was "extremely good," but that it "would have been better still without abusive terms." Mann responded that he was

60   S. Valentin, *"Steine in Hitlers Fenster,"* 304.
61   See Winfried Halder, *Exilrufe nach Deutschland: Die Rundfunkreden von Thomas Mann, Paul Tillich und Johannes R. Becher, 1940–1945; Analyse, Wirkung, Bedeutung* (Münster: LIT Verlag Münster, 2002), 65; Hoffschulte, *"Deutsche Hörer,"* 58–59.
62   Thomas Mann, *Listen, Germany! Twenty-five Radio Messages to the German People over BBC* (New York: Alfred A. Knopf, 1943), v. Reprinted in this volume.
63   Draft letter by Lindley Fraser to BBC New York Office re Thomas Mann, dated December 4, 1942. Slattery, "Thomas Mann und die B.B.C.," 164.
64   Letter by Basil Thornton to W. M. Newton, dated December 7, 1942. Slattery, "Thomas Mann und die B.B.C.," 165.

"glad to keep these objections in mind," and that he hoped to succeed in "restraining [my] temperament."[65]

In this he was not fully successful. To Mann, attempting to be objective about Hitler and the Nazi rulers was a thoroughly unappealing proposition. After the respectful reprimand by the BBC, he did largely avoid crude insults, such as "fanatical idiot," "apocalyptic thugs," and "Gorilla." But he saw no reason to temper his outrage and criticism as the war progressed towards its cataclysmic end. On the contrary, his anger only deepened as it inevitably blended with shame and mourning.

The Decisive Battle of Mankind

Beyond the taunts and invectives, Mann's radio work was for him a deadly serious business. He had to explain this to Agnes Meyer, who, like Alfred Knopf, feared that Mann's dedication to the fight against Hitler was distracting him from his true mission—to write great novels. She felt that the author of the *Joseph* novels "was too good" for mere politics. So he decided to italicize it for her: "*Je fais la guerre* [*I am making war*] [...] this is a decisive battle of mankind and everything will be decided here and now, including the fate of my life's work [...]. You don't know what I have suffered in these eight years, and how intensely I wish that the most repulsive riff-raff that has ever made 'history' will be destroyed—and that I live to see it happen." He added that "people's regard for my literary work is not complete and in the final analysis cannot make me happy if it is not partly governed by sympathy with this other cause"—the fight against Hitler.[66]

Mann's "Je-fais-la-guerre" letter was written shortly after his second personal encounter with Franklin Delano Roosevelt (1882–1945), which may explain its tone of determination and self-confidence. Thomas, Katia, and Erika Mann had stayed at the White House over the weekend of January 12–14, 1941, and Mann was eager to let Agnes Meyer know how impressed and, once again, how charmed he was by FDR. Invoking Old Testament imagery, he told her: "there is something like a blessing upon him, and I am drawn to him as the born opponent [...] of what must be toppled [...]. I felt strengthened afterward."[67]

The timing of the January 1941 visit to the White House, which Mann himself instigated, suggests that he was seeking a kind of blessing for his own war of the airwaves. He had written his first address to the German people in October of 1940. In November, Roosevelt won

---

65 Slattery, "Thomas Mann und die B.B.C.," 166.
66 Letter to Agnes Meyer, dated January 24, 1941, *Letters of Thomas Mann*, 354; German original in BrAM, 253–54.
67 *Letters of Thomas Mann*, 355; German original in BrAM, 254.

reelection for the second time. In December, Mann wrote to Hendrik Willem van Loon (1882–1944), a popular writer and radio commentator of Dutch origin and a friend of the Roosevelts who had brought about Mann's earlier invitation to the White House in 1935, asking him to work his magic one more time. Mann gave as his reason his deeply felt desire to once again see the man he revered, especially under the present circumstances now that the war was in progress.[68] The jovial Dutchman obliged; First Lady Eleanor Roosevelt (1884–1962) issued the desired invitation.

Strictly speaking, there was nothing that needed to be discussed between the American president and the German exile. The president talked to him about the speech he was going to deliver at his third inauguration, and Mann noted with satisfaction that Roosevelt was going to emphasize the paramount importance of "the political-moral viewpoint over economic considerations." Aside from this, their "lively conversation" probably did not rise above pleasant small talk.[69] At the customary cocktail hour Mann presented a copy of his privately printed essay *The War and Democracy*, inscribed: "To F.D.R., President of the U.S. and of a coming better world." It is not known if Roosevelt ever read it.

The available evidence suggests that Mann was animated to seek this second encounter with Roosevelt by a strong element of magical thinking. He evidently believed that what he called "Kontakt"—personal and direct contact—to a great historical figure such as Roosevelt would have a beneficial effect on himself, the contact-seeker. He ascribed this touching superstition to his Goethe figure in *Lotte in Weimar*. In light of his habit to identify with Goethe playfully and ironically—a habit that became more pronounced as he advanced in age—we may safely conclude that the superstitious belief in the magical effect of "Kontakt" was very much his own. In his view, renewing contact with the "blessed man" in the White House established a kind of imaginary brotherhood in arms in the common fight for the better world that he mentioned in his inscription to FDR. And it was this strong emotional connection to the most powerful man in the world, above all, that gave him, the man of peace, the confidence to proclaim "Je fais la guerre."

It seems entirely congruent with Mann's cultish relationship to Franklin Roosevelt that throughout his radio addresses he fashioned the American president as the mightiest opponent of Hitler—mightier than Churchill, mightier than Joseph Stalin (1878–1953). Upon the death of Roosevelt on April 12, 1945, in the Municipal Auditorium of Santa Monica, Mann delivered a eulogy in which he celebrated FDR as the embodiment of goodness and goodwill. In his radio address of April 19, 1945, he contrasted, for the

---

68   Letter to W. H. van Loon, dated December 16, 1940. *Regesten*, vol. II, 40/660.
69   Entry of January 14, 1941, Thomas Mann, *Tagebücher 1940–1943*, ed. Peter de Mendelssohn (Frankfurt am Main: Fischer, 1982), 210–11.

final time, the American president with Hitler. His deeply felt tribute to the great winner of the decisive battle of mankind must have stunned his listeners in Germany, where FDR was routinely maligned as a war criminal and a mere tool manipulated by the great Jewish world conspiracy. Mann concludes the address with the lament that Roosevelt is gone, but Hitler is still alive: "How dare you!" Addressing Hitler directly, he exclaims: "Your days are numbered; they have been numbered from the day He rose to oppose you; even in death He will terrify you." Hitler's days were indeed numbered. Eleven days later he put an end to his life.

Given the sheer extent of Mann's multifarious activities, it seems plausible that in the economy of his creative output his radio work acquired a kind of self-healing function simply by allowing him to let off steam. To the extent that his monthly radio talks were driven by hatred, they simultaneously helped him to compartmentalize that negative energy and keep it off his desk, while, seemingly unperturbed, he was weaving his intricate narratives. He increasingly felt that if he did not engage in the war, everything else, including his novels, would be tarnished and diminished. As he explained to Agnes Meyer, he took pride in his ability to not permit "hatred to degrade and paralyze me. I have written *Joseph in Egypt*, *The Beloved Returns*, and *The Transposed Heads*, works of freedom and gaiety and, if you will, self-control. I am rather proud that I have brought all that off, instead of joining the ranks of the melancholics, and I feel my friends should regard the fact that I also go on fighting as a sign of strength [...]."[70]

Mann's Sources

At the beginning of his collaboration with the BBC, as we have seen, Mann was given some suggestions for the kinds of topics he might want to address. In essence, however, they let him choose the events and topics on which he wanted to comment. It is not clear, though, to what extent the BBC provided him with information gained from the British intelligence services, because for much of his radio work Mann used sources that would have been easily accessible to any avid consumer of political news. His most trusted sources were *The Nation* ("America's Leading Liberal Weekly since 1865") as well as the *New York Times* and the *Los Angeles Times*. Also, he faithfully listened to the radio whenever the president addressed the nation, and he listened regularly to Raymond Gram Swing (1887–1968), the CBS commentator, who was an expert on German and European affairs and an outspoken critic of fascism. In addition, he drew

---

70 *Letters of Thomas Mann*, 354; German original in BrAM, 253–55.

on a personal collection of newspaper clippings, dating back to 1934, that documented the advance of fascism ("Fascisierung") in Europe.[71]

Another important source Mann was able to use was the collection of notes and aphorisms, drawn from his diaries of 1933 and 1934, that he had compiled in 1935 in preparation for that above-mentioned major political article that he never completed. In 1945 he decided to publish those notes in a private printing by the short-lived Pazifische Presse, which specialized in works by German exile writers living in California— Lion Feuchtwanger (1884–1958), Alfred Döblin (1878–1957), and Franz Werfel (1890–1945) among them.[72] Under the title *Leiden an Deutschland*, those fragments were meant to document two things: his true attitude towards Nazi Germany during the years of his public silence, and his prescience from the start of the Third Reich in predicting war and catastrophe as its inevitable outcome. In retrospect, those notes read like a warmup exercise for the prolonged engagements of Mann's war of the airwaves.[73] Most of the major themes of *Listen, Germany!* are sounded first in *Leiden an Deutschland*—the fundamental mendacity of the Nazi regime, the "bestiality" of their behavior, the genocidal potential of their "idiotic racial theories," their insular frame of mind, and several others.

As for information from British intelligence, Mann's diaries reveal little. We can nonetheless be quite certain that he was supplied with secret information from the BBC's Monitoring Service at regular intervals. We are led to this conclusion by a remark in his address of January 1942, in which he reports on the fate of "four hundred young Dutch Jews" who had been taken to Germany "as objects of research on poison gas." He assures his listeners that the information was reliable, using the phrase "so I have been told." Furthermore, he tells his German listeners: "The news sounds unbelievable, but my source is good." This is the first indication we have that he was indeed fed secret information that was not available elsewhere.

Five months later, in his message of June 1942, Mann reports that he must correct his earlier information. The number of Dutch victims was almost twice as high as he had reported. He was newly informed that they had been taken to the concentration camp at Mauthausen (near Linz, Austria), and that they had been gassed. Again, he emphasizes the trustworthiness of his sources, asserting that he received this information

---

71 Entry of January 5, 1934, *Tagebücher 1933–1934*, 285. Hoffschulte, "Deutsche Hörer," 404–36.

72 Roland Jaeger, *New Weimar on the Pacific: The Pazifische Presse and German Exile Publishing in Los Angeles 1942–1948*, trans. Marion Philadelphia and ed. Victoria Dailey (Los Angeles: Victoria Dailey Publisher, 2000).

73 Thomas Mann, *Leiden an Deutschland: Tagebuchblätter aus den Jahren 1933 und 1934* (Los Angeles: privately printed by the Pazifischen Presse, 1946).

"through indirect channels" from Holland. This was information that had in the meantime been confirmed by the Dutch government-in-exile—an entity with which Mann had no contact. The additional information on this matter was received "privately," which is to say, through the BBC's Monitoring Service.

Bringing up the matter of Mauthausen shows that the subject of genocide emerged early in his radio work as a central topic. It very much remained on his radar and, as we shall see, surfaced in a major way three years later, provoking him to one of his most insightful reflections on what today we call the Holocaust. He began to realize that Germany's emerging policy of systematic extermination was a logical consequence of the official antisemitism. Starting in 1933 he recorded in his diary the step-by-step marginalizing of Jews beginning with the dismissal of Jewish members of the civil service, including from the universities, and leading in 1935 to the promulgation of the infamous Nuremberg racial laws. Those anti-Jewish measures struck close to home because they applied to his Jewish wife, Katia; to her brother, the physicist Peter Pringsheim (1881–1963); as well as to their parents, Alfred (1850–1941) and Hedwig Pringsheim (1855–1942), who were driven out of their magnificent house on Munich's Arcisstraße, which had to make room for a new structure that was part of the Nazification of Munich's cityscape. Had Thomas Mann and his family remained in Germany, his own six children would have been categorized as "Mischlinge" (mixed-breeds, mongrels) and would have been dealt with in accordance with those laws.

What Mann reported about Mauthausen occurred virtually contemporaneously with the secret Wannsee Conference of January 20, 1942, at which the complete eradication of the Jewish population in German-controlled Europe was adopted as a matter of government policy. Even without knowledge of the Wannsee Conference, Mann could tell that something monstrous was being perpetrated in Nazi-occupied Europe, and he was determined to inform his listeners about it. In his address of September 1942, Mann reminds his listeners of the Nazis' true goal, citing Goebbels's statement that it was their intention "to exterminate the Jews," whether they win or lose the war. He presents two particularly horrific examples of that policy: the rounding up of 16,000 Jews in Paris and their transport to the camps in the East, and the gassing of 11,000 Polish Jews locked in airtight boxcars in Konin near Warsaw.

Given the often-unreliable nature of wartime reporting both in the press and on the radio, it comes as no surprise that not all information that Mann used in his addresses was correct. Some of it turned out to be based on mere rumor. A more characteristic and problematical feature of his radio speeches and of his political outlook in general is a sometimes conspicuous layer of wishful thinking. For example, on the first anniversary of the start of hostilities, he writes in his diary: "America's entry into the war would almost certainly result in the immediate fall of the Nazi regime, perhaps with a revolution in Italy as a prelude."[74] Nothing of the sort came to pass. When in the wake of Pearl Harbor, the United States declared war on Japan, Germany's ally, it was Germany that declared war on the United States. The result was the opposite of what Mann had wished would happen. The regime's grip on the population became even tighter, as the Nazi government could now claim that Germany was fighting for its very survival. In another example of futile hopes expressed in his early broadcasts, Mann unrealistically suggests that his listeners in Germany should stop obeying their oppressors, overthrow the Nazi regime, and thus "save [their] souls." Only wishful thinking could lead him to believe that this was simply a question of wanting and not wanting. It is surely one of the saddest aspects of Mann's radio talks to see him gradually and reluctantly come to the realization, and to accept, that under a Fascist dictatorship his compatriots, misinformed and intimidated as they were, proved to be unable—perhaps even unwilling—to free themselves.

Facing the Darkest Chapter of German History

Mann's radio talks followed, roughly speaking, the changing course of the war all the way to, and beyond, Germany's unconditional surrender on May 8, 1945. Because he spoke about changing events and diverse topics, his addresses can, if read today as a continuous whole, easily leave the impression of haphazardness. But close examination reveals that his messages are held together by his core political beliefs and by an underlying concern for the eventual spiritual recovery of Germany from the impending catastrophe. Viewed in their entirety, Mann's radio addresses over a span of almost five years represent the most sustained attempt by a German exile to confront his isolated and deluded former compatriots with the terrible truth about the darkest chapter in their history, and to remind his listeners that the unreserved and sincere acknowledgment of the enormous crimes committed in the name of Germany was the indispensable precondition of any thought of recovery and healing.

 One of the most fascinating aspects of reading *Listen, Germany!* is to observe the gradual shifts in Mann's attitude towards his native country resulting from a political learning process that gained pace during his exile years. For example, he initially acted in the belief, idealistic but erroneous, that the better Germany, suffering under the yoke of dictatorship, would want to rise up and rid itself of an ideology that he deemed base, inhumane, and fundamentally un-German. Reluctantly, and with much pain and shame, he came to realize that liberation would have to come

---

74 Entry of September 1, 1940, *Tagebücher 1940–1943*, 142.

from outside, leaving in its wake immense destruction and suffering. In the end he came to see and to accept that for Germany to be thoroughly denazified, it would have to suffer military defeat. As it gradually dawned on him that his exhortations were unrealistic and futile, particularly after Reinhold Niebuhr (1892–1971), the highly regarded ethicist and a personal acquaintance, pointed out in a review that Mann's entreaties to his fellow Germans living under the Nazi tyranny lacked empathy (more about that later), he modified his tone. Rather than berating the Germans for their failures, he began to fashion himself increasingly as an educator and moral leader. As Tobias Boes has argued, by positioning himself as an antidote to Nazism, Mann "transformed the social role of the author into something that it had never been before," namely a "teacher of Germany."[75]

In addition to his educational tone, Mann increasingly chose to strike a distinctly pastoral tone, resorting to biblical language. Thus, in his address of January 1942, he admonished the Germans, "You need to *purify* yourselves. The atonement that you struggle to avoid must be your own work, the work of the German nation … A purification, rectification, and liberation must and will occur in Germany, so fundamentally and with such determination that it will be commensurate with evil deeds, the like of which the world had never seen before." The ultimate goal of such self-purification was to assure "that the great German nation can look humanity in the eye again and freely extend its hand in search of reconciliation."

Another issue that resolved itself during his engagement in the war of the airwaves was the question of the true character of Germany as a nation. Was there one Germany, unified in spirit, or were there two Germanys? If two, was one good, the other evil? For a long time, Mann operated on the belief that there were indeed two Germanys, the patently evil Germany and the other, different Germany that he represented—the Germany of Goethe, Schiller, and Beethoven. His initial appeals to overthrow the Nazi regime presupposed the existence of such a Germany—a Germany that was good and decent at its core. Given this frame of mind, he waited eagerly for signs of life from that other Germany existing within Nazi Germany. He was deeply moved, therefore, and felt strengthened in his belief in that "other" Germany, when he learned from an article in *The Nation* of the "rebellion at the University of Munich."[76] Members of a resistance group known as "The White Rose" led by Sophie (1921–1943) and Hans Scholl (1918–1943) were caught distributing pamphlets that denounced the regime's lies and called for an end to the war. This

---

75   See the chapter "The Teacher of Germany" in Boes, *Thomas Mann's War*, 19–45, 22.

76   Entry of June 12, 1943, *Tagebücher 1940–1943*, 588. Mann's source was "Behind the Enemy Lines," *The Nation*, June 12, 1943, 810.

happened in the university's atrium, right next to the lecture hall in which Mann in 1933 had delivered his fateful lecture on Wagner. Hans Scholl, his younger sister Sophie, and several of their co-conspirators paid for their courage with their lives.

This presented Mann with a welcome opportunity to address the vexed question of Germany's true character and specifically to contest the claim of Germany's unmitigated evil promoted by Sir Robert Vansittart (1881–1957), a high British government official. During the bombardment of London known as the "Blitz," Vansittart delivered a series of radio addresses that were published as a pamphlet under the telling title of *Black Record*. It was a runaway success and led to the formulation of a doctrine known as "Vansittartism." This view of Germany holds that since unification of the country in 1871 the Germans had been acting as an incorrigibly militaristic and belligerent people, with no significant exceptions.[77] Mann was not willing to let that stand. In his address of June 1943, he refers to the two hundred thousand German political prisoners who had suffered torture and death at the hands of the Nazi state for their unshakable belief in law and liberty, and in particular to those courageous students at Munich University. Mann argued that there was far too much evidence to the contrary to hold as tenable the monolithic view of Germany propagated by Vansittart. Those "brave, glorious young people" died for "Germany's honor," Mann asserts, adding that they "shall not have died in vain, shall not be forgotten." He predicts correctly that after the demise of the Third Reich their names—"die Geschwister Scholl"—will be memorialized, as those of the Nazi leaders will not.

It is entirely possible, as some scholars have speculated, that the Scholls, or other members of the White Rose circle, were directly inspired by Mann's radio broadcasts.[78] We have no proof, but the echoes of Mann's campaign in their own incendiary broadsheets against the mendacity of the Nazi regime do make this a plausible assumption. Like Thomas Mann, the members of the White Rose were trying to spread information with the intention of undermining the fighting morale of the German people and promoting resistance. Furthermore, it is striking that the very first broadsheet distributed by the White Rose in the summer of 1942 concludes with a quotation from Goethe's play of 1814, *Des Epimenides Erwachen*—the same work from which Mann quotes in his message of September 1941. This is by no means a well-known work from the Goethe canon. What made it relevant to both Mann and the

---

77 Sir Robert Vansittart, *Black Record: Germans Past and Present* (London: Hamish Hamilton, 1941). See Hans Rudolf Vaget, "Vansittartism Revisited: Thomas Mann, Bertolt Brecht and the Threat of World War III," *Publications of the English Goethe Society* 82 (2013): 26–41.

78 See Hoffschulte, *"Deutsche Hörer,"* 307–08; Dieter Borchmeyer, *Thomas Mann: Werk und Zeit* (Berlin: Insel, 2022), 1079.

White Rose is its spirit of opposition to the then-oppressor of Germany, Napoleon.[79]

Looking at the entire body of Mann's propaganda work, it is moving to see that his belief in the hypothesis of the two Germanys began to crumble under the sheer weight of the German crimes. In particular, the mass murder of the Jews of Europe began to overwhelm his belief in the significance of the "other" Germany. He came to see that it was asking too much of other nations, many of them the victims of German aggression, to make any fine distinctions between good and bad Germans. Those crimes were committed in the name of Germany as a nation. In reminding his compatriots of Germany's guilt, however, he was careful to distinguish between the responsibility of particular individuals and the guilt of the collective.

By the time the war ended, Mann had entirely let go of the comforting notion of the two Germanys. Reluctantly he embraced the reality that there was only one Germany, albeit one with two very different faces, reminiscent of Dr. Jekyll and Mr. Hyde in Robert Louis Stevenson's (1850–1894) gothic parable. This comparison was first suggested by Sebastian Haffner (1907–1999), a German lawyer who fled Germany in 1938 and became a successful journalist at the *Manchester Guardian*. Haffner had recently authored *Germany: Jekyll and Hyde*.[80] Mann read it with approval.[81] Three weeks after the end of the war in Europe, Mann used the occasion of his third annual lecture at the Library of Congress, where Agnes Meyer had created a sinecure for him as a consultant in Germanic Literature, to address the question of the true character of the Germans.

In that Washington lecture, the creator of *Doctor Faustus* sets forth his belief that in the last analysis "there are *not* two Germanies, a good one, and a bad one, but only one [...]."[82] Nazi Germany grew out

---

79 There is no mention in Mann's radio talks of the failed coup attempt against Hitler on July 20, 1944, by German army officers led by Claus Schenk Graf von Stauffenberg (1907–1944). That attempt, which ended with the prompt execution of Stauffenberg and his co-conspirators, occurred during the hiatus in Mann's monthly messages during the second half of 1944. Of course he followed those developments in his diary, viewing them as "the beginning of the end." Entry of July 21, 1944, *Thomas Mann, Tagebücher 1944–1.4.1946*, ed. Inge Jens (Frankfurt am Main: S. Fischer Verlag, 1986), 79.

80 Sebastian Haffner, *Germany: Jekyll and Hyde* (London: Secker and Warburg, 1940). For a more detailed treatment of the Mann–Haffner relationship, see Hans Rudolf Vaget, "Germany: Jekyll and Hyde. Sebastian Haffners Deutschlandbild und die Genese von *Doktor Faustus*," in *Thomas Mann und seine Quellen: Festschrift für Hans Wysling*, eds. Eckhard Heftrich and Helmut Koopman (Frankfurt am Main: Klostermann, 1991), 249–71.

81 Entry of May 15, 1940, *Tagebücher 1940–1943*, 76.

82 Thomas Mann, "Germany and the Germans," in *Thomas Mann's Addresses Delivered at the Library of Congress, 1942–1949* (Washington, DC: Library of Congress, 1963), 64–65. Also in *GW* XI, 1146.

of its antecedent, the presumably "good" Germany: "Evil Germany is merely good Germany gone astray," the result of a mutation which Mann ascribes, speaking metaphorically, to "devilish cunning," such as Nazi propaganda. Elsewhere, including in his radio talks, he explains that mutation by using the term "verhunzen," meaning to let something worthy go to the dogs. Even more disquieting is Mann's belief that it was Germany's "best" that turned into something evil; the "best" being its culture of "Innerlichkeit"—of inwardness, of introspection—that produced the flowering of German Romanticism and of music of universal appeal. Concomitantly, however, "Innerlichkeit" produced the purportedly nonpolitical attitude of contempt for the political arena and neglect of the public sphere. This, of course, is one of the grand and provocative themes of *Doctor Faustus*, a novel that may be described as a melancholy and mournful reflection on the hidden correspondences between the striving of German music for worldwide hegemony and Germany's striving for supremacy by attempting to become a great power and rule the world.[83]

Mann's embrace of the "One-Germany" theory undergirds the later radio speeches, which were given at a time when Germany was facing defeat and humiliation. But its presence can be felt earlier in his radio messages to the Germans. As he explains in his address of August 1941, the present evil of National Socialism and racism has deep roots in German history: "It is the virulent degenerate form of ideas that always carried the seed of murderous corruption in them, but that indeed were in no way foreign to the old, the good, Germany of culture and refinement."

Mann's search for answers—his very own "Ursachenforschung"—stands out from the mushrooming theories and speculations about the rise and fall of fascism by dint of his deep-focus view of the matter. Convinced that the emergence of Nazism cannot be traced back to the Versailles Treaties of 1919 alone, or to the world economic crisis of the late 1920s, Mann searched for the seeds of the present evil in the more distant past. He found them buried in Romanticism, in the age of Reformation, even in the late Middle Ages, which had witnessed various forms of mass hysteria. He believed that those seeds proved resistant to the surface changes of history and found their most virulent articulation in the twentieth century. The foremost meaning of "One Germany," then, was this: Nazism was not something alien that entered the body politic out of nowhere at a late stage of German history; rather, it was a homegrown disease with a long period of incubation.

---

83 For a sustained argument in support of this reading, see Hans Rudolf Vaget, "'German' Music and German Catastrophe. A Re-reading of *Doktor Faustus*," in *A Companion to the Works of Thomas Mann*, eds. Herbert Lehnert and Eva Wessell (Rochester, NY: Camden House, 2004), 221–44.

"One Germany" also implies that Mann would not claim any exception for himself. Accordingly, in "Germany and the Germans," he ceased to present himself as representing the other, "good" Germany. Unflinchingly, he now declared that his diagnosis of Germany's malady also applied to himself: "[…] it is all within me, I have been through it all."[84] By including himself, Mann greatly increased his credibility in postwar Germany as a moral leader, at least with part of the German population. But only up to a point. The flipside of the "One Germany" hypothesis, insofar as it implies that the scourge of Nazism had deep roots and a long period of incubation, proved unacceptable both to many opponents of Nazism and to the sea of sympathizers. After 1945, criticizing Hitler and Nazism had become acceptable and was perfectly in order. Implicating the historic old Germany of culture and *Bildung* was not.

After the German surrender at the Battle of Stalingrad on February 2, 1943, Mann believed, as most observers did, that the demise of Hitler's Third Reich was only a question of time. With the Allied forces preparing for the invasion of the European continent and himself embarked on a major new work, *Doctor Faustus*, he decided to suspend his radio talks until the actual end of the hostilities was at hand. In his penultimate address before signing off, in his message of May 1, 1944, he again spoke to his compatriots as a healer by putting his finger on one of the psychological roots of the Nazi mentality and by pointing out how it might be rooted out in a postwar world. He singles out a certain exceptionalism as a fateful deformation of the German mind, nourished over a long period of time and exploited by National Socialism. Mann defines it as "Superioritätswahn," the illusory belief in the superiority of the Germans, in racial and cultural terms, over the rest of the world. He reminds his compatriots that German culture, the prestige of which was routinely misused by Hitler and the Nazis to justify their policy of expansion and aggression, is neither the highest nor the only culture. Germans are neither devils nor angels. They have been misled by false teachers and must learn anew how to live in peaceful brotherhood with their neighbors. And that means accepting democracy—a concept that "we Germans have foolishly treated with contempt for too long."

When in the winter of 1944/45, during the Battle of the Bulge on the Western Front in Belgium, hope for a turn in Germany's military fortunes and perhaps a separate peace with the Western allies once again began to glimmer, Mann agreed to resume his radio addresses, even to speak twice a month, as he was urged to do by the BBC.[85] Much had changed since Mann had last spoken to the Germans. The Allied forces had reached the Western border of the *Reich*, and on October 21, 1944,

---

84 "Germany and the Germans," *Thomas Mann's Addresses*, 65.
85 Letter to Agnes Meyer, dated January 7, 1945, BrAM, 612.

the historic city of Aachen (Aix-la-Chapelle) had become the first German city to be liberated. Reminding his German listeners of their imminent liberation was thought to further undermine the Germans' willingness to defend their homeland to the death, as they were being told to do by their increasingly desperate rulers.

Addressing his listeners in Germany on January 1, 1945, Mann immediately dashes their mistaken hopes for a separate peace by reminding them that the temporary successes in the woods of the Ardennes are deceptive—as were the highly touted victories of the German *Wehrmacht* during the early phases of the war—because the civilized world cannot and will not tolerate the survival of Nazism in any shape or form. As if to compensate for the bitterness of his prediction, he reminds them of the changed outlook of the people in the limited areas of Germany over which the Allies had gained control, as Erika, always close to the action, had reported. Those Germans were enjoying peace and were turning their thoughts to the task of rebuilding.

As he admitted to Agnes Meyer, Mann was not quite certain what he should tell the Germans so close to the end, because he was unsure of what was going on in their minds. Some of them absurdly believed that the Allies would have to finance the reconstruction of the very cities they had destroyed.[86] He did not have to wonder for long, because the news coming in from the Eastern Front laid bare the gravest of the German crimes. On its march to the river Vistula, the Red Army had reached the sites of the German death camps, although their operators, before abandoning them, had tried to destroy the evidence of their true, gruesome purpose. Mann took up the painful topic in his addresses of January 14 and 16, 1945, well before the official date of the liberation of Auschwitz, January 27. He confirmed what his listeners secretly suspected—or knew but suppressed—that the concentration camps in the East were in fact enormous death camps, which is to say, one giant murder facility: "eine riesenhafte Mordanlage." His comments in those two speeches mark the culmination of his preoccupation with the genocidal dimension of Nazi Germany throughout his radio addresses.

Thomas Mann was the first to observe that the camps would be viewed as "*the* monument of the Third Reich," the unmistakable emblem of its comprehensive criminality. That criminality was by no means restricted to the death camps. It included war crimes on a large scale committed against civilians throughout Europe. Addressing his compatriots personally—"du, deutscher Landsmann, du, deutsche Frau"—Mann assumes again the role of therapist and instructs them to accept the truth, unimaginable though it may appear to be. That truth must be faced unreservedly and must be allowed to enter "your conscience." He provides accurate figures based on the camp's internal bookkeeping: one million seven hundred and fifteen

86 Ibid.

thousand Jews from twenty-two different countries murdered in Auschwitz-Birkenau alone. And he cites some of the graphic particulars found in that "death factory": the barrels of lime, the gas pipes, the crematoria, the piles of bones, and the mountains of clothes and shoes, including those of children. What he expects of his compatriots—what is in fact needed, he says—is a sense of horror and shame, is repentance, is hatred of the villains who have made Germany an abomination in the eyes of God and the world.

Mann is particularly concerned, as he is throughout the war, about the irreparable damage done by the Nazis to Germany's reputation and to the prospects for her return to the family of civilized nations. He reminds his listeners that any thought of "reconciliation with the world" will require as an iron precondition that they acknowledge the full extent of the crimes committed in the name of Germany and accept their responsibility. Revulsion and shame must not cause them to avert their eyes. The Germans must become knowing. To that end he urges them to undertake a tremendous project of investigating, educating, and enlightening. Ignorance can be neither an excuse nor an option.

What Mann set out as a precondition for healing and reconciliation amounted to nothing less than what today is known as Holocaust research. At the time when everybody's overriding concern was with survival, Thomas Mann's call for a full accounting remained unheeded; the mass murder of Jews remained a taboo for a long time. The German Holocaust research that he demanded did not get under way until the late 1970s, and when it did, no one seemed to be able, or willing, to recall and credit the prescient voice of Thomas Mann.

Congruent with the gravity of the revelations about Auschwitz in the radio addresses, the liberation of the camps also figures in the great reckoning that is *Doctor Faustus*. In the novel's penultimate chapter, Mann uses the liberation of the camp at Buchenwald, located in the center of Germany, next to Weimar, to make the same point about German responsibility and guilt that he made when addressing his German listeners. He has the narrator report about the dramatic gesture made by US General George Patton that got wide coverage in the American press: "Meanwhile a transatlantic general has the inhabitants of Weimar file past the crematoria of their local concentration camp and declares (should one say, unjustly?) that they [...] share in the guilt for these horrors that are now laid bare and to which he forces them to direct their eyes." To make clear what constitutes their collective guilt, the narrator identifies them as "citizens who went about their business in seeming honesty and tried to know nothing, though at times the wind blew the stench of burned human flesh up their noses."[87]

---

87 Mann, *Doctor Faustus*, trans. John E. Woods (New York: Alfred A. Knopf, 1997), 505.

Mann's War of the Airwaves in the Rearview Mirror

All of this raises a crucial question about the reach of Mann's voice. How many Germans were actually willing and, given the existing prohibitions and the risk in violating them, sufficiently courageous to tune their radios to the BBC? Given the immaterial nature of the medium of radio, no hard data about the reception of Mann's addresses can be had. In the fall of 1944, the BBC estimated that approximately four million listeners tuned in to their German program.[88] But that number includes those in the less severely jammed areas of Europe occupied by Germany. Thomas Mann, for his part, was under no illusion about the size of his audience in "Germany proper." He knew from letters he received that many of his listeners were located in Switzerland, Sweden, Holland, and the Czech "Protectorate."[89]

In his very last address, dated December 30, 1945, Mann takes a rather dim view of the success of his radio talks. Referencing Shakespeare's play *Love's Labour's Lost*, which figures prominently in *Doctor Faustus*, he bitterly dismisses his radio work as "love's labor for Germany foolishly lost."[90] At the time, he was incensed by the hypocritical reaction to his addresses by the so-called "inner emigration" made up by colleagues who opted to remain in Nazi Germany. Barely a few months after the end of the war, in an open letter, Walter von Molo, the author of nationalist historical novels, called on Thomas Mann to return to Germany as "the good doctor" and to help to heal the nation's wounds. The letter hinted that he was uniquely qualified to fill that role, having acted as their spiritual and moral leader in his wartime radio addresses.[91] Mann distrusted this show of remorse and sincerity and declined the invitation, leaving open the possibility of a visit at a later date. In an open letter of his own, written with barely controlled indignation, he reiterated for the benefit of his critics the pain of exile and reminded them of their sins. And he flatly rejected the insinuation that he should give up his American citizenship.[92]

His instincts did not betray him. As Leonore Krenzlin has shown, this entire clash between a handful of pretend exiles and real exiles, grandly named in retrospect "die große Kontroverse," was initiated by a former press officer of the German Wehrmacht, Johann F. G. Grosser, and most

---

88 Slattery, "Thomas Mann und die B.B.C.," 168.
89 *Listen, Germany!*, foreword, vi. Also reprinted in this book.
90 See also Thomas Mann, "Brief nach Deutschland," in *Große kommentierte Frankfurter Ausgabe* (Frankfurt: S. Fischer, 2009), 19.1, 115.
91 Walter von Molo, open letter to Thomas Mann, dated August 4, 1945. Thomas Mann, *Briefwechsel mit Autoren*, ed. Hans Wysling (Frankfurt: S. Fischer, 1988), 365–68.
92 "Brief nach Deutschland," GKFA, 19.1, 72–82.

vigorously argued by Frank Thiess (1890–1977), a novelist and author of film scripts.[93] Its ultimate goal was to disqualify the author of *Deutsche Hörer!* as an interpreter of the Third Reich.[94] The position that Thiess, Von Molo, and their likeminded colleagues took was that no person who had not experienced the Nazi years first-hand should pass judgment on them, as Mann, in their view, had done quite recklessly.

Only once did Mann comment on the controversy surrounding his radio addresses. The occasion was a momentous one, as was the venue. This was his first speech on German soil after leaving the country in 1933. In the summer of 1949, he had agreed, with much trepidation, to go to Frankfurt—also to Weimar—to mark the two-hundredth anniversary of the birth of Goethe, and to do so in Frankfurt's Paulskirche, the birthplace in 1848–1849 of the stillborn German democracy. He prefaced his remarks about Goethe by reflecting at length upon the gulf that had opened between Germany and the rest of the world during the twelve years of the Nazi dictatorship. Noting how very strange it was that his children—Erika, Klaus, and Golo Mann (the historian; 1909–1994)—had joined the war wearing American uniforms, he frankly confesses that he, too, fought in that war when he addressed the German people over the BBC to assure them that Hitler's victories meant nothing and predicted that his regime was predestined to end in utter shame. Trying to justify his contribution to the Allied war effort, he assured his audience that his "allocutions" had brought consolation, inner strength, and belief to "many, many distraught and suffering souls all over the world and, as I know for sure, in Germany."[95]

Although Mann made an effort to strike a conciliatory tone, he was hardly entirely sincere. We have to wonder how some in his audience felt when he told them, contrary to the massive evidence on display in his radio addresses, that every word of anger and loathing was directed "only" at the people in power who had seduced and misled the German people. In 1949, when he visited Weimar, situated in the newly founded German Democratic Republic, Mann could bathe in the official,

---

93 Johann F. G. Grosser, *Die große Kontroverse: Ein Briefwechsel um Deutschland* (Hamburg: Nagel Verlag, 1963). This is an anthology of the various contributions to the debate of 1945/1946. On Grosser, see Leonore Krenzlin, "Geschichte des Scheiterns—Geschichte des Lernens? Überlegungen zur Lage während und nach der 'großen Kontroverse' und zur Motivation ihrer Akteure," in *Fremdes Heimatland: Remigration und literarisches Leben nach 1945*, eds. Irmela von der Lühe and Klaus-Dieter Krohn (Göttingen: Wallstein, 2005), 57–70.

94 See Hans Rudolf Vaget, "Das Erbe des 'Unpolitischen.' Thomas Mann und die politische Kultur Nachkriegsdeutschlands," in *Praeceptor Germaniae: Thomas Mann und die politische Kultur der Deutschen*, ed. Heinrich Oberreuter (Baden-Baden: Nomos Verlag, 2019), 101–20.

95 "Ansprache im Goethejahr," *GW* XI, 481–97, 484–85.

government-staged welcome, no criticism of him was allowed to surface. In Frankfurt, located in the Federal Republic of Germany, Mann encountered a rather mixed reception. The atmosphere in postwar West Germany remained filled with open and hidden resentment of Thomas Mann, now a proud US citizen, who was viewed by many as the mouthpiece of the victorious new superpower. Mann's relationship to West Germany remained fraught because he remained convinced that under the leadership of Chancellor Konrad Adenauer (1876–1967; 1949–1963) denazification did not nearly go far enough.

Shortly after his reencounter with Germany, Mann wrote to his friend Theodor W. Adorno (1903–1969), his musical advisor on *Doctor Faustus*, who had returned to the University of Frankfurt, from which he had been barred as a young academic: "As for me, no ten horses could drag me to Germany."[96] When the post-FDR United States changed its course from antifascism to anticommunism, Mann decided to leave America. But instead of "coming home," he returned to the land of his first exile, Switzerland, where he died on August 12, 1955, as an American citizen.

Reception

As stated previously, there is no way to reliably gauge how many Germans listened to Mann's radio addresses, let alone gauge their impact on those who did listen, given the ephemerality of the medium of radio and that doing so was a punishable crime. We do have some indication, however, even if scant, of reactions to the published editions of the addresses. Uncharacteristic of Mann's books, but not surprising considering the historical circumstances, neither *Listen, Germany!* (1943) nor *Deutsche Hörer!* (1945) drew many reviews. Of the few we know, three are worthy of note.

Writing in the *Yale Review*, Sigmund Neumann (1904–1962) discusses both Mann's *Listen, Germany!* and the star American journalist Dorothy Thompson's (1893–1961) book of letters to a fictitious German friend, *Listen, Hans!*[97] emphasizing the extraordinary importance in the

---

96 Letter to Adorno, dated July 1, 1950, in Theodore W. Adorno and Thomas Mann, *Correspondence 1943–1955*, eds. Christoph Gödde and Thomas Sprecher, trans. Nicholas Walker (Malden, MA: Polity, 2006), 61.

97 Dorothy Thompson, *Listen, Hans!* (Boston: Houghton-Mifflin, 1942). Thompson was a staunch antifascist who had conducted a prominent interview with Hitler even before he became dictator—*I Saw Hitler* (New York: Farrar and Rinehart, 1932)—and had been expelled from Germany in 1934. In somewhat of a parallel to Mann's addresses, the "letters" in *Listen, Hans!* had been broadcast in weekly installments by CBS in the spring and summer of 1942. Though aimed at a different audience, they have in common with Mann's addresses the intent to inform about the evils of Nazism, counter Nazi propaganda, and encourage resistance. Mann and Thompson had personal and professional contacts; in a 1934 review of his novel *The Tales of Jacob* she had saluted him as "The Most Eminent

ongoing war of "the second front of civilian morale."[98] He notes the religious coloring of Mann's addresses and the voice of despair that speaks from them, but also the disdain of a prophet whose warnings have been ignored. Neumann admires the "strong moral fiber, the uncompromising clarity and serenity" of Mann's "revolt against the world of Hitler" in what he sees as the broadly educational effort to return Germany to a "dignified place in the Western world."[99]

In a terse review for *The Nation*, the highly regarded ethicist and theologian Reinhold Niebuhr takes a much more critical view of Mann's radio talks. He acknowledges the "eloquent scorn of a great humanist for the Nazis and all their works."[100] But he expresses strong doubts about the efficacy of the talks, given their tone and lack of empathy: "Dr. Mann frequently allows himself to taunt the German people for their political ineptness and docility. His taunts may be justified, but that does not make them helpful to a people facing such desperate alternatives." Niebuhr points out that Mann's prediction that after defeat "the vindictiveness of the whole world will break loose" against all Germans actually strikes the same note as Goebbels and is therefore unhelpful as anti-Nazi propaganda. He brands as "naïve" Mann's grasp of the "tragic realities of history," specifically the "dilemma" that "millions of anti-Nazis in Germany" face as they contemplate the German defeat. "The most stouthearted among them still find defeat preferable to victory and continued enslavement. But it is idle to regard this choice as an easy one."

This criticism came as a shock to Mann because the previous year Niebuhr had reviewed his political writings in *Order of the Day* very favorably.[101] Mann had made Niebuhr's acquaintance in 1939 when he premiered his lecture, "The Problem of Freedom," at the Union Theological Seminary in New York in the presence of both Niebuhr and Paul Tillich (1886–1965), another theological luminary. Thereafter, Mann and Niebuhr had cooperated at the landmark "City of Man" conference in Atlantic City in May 1940. Writing to Agnes Meyer, Mann tried to persuade himself that the malevolence of Niebuhr's review of *Listen, Germany!* was caused by his own failure to acknowledge Niebuhr's review of *Order of the Day*: "Such human failings

---

Living Man of Letters." Dorothy Thompson, "The Most Eminent Living Man of Letters. Thomas Mann Gives an Old Tale Beauty and Significance," *New York Herald Tribune*, June 10, 1934, Books section, 1.

98 Sigmund Neumann, "To the Other Germany," *Yale Review* 32 (1943): 594–97.

99 Ibid.

100 Reinhold Niebuhr, "Mann Speaks to Germany," *The Nation* 156, July 13, 1943, 244.

101 Reinhold Niebuhr, "Mann's Political Essays," *The Nation*, November 28, 1942, 582–84.

always come back to haunt you."[102] Yet there are reasons to believe that Mann took Niebuhr's criticism to heart and saw its validity, because in the ensuing addresses to the German people we find more signs of empathy, as they take, broadly speaking, a more educational turn.

Finally, an anonymous and sympathetic reviewer of the German-language edition of *Deutsche Hörer!* in a Swiss newspaper, Basel's *National-Zeitung*, took an intriguingly comparative look at Mann's radio messages. Characterizing him as a political "agitator" in the positive sense, the reviewer asserts that the feeling of revulsion that Hitler evokes in anyone steeped in European thought has perhaps never been expressed with greater rhetorical power than here. In this regard the reviewer draws an enlightening parallel to the imposing French writer Victor Hugo (1802–1885), who during his eighteen years of self-imposed exile in reaction to Napoleon III's (1808–1873) coup d'état in December of 1851, hurled poisonous invectives and denunciations at the French emperor with uncompromising severity. Like Hugo's inspired polemics, Mann's antifascist radio addresses should, in the final analysis, according to this reviewer, best be viewed as "châtiments," Victor Hugo's own label for his polemics, that is to say, as castigations of a corrupt and criminal regime by an exile of unimpeachable moral authority.[103]

A final observation: *Deutsche Hörer!* failed to do what it unrealistically had set out to achieve—to foment the overthrow of the Nazi dictatorship by the Germans themselves. It also failed in its unrealistic desire to shorten the war by even one day, to reduce the sacrifices of the countries attacked and occupied by Germany, and to mitigate the suffering of those Germans who sat in their bomb shelters while their houses were reduced to ruins. And yet Mann's radio talks during the Second World War deserve an honorable mention in the cultural memories of both Germany and the US. They exemplify an essential feature of Mann's identity as a writer: his outsize sense of responsibility for the political soundness of the land of his birth, the land of the culture that formed him. He acknowledged that bond most memorably in the Bonn manifesto, as he broke with the disastrous course that Germany was taking and prepared the way for going to war against her. He asserted the "mutually educational bond between nation and author"—a bond that is "delicate and of high importance," yet indestructible.[104] Such sense of responsibility is abundantly manifest in Mann's radio addresses to the German people in both their castigating and educational modes. They are impressive testimony to his own high-minded notion of what it means to be a writer in the world in which one lives.

---

102 Letter to Agnes Meyer, dated February 17, 1943, BrAM, 464–65.
103 Anon., "Thomas Mann als Agitator," *National-Zeitung*, Basel, December 7, 1945.
104 *The Order of the Day*, 108; translation adjusted.

Foreword to the Book Edition of 1943[1]

Thomas Mann

In the autumn of 1940 the British Broadcasting Corporation approached me with a request to broadcast regularly short messages over their system to my compatriots, commenting on the events of the war, with the purpose of endeavoring to influence the German public in the direction of the convictions that I have often uttered.

I believed that I should not miss the opportunity of making contact, however loose and precarious, with the German people and also with the inhabitants of the subjugated territories, behind the back of the Nazi Government, which had deprived me of all means of exerting intellectual influence in Germany as soon as it had the power to do so. The suggestion was particularly attractive because my words were not to be broadcast from America by short wave, but from London by long or medium wave, and thus could be heard on the only type of radio the German people were permitted to have. It was also enticing to write German once again in the knowledge that the written words would be allowed to fulfill their purpose in the form in which they were conceived—in German. I agreed to send monthly messages, and after a few trials I asked for a prolongation of my speaking-time from five to eight minutes.

The broadcasts at first were transmitted in this way: I cabled my texts to London, where they were read by a German-speaking employee of the BBC. At my suggestion, a more complicated but more direct and therefore more attractive method was soon adopted. Whatever I have to say is now recorded by the Recording Department of the NBC in Los Angeles; the record is sent to New York by air mail, and is then transferred by telephone to another record in London, where it is played before the microphone. In this way not only my words but my own voice is heard by those over there who dare to listen.

More people listen than one might expect, not only in Switzerland and in Sweden, but also in Holland, in the Czech "Protectorate," and in Germany proper, as has been frequently proved by the most strangely

---

1   Thomas Mann, *Listen, Germany! Twenty-five Radio Messages to the German People over BBC* (New York: Alfred A. Knopf, 1943), v–viii. Thomas Mann himself rendered this foreword into English.

coded replies from these countries. By roundabout ways such replies, indeed, come even from Germany. Evidently there are people in this occupied territory whose hunger and thirst for free speech are so great that they brave the dangers connected with listening to foreign broadcasts. The most striking proof that this is so—proof which is amusing and disgusting at the same time—is provided by the fact that my allocutions have been referred to, in an unmistakable fashion, by my Führer himself, in a beer-hall speech in Munich, in the course of which he mentioned me as one of those who attempt to incite the German people against him and his system. But these rabble-rousers, he roared, were greatly mistaken: the German people were not that way, and to the extent that they were that way, they were, thank God, behind lock and key. — So much filth has come out of this mouth that it causes me slight feelings of nausea to hear my name come from it. Yet the utterance is valuable to me though its lack of logic is evident. Often the Führer has expressed his contempt for the German people and his conviction of the cowardice, submissiveness, and stupidity of these people, of their infinite ability to swallow lies; he forgot, though, each time to add an explanation of how he succeeds simultaneously in seeing the Germans as a master race destined to world domination. How can a nation spiritually incapable of ever revolting *even against him* be a master race? I beg the hero to examine this question some day between planning one battle and the next.

Perhaps he is right in his confidence that the German nation "is not that way"—he has always been most revolting when he was right. Moreover, to call a people to revolt does not yet mean to believe, deep down in one's heart, in their ability to revolt. What I believe unshakably is that Hitler cannot win his war—this is a belief based much more on metaphysical and moral reasons than on military ones, and wherever I express it in the following pages it is completely sincere. But far be it from me to wish to fortify thereby the dangerous conception that the victory of the United Nations[2] is self-evident and assured, and that in view of this self-evidence and this certainty one can afford not only every mistake, but also every division of the will, every half-heartedness, every "political" reservation concerning one's allies and the kind of peace to be gained. One can

---

2 In *Deutsche Hörer*, Mann uses the English term "United Nations" in speaking of the allies. The charter for the international organization the United Nations was adopted by fifty nations on June 26, 1945, in San Francisco, and the charter took effect and the UN came into being on October 24, 1945. However, the name for the successor organization to the League of Nations had long been a part of political debates, especially after the so-called ARCADIA Conference in Washington (December 22, 1941–January 14, 1942). This event, in which Roosevelt and Churchill both participated, was specifically dedicated to plans for this future world organization.

afford *nothing*, nothing at all any longer after all that has been omitted and committed in the past. After all, this war could have been prevented, and the fact itself that it had to come is a heavy moral mortgage on our side. The war has sinister antecedents, whose determining motives are by no means dead, but continue to work underground, endangering the peace and with it the victory. We shall lose the war if we wage a wrong war and not the right one, which is a war of the peoples for their liberty.

September 15, 1942

Translators' Note

Jeffrey L. High and Elaine Chen

THE FOLLOWING TRANSLATION of Thomas Mann's *Deutsche Hörer!* radio addresses is based on the reading edition of *Deutsche Hörer!* published by S. Fischer Verlag in 1987. In keeping with H. T. Lowe-Porter's dictum in the preface to her translation of Thomas Mann's *Buddenbrooks* to transfer "the spirit first and the letter so far as it might be," we have made every effort to render Mann's prose as faithfully as is prudent while privileging the author's characteristic spirit and style. His style will appear at times as unusual in English as it does in the original German, including Mann's rhetorically distinct code-switching between innovation, allusions to relevant stylistic precedents, and intentionally platitudinous expressions. We have made every effort to maintain elements of Mann's idiosyncratic and innovative uses of syntax—including long and complicated sentences, paratactic lists and appositions without the use of "and," frequent commas, semi-colons, and *Gedankenstriche* (here rendered as em-dashes)—and a characteristic preponderance of neologisms.

The translation of Mann's word creations result in English terms as unprecedented as the originals, including, e.g., "Gassenhistoriker," or "populist gutter historians"; "Hysterikerklaue," or "this hysteric's clenched claw"; and "Propagandageblök," or "propaganda-bleating." His texts present particular challenges in achieving a faithful balance between consistency and contextual flexibility in the cases of a number of his preferred terms. Two of the most systemic challenges have been translations of Mann's use of singular nouns that imply plural possessive pronouns (e.g., Germany/it/its/their), his frequent use of the noun "Mensch," and his repeated description of the Nazis as "Abenteurer," literally "adventurers." "Mensch," although grammatically a masculine noun in German, is a gender-inclusive term meaning "human being" or "person" more often than the historical English default translation "man." As a masculine noun, "Mensch" requires masculine pronouns in German, which are nonetheless gender-neutral in their meaning to the German ear. In these cases, the pronouns for "human being" are rendered as "they/their" throughout, in an effort to retain the inclusivity of the term "Mensch," and to avoid a slavish convention that makes as little sense as rendering the pronouns of "obedience" (*der Gehorsam*) as "he/him/his." In other cases, the challenge lies in rendering Mann's distinctive word choices; e.g., his use of the term "Abenteurer" to describe the Nazis implies at once some combination of "adventurer," "carpetbagger," and "freebooter," and has been translated here as "marauder" throughout. Among the many colorful adjectives Mann employs in his description of the Nazis and their crimes, those requiring particular contextual flexibility include descriptions of behaviors that are "himmelschreiend" (unholy, outrageous, abominable) and acts of "Verhunzung" (defilement) that "zum Himmel schreien" (cry out to heaven). We have maintained Mann's nuanced usages of "America" and "the United States," have translated both the continent and the concept of "Europa" as "Europe" throughout, and have adjusted Mann's usages of the terms "United Kingdom," "Great Britain," "British," "England," and "English" to conform with English-language conventions.

Except in those cases where authoritative translations already exist, translations of texts by other authors cited by Mann are our own, and in the case of his frequent translations or paraphrases of English texts into German we have supplied references to or cited the originals, or provided Mann's German renderings and paraphrases in the annotations.

We have had the good fortune of being permitted to access the annotations to *Deutsche Hörer!* in the forthcoming vol. 18 of Fischer Verlag's *Große Kommentierte Frankfurter Ausgabe*, edited by Kai Sina and Hans Rudolf Vaget, in drafting our own more concise annotations, as appropriate for an edition meant for less specialized readers. The annotations provide necessary historical and biographical context for Mann's discussions of the events of the war.

Figure 1. Members of the Mann family at Pacific Palisades, California, 1945. From left: Frido Mann (1940–); Thomas Mann's wife Katia Mann (1883–1980); Frido Mann's younger brother, Toni Mann (1942–); Thomas Mann. TMA_3072 - ETH-Bibliothek Zürich, Thomas-Mann-Archiv / Photograph by Florence Homolka. Public domain.

Figure 2. Erika Mann (1905–1969) with her father Thomas Mann in Los Angeles. *Los Angeles Daily News* Negatives, UCLA Library Special Collections. Public domain, Creative Commons Attribution 4.0 license.

Figure 3. 1936 poster featuring the Volksempfänger ("people's radio"), advertising that "All of Germany hears the Führer with the people's radio." Courtesy of Bundesarchiv (German Federal Archive), Plak 003-022-025 / Designer: Leonid.

Fig. 4: The old NBC building (1938–1964) at the corner of Sunset Boulevard and Vine Street in Hollywood, California, where Thomas Mann recorded his addresses. Photograph by the Works Progress Administration, 1938. © Works Progress Administration Collection, Los Angeles Public Library, used by permission.

Figure 5. The BBC Broadcasting House, bombed on 15 October 1940, was one of the buildings that the Luftwaffe specifically targeted during the Blitz. BBC Broadcasting House: Bomb Damage, 1940 © BBC.

Figure 6. First German edition of *Deutsche Hörer!* (Frankfurt am Main: S. Fischer Verlag, 1942). Photo from Wikimedia Commons, by H.-P. Haack, Antiquariat Dr. Haack, Leipzig.

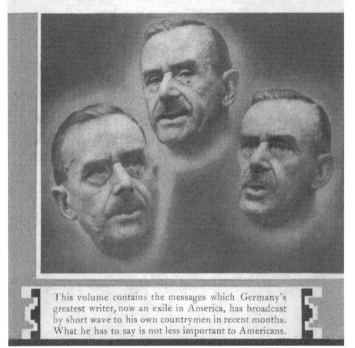

Figure 7. The 1943 English edition of *Listen, Germany!* (New York: Alfred A. Knopf, 1943). Courtesy of Professor Tobias Boes.

Figure 8. The second, expanded German edition of *Deutsche Hörer!* (Frankfurt am Main: S. Fischer Verlag, 1945). Photo from Wikimedia Commons, H.-P. Haack, Antiquariat Dr. Haack, Leipzig.

Figure 9. Thomas Mann at radio station WQXR in New York in 1937. Photograph by Eric Schaal, Porträtaufnahme Thomas Mann, 1937, New York © Wallstein Verlag

Figure 10. Thomas Mann working at his desk in Pacific Palisades, 1945. Library of Congress LC-USZ62-57783.

The Addresses

1940

October 1940

German Listeners!
A German author speaks to you, whose work and person are outlawed by your rulers, and whose books—even when they deal with the most German matters, with Goethe for example—can only speak to foreign, free peoples, in their languages—while they must remain silent and unknown to you. My works will return to you someday, this I know, even if I myself no longer can. As long as I live, however, and even as a citizen of the New World, I will be a German, and will suffer under the fate of Germany, and under everything that Germany has inflicted on the world for the past seven years, morally and physically, through the will of criminal, violent brutes. During these years, the unshakeable conviction that this can come to no good end has time and again inspired me to deliver words of warning, some of which, I believe, have reached your ears.[1] In the present state of war it has become impossible for the written word to penetrate the rampart that tyranny has erected around you. Therefore, I gladly embrace the opportunity offered to me by the British authorities to report to you from time to time on what I see here, in America, the great and free nation in which I have found a home.

When five months ago German troops invaded Holland,[2] and when, in Rotterdam, bombs took the lives of tens of thousands of human beings within a few minutes, the editor of the American magazine *Life*, an illustrated magazine that otherwise never takes positions on political questions, and which everyone reads, wrote: "This is the greatest challenge that America has faced as a land of freedom in eighty years ... Powerful, nefarious military nations have attacked what is our American way of life ... Whether we will ever have to stand armed and fight alongside Great Britain, we do not yet know; but this much we do know, that Great

---

1   Mann's *Ein Briefwechsel* (A Correspondence, 1937) was his first published indictment of the Nazi regime. It was written in Zurich after his exile and circulated in Germany as covert letters.
2   On May 10, 1940, the Wehrmacht began its western offensive against Holland, Belgium, Luxembourg, and France.

Britain's fight is also in a very deep sense our own."[3] That was the conviction then, after the tenth of May, and that is the conviction still today. That is what the workers and the business people, the Republicans and the Democrats, the supporters of Roosevelt and the supporters of his opponent believe. Little remains of the old America that believed that it was capable of living for itself, without any need for concern about the world beyond the ocean.[4] What brought about this deep transformation? You know very well. One hundred and thirty million benevolent, friendly people live in this country. They want to work and to build in peace. They actively engage with the major questions, which they address collectively, as each sees fit. War, conquest of foreign lands, alliances, axes, secret meetings, the breaking of treaties seem unnecessary and insane to them. But then along come their newspapers and radio reporters and tell them what is happening in Europe. How in Norway, in Holland, Belgium, Poland, Bohemia, how everywhere the picture is the same, how German troops that no one invited are stationed in these countries—countries that have in no way provoked them—and oppress and plunder them. And how those who love their fatherland and don't want to forge weapons for the foreign intruder are shot dead as criminals. Of course, an American is above all an American citizen; however, it is often so that they or their father or grandfather were born in Norway, in Holland, in Belgium, in the Danish Protectorate, in the General Governorate of the Occupied Polish Regions, and the Protectorate of Bohemia and Moravia,[5] that they still have relatives in

---

3   The original text of June 3, 1940, written by politically engaged *Life* editor Henry R. Luce (1898–1967), reads as follows: "America is now confronted by a greater challenge to its survival as a land of liberty than any it has had to face in eighty years ... The American way of life is bitterly opposed by mighty and ruthless military nations ... We may never fight side by side, comrades in arms of France and Britain. But we know now that, fundamentally, their struggle is our struggle." Henry R. Luce, "America and Armageddon: Henry R. Luce, Editor of *Life*, Defines the Challenge to the Democratic Way of Life," *Life: America and the World* (June 3, 1940), 40 and 100, 40.

4   Mann refers here to an article in *Life* of May 27, 1940, "50,000 Airplanes: U.S. to Multiply Fleets and Factories" (83–93), which documents the outrage in the US over the German blitzkrieg against the Low Countries. Contrary to what Mann suggests here, the debate between isolationists and interventionists about American involvement in Europe continued until the US entered the war in December 1941 after the Japanese attack on Pearl Harbor.

5   The General Governorate for the Occupied Polish Region and the Protectorate of Bohemia and Moravia were occupational administrative zones established by the National Socialist regime after the invasion of the Czech lands in March 1939 and Poland in September 1939. On April 9, 1940, the National Socialists invaded Denmark, establishing the Danish Protectorate, which became

one of these countries and hold fond memories of it. And even if this were not the case—even then, indeed especially then—if their family comes from Germany,[6] then, as a straight-thinking human being, they nonetheless have to be outraged by all the injustice, all the violence that they hear of. No, I have not found any difference between German-Americans and Anglo-Americans and Italian-Americans. All of them feel that this is not the right way to unite Europe, and that, sooner or later, so many criminal acts will necessarily result in retribution.

Thus the American citizen has above all three hopes. The first is America itself, its tremendous economic power, its good and proven leaders. The second is Great Britain. It may be that the Americans previously looked upon the British with some mockery. One deemed them tired, overrefined. Today however, in light of the defense of London,[7] there is only one voice of common admiration. Great Britain carries the banner of freedom. It speaks and it fights for all of the suffering peoples who resist only in secret;[8] that is why the wish to help Great Britain is so great here. The third, unfortunately no longer very strong, hope rests upon the German people. Will the Germans not finally realize, so people ask themselves here, that with their victories they only tread further into an endless quagmire? That, if their soldiers now invade three more countries, their U-boats sink three more ships filled with refugee children,[9] if they drive still more people into misery, exile, and suicide, and bring down the hatred of the world upon themselves, that still brings them no closer to the desired end? That there exist far better paths to the end that we all desire: a just peace for the entire world?

---

an occupational dictatorship on August 29, 1943. All three of these countries were occupied until 1945.

6   In a 1942 broadcast, Mann addressed Americans of German descent in order to convince them of the importance of America's fight against Nazi Germany. See pages 64–66 in the present volume.

7   During the Battle of Britain (July to October 1940), the German Luftwaffe intensively bombarded London, Birmingham, and Coventry in an unsuccessful attempt to force Great Britain to surrender.

8   In his December 1940 radio address "Gruß an Norwegen" ("Greetings to Norway"), Mann employs similar rhetoric in an appeal to the Norwegian people to continue the fight against the occupation.

9   During the war, German submarines routinely attacked passenger ships in the North Atlantic, under the pretense that they were transporting weapons. One ship, the *SS City of Benares*, which was evacuating ninety children from Britain to Canada, was sunk on September 17, 1940 while en route from Liverpool to Montreal. Also on board were Mann's daughter Monika (1910–1992) and her husband, the art historian Jenö Lányi (1902–1940). Of the 408 people on board, 258 perished, including Lányi.

November 1940

German Listeners!
The reelection of Franklin D. Roosevelt as President of the United States is an event of the very highest order,[10] possibly decisive for the future of the world, and so it has also undoubtedly been received by those in Europe who have acted as if they considered the election and its result to be a purely domestic American affair. In Roosevelt, the destroyers of Europe and the desecrators of the rights of nations see their most powerful adversary, and rightly so. He is the representative of democracy at war, the true bearer of a new, socially bound idea of freedom, and the statesman who, arguably all along, distinguished most clearly between peace and appeasement.[11] In our age of masses, which as such is connected with the concept of a Führer, the task fell to America to bring forth the happy phenomenon of a modern Führer of the masses who wants goodness and intellectual engagement, that which is truly progressive, peace and freedom; and Great Britain's heroic resistance against the most infamous tyranny that has ever threatened the world, this resistance, for which admiration here grows daily, gives Roosevelt time to mobilize the tremendous, latent power of his country in the struggle for the future.

This will be a protracted struggle, nobody harbors any illusions about it. But the longer it goes on, the more certain is its outcome. The depraved marauders who pursue the enslavement of the world can sense at bottom that they have already gambled away the moment—they sense it as deeply as their muzzled peoples, who are held in a state of terror through a series of pathetic sham successes. Nobody in the world believes that the German people approve of their oppressors' monumentalist strivings, which amount to a miserable humbuggery of blood and tears. Their leaders, it goes without saying, feign confidence. In a speech of particularly pathological hypocrisy that Hitler recently held in his Munich coup-cellar,[12] he assured you that the highest military authorities in Germany

---

10 Per the BBC's request, Mann regularly begins his speeches with references to current events in politics. On November 5, 1940, Franklin D. Roosevelt (1882–1945) was elected to office for the third time by a large majority (449 to 82 votes in the electoral college), beginning a norm-breaking third term in office, which was later followed by a fourth.

11 Neville Chamberlain (1869–1940), the British Prime Minister from 1937 to 1940, hoped to reach a compromise with Adolf Hitler (1889–1945). His policy of appeasement culminated in the Munich Agreement of September 30, 1938, forcing Czechoslovakia to cede the German-speaking Sudetenland to Germany. Mann perceived this agreement as a betrayal of Czechoslovakia, a democracy that he admired and that had granted him citizenship in 1936.

12 Mann is referring here to Hitler's November 8, 1940 speech in Munich's Löwenbräukeller on the occasion of the anniversary of the so-called Hitler Putsch on November 9, 1923, which had actually taken place in the Bürgerbräukeller.

consider victory to be certain. In the first place, it is bizarre that he invokes a higher authority than his own. Is he not Caesar, Frederick the Great, and Napoleon all in one, and Charlemagne on top of that? The populist gutter historians of National Socialism have provided him, the pathetic historical imposter, with a script to read in black and white. How can he fall so far out of his role that he invokes the judgment of the same generals who merely execute his inspired visions?—But not all of these generals are mere gray-haired cadets and narrow-minded engineers of the military moment. I was told the story of how a German high officer in Paris said to a group of Frenchmen: "Pauvre France maintenant. Pauvre Allemagne—plus tard!"[13] He could not speak much French, but it was enough for him to make himself understood: and I am convinced that it is enough to make large numbers of the German people understand.

What is to become of the European continent, what of Germany itself, we all ask ourselves here, if the war lasts three, if it lasts five more years; and, without any doubt the German people, in horror, ask themselves the same. The misery that already prevails provides only a faint glimpse of that which must follow. And why must this follow? Because a handful of stupid criminals is exploiting the process of economic and social transformation, in which our world finds itself, in pursuit of a senseless and anachronistic Alexandrian march of world conquest?[14] Yes, for this reason alone. What must and will result from the conclusion of this war is clear. It is the beginning of a world federation; the creation of a new equilibrium between freedom and equality; the safeguarding of individual values as part of the promotion of collective life; the dismantling of national state sovereignty and the establishment of a society of free yet collectively responsible nations with equal rights and equal obligations. Our nations are ready for such a reorganization of the world. If they were not ready twenty-two years ago[15]—then the experiences of the last decade have made them ready for it. However, they are probably more ready for it today than they will be after the destruction, after the pestilential and devastating effects of a war lasting many years. If we were to end this war today and to proceed to the common task at hand—there would be no people whose prospects for a happier future would not be better than if we were to allow it to continue.

13   "Poor France now. Poor Germany—later!" The origin of the anecdote is not documented.
14   Mann alludes to the ten-year campaign of the Macedonian king Alexander the Great (356–323 BCE).
15   Mann is referring to the signing of the Treaty of Versailles on June 28, 1919.

The German people must and will take their "place in the sun" in the world that is to come.[16] If, however, they continue to obey their seducers, passively and actively, through thick and thin, then they will realize too late that a people does not take its place in the sun by shrouding the world in night and horror. Away with the agents of ruin! Away with the National Socialist defilers and tormentors of Europe! I know that I am only giving voice to the deepest longing of the German people themselves when I call to them: Peace! Peace and Freedom!

December 1940

Germans—The Christmas celebration comes once again, a beloved celebration, a celebration of love, and the dearest to you, a celebration filled with light and fragrance and childhood dreams. One is tempted to call it the most German of all celebrations, and it is likely that no people celebrates it with such fervor as do you. Why? Possibly, because, in its cosmic and spiritual profoundness, it is a symbol of your becoming a people, and because it mirrors the history of your becoming civilized. In the prehistoric heathen-Germanic times, it was the celebration of the winter solstice,[17] the rebirth of the light from winter night, the dawning of a new day in the world. Then, however, the young light became the child in the cradle, in the manger of Bethlehem; the festival became the birthday of the Son of Man and savior, whose great and tender heart brought a new feeling of humanity, a new morality to the world, who called his father in heaven the father of all human beings, and in whose annunciation the tribal god of the Jewish people rose anew as the transcendent-spiritual and all-loving god of the universe.

The history of this celebration is your history. There was no Germandom before the light in the East appeared also for you, before Christian humanity penetrated the Germanic-pagan primal state, and united your moral and spiritual sensibility with Christian-occidental civilization. You belong to this community, you celebrate your membership in it when you set up the manger of the sun-child beneath the tree of lights and place images of the shepherds and kings who pray to him around it. You celebrate, too, the glorious contributions that the German spirit has made to and by virtue of Christian-occidental culture: the works of Dürer

---

16 In a Reichstag debate on December 6, 1897, Bernhard von Bülow (1849–1929), Secretary of State for Foreign Affairs, used the image of a "Platz an der Sonne" to justify the expansion of Germany's colonial policy under Wilhelm II.

17 Mann traces the progress of Northern European civilization from the Scandinavian festival of the winter solstice, or Yule, to the German Christian celebration of humanity and morality embodied in Christmas. By contrast, the National Socialists attempted to define Christmas exclusively in terms of a quasi-mythical Germanic tradition.

and Bach, the freedom poems of your Schiller,[18] Goethe's *Iphigenie*, *Fidelio*, the *Ninth Symphony*.[19]

Now you prepare yourselves again to observe the Christian, the German festival—for the second time during the war that your present Führers have imposed upon you and the world—many of you in mourning for sons and fathers who perished in attacks on neighboring peoples, certainly with anguished hearts, all of you, at the thought of how long all of this yet should last, where all of this yet should lead. You set the table of presents—it will be in a miserable state, because good things are not procurable, even though your masters have plundered the devastated continent in your name. Yet the Christmas candles burn. I would like to ask you, how, reflected in their light, do the deeds appear to you that your Führers have led you as a nation to commit over the past year, the acts of insane violence and destruction in which they have artfully made you complicit, all of the atrocities that they have piled high in your name, the unfathomable misery and human suffering that National Socialist Germany, that is to say: a Germany that is now allowed to be neither German nor Christian, has spread all around itself. Would you tell me how the beautiful old songs that you now sing with your children harmonize with these deeds, songs themselves filled with the feelings of childhood—or do you no longer sing them? Have you been ordered to sing, instead of "Silent Night," the bloody party anthem,[20] a cross between a headline in a local rag and a substandard pop song, lies that some outlandish ne'er-do-well offers up to a mythical hero? If so, I have no doubt that you would obey, because your obedience knows no limits, and, I just want you to know, with each passing day, your obedience becomes more unforgivable.

Unending and unforgivable is your trust, that is to say, your credulity. You believe a miserable historical swindler and pseudo-conqueror that through him and through you a world dawns, in which it is all over for any values that not only make the Christian a Christian, but even simply make the human being a human being; for truth, freedom, and justice. You believe him that he is the man of the millennia, come to take Christ's seat, and to displace the doctrine of the redeemer of human brotherhood

---

18 Mann is probably referring less to the poetry than to the dramas, for example, *Don Carlos* (1787) and *William Tell* (1804).

19 Here, Mann refers to: painter Albrecht Dürer (1471–1528); composer Johann Sebastian Bach (1685–1750); author Friedrich Schiller (1759–1805); the tragedy *Iphigenie auf Tauris* (1779) by Johann Wolfgang von Goethe (1749–1832); and the opera *Fidelio* (1805) and the *Ninth Symphony* (1824) by composer Ludwig van Beethoven (1770–1827).

20 "The Horst Wessel Song" was initially used as the battle song of the SA, later as the party anthem for the NSDAP. The author of the song's lyrics, Wessel (1907–1930), was a member of the SA. He was shot by a communist in 1930 and subsequently glorified as a martyr in Nazi propaganda.

under God with the doctrine of violence that murders bodies and souls. You believe him, that you are the master race that is chosen to bring forth a so-called 'new order,'[21] in which all other peoples have to toil for you as slaves. And as slaves of his wretched fanaticism you carry on fighting like berserkers for this horrendous 'new order,' for a world, then, in which observing the Christmas celebration, the celebration of peace and love, would be a much worse falsehood and blasphemy than it already is today. What you believe above all, however, is that it would be the end of the German people, that it would be over for you forever, if you did not 'triumph,' that is, if you did not follow an infamous demoniac through thick and thin to the extreme—to an extreme that will look like anything but a victory. He tells you that, so that you consider your fate to be indissolubly bound to his own—which, to be sure, is sealed, if, as can be predicted with certainty, his well-laid plans fail. Oblivion will be the mildest fate to befall his name in this more than likely case. But you? Should it be your end, the end of Germandom, if not he, but reason and human decency, should carry the day? It will be the new beginning of Germandom, its winter solstice, new hope, new happiness, and new life! In the order of nations, for which the socially rejuvenated Great Britain fights,[22] and fighting at her side a world armed with rich resources,[23] an order of justice, of common welfare, and of responsible freedom for all, you will be assigned the place you are worthy of—that "place in the sun" that you cannot conquer by engulfing the world in night and terror.

Completely different possibilities for personal development and the satisfaction of your deepest spiritual needs would be offered to you in *this* new order, in contrast to this world of servitude in which you are expected to play the role of supreme servant: the satisfaction for example of the very German need to be loved. Do you not know that beneath all the crimes to which you have been seduced this deep wish remains ever alive: to be loved? Do you not know that it does not make you happy in the very least, that it is in principle a horror and a desperate misery for you to play the villain of humanity?

---

21   Mann is referring here to a speech of July 25, 1940 given by Walther Funk (1890–1960), Reich Minister of Economics and President of the German Reichsbank. In that speech, Funk outlines his ideas about restructuring Europe after a National Socialist victory.

22   Mann appears to be referring to the revitalization of the Labour Party under the leadership of Clement Attlee (1883–1967) during the 1935 elections.

23   Winston Churchill (1874–1965), who succeeded Chamberlain as British Prime Minister on May 10, 1940, campaigned intensively with Roosevelt for US armaments and supplies in the struggle against European fascism. In March 1941, the US Congress passed the Lend-Lease Act, which promised comprehensive support to Great Britain as well as to the USSR and China, thus making the United States a de facto participant in the war.

Germans, save yourselves! Save your souls by renouncing your oppressors, who think only of themselves and not of you; renounce your belief in them and your obedience to them! I live in the world from which you are cut off, even though you belong to it, and I know, and I am telling you: Never will this world tolerate nor suffer the 'new order,' the subhuman utopia of terror, for which your seducers let you bleed and wither away. These great Christian peoples will never accept that the peace for which even you long should be a peace over the graves of freedom and human dignity. In the coming years, you can, if you so choose, increase by tenfold the misery that you have already caused out of obedience and credulity, but in the end, measure for measure, it will be your own misery, and how things will look, how things will unfold in Germany at the end of this outrage, no one wants to imagine.

It is Christmas, people of Germany. Let yourselves be moved and outraged by the meaning of the bells when they proclaim peace, peace on Earth!

1941

February 1941

German Listeners!
The most recent address by the German head of state in the Berlin Sportpalast made a particularly repugnant impression in America[1]—not so much through its content, which was of the lowest rank of wretchedness and only proved the incapacity of this defective brain to make any useful contribution to the burning questions of the day, but much more through its mirth, the unhealthy cheerfulness that rang from it, and which was evidently the main reason why in Great Britain, too, the address was perceived as "paranoic," as insane. "Hitler frequently made jokes," wrote the American press. "There were more bursts of laughter than there usually are when he delivers an address." What was the nature of these witty remarks? "A British politician calculated," said the Conqueror, "that I had made seven mistakes in the year 1940. I made 724 mistakes, but my opponents made four-million-three-hundred-and-eighty-five-thousand."—Unsurpassable. The centuries will pass on this humoristic treasure from one to the next, along with the other gems that unleashed the howls of delight of the Myrmidons who filled the Sportpalast[2]—provided only that a human sense of shame does not prevent it. For is there not really something excruciatingly offensive to one's sense of shame, something idiotic-obscene about being so funny under the world-circumstances of the present, for which Herr Hitler may understand himself to be blameworthy as their originator? Truly, now is exactly the right moment to make crappy jokes! Misery and sorrow, the hunting down of human beings, homelessness, despair and suicide, blood and tears fill the Earth. Nations of proud history,[3] whom humankind has much to thank for, and who

---

1   On January 30, 1941, Hitler spoke at the Berliner Sportpalast on the eighth anniversary of the National Socialists' "Machtergreifung" (rise to power; January 30, 1933).

2   The Myrmidons were an ancient Greek tribe from Thessaly that derived its origin from the mythological King Myrmidon, a son of Zeus, who transformed himself into an ant to seduce Eurymedusa. In Homer's *Iliad*, Book XVI, Achilles commands an army of Myrmidons, "ant warriors," who obey him unconditionally. In more recent usage, the word refers to those charged with robotic and brutal execution of orders.

3   Mann means France, the Netherlands, Denmark, and Norway.

once lived in prosperity, now lie broken, defiled, and plundered. Others are engaged in a life-and-death struggle to avert this fate.[4] Still others are forced to sacrifice their freedoms for the sake of freedom itself, and to summon all of their resources in order to arm themselves for the same fight.[5] In silent dread, amid a shattered continent, threatened by starvation and famine, the German people themselves—who have lived through war and worse for eight years—await a future that promises only war, one war after another, unforeseeable war, unforeseeable abstinence from joy and therewith the hatred and curses of the world. Their Führer, however, is cracking jokes about it.

That was one thing that made the address ring so repulsively here. A further cause of disaffection has long been the laughable degree to which this character is full of himself, one that causes him to say "I" and "I" time and again, entirely oblivious to the question of whether, in the case of *his* person, this emphasis on the first-person does not amount to an insufferable aesthetic and moral tact- and tastelessness. For it is insufferable when someone, in whose skin no one wants to be, constantly says "I." Herr Hitler sees the juncture of world history that he initiated—by entering into alliances with Russia and Japan[6] and thus betraying the two basic tenets of his political religion, anti-Bolshevism and the idea of race—as a mere means to scam the entire world—he evidently sees this history from a highly personal perspective, from the perspective of his biography, the career of a swindler that he thinks is the life of a hero, and the adventurousness of which beguiles his weak mind. Would that he could be convinced that this individual, Hitler—in his unfathomable dishonesty, his sleazy savagery and vindictiveness, with his never-ending bellowing of hatred, his butchering of the German language, his shoddy fanaticism, his cowardly asceticism and pathetic artificiality, his entire defective humanity, which lacks even the slightest trace of unselfishness and a higher life of the soul—is the most repulsive figure on whom the light of history has ever fallen. At best he is a tool that the will of the world operates for purposes and goals that lie totally beyond his own dull awareness. If they are fulfilled, then this tool suitable only for destruction

---

4   Mann means Great Britain, among others.

5   Mann means the US, which had already provided massive aid to Britain through the Lend-Lease program prior to its entry into the war. Roosevelt signed that military aid program, which he had championed, into law on March 11, 1941.

6   On August 23, 1939, Germany and the Soviet Union concluded the tactical non-aggression "Molotov-Ribbentrop Pact"; in a secret additional protocol, it was agreed that Poland and the Baltic states would be divided into German and Soviet spheres of interest. On September 27, 1940, Germany, Italy, and Japan concluded a ten-year Tripartite Pact (also known as the Three Power Pact), which codified the reciprocal military support among the Axis powers.

will be thrown away and swiftly forgotten. The day of his fall, however, the day on which this angry attack dog's voice no longer echoes around the globe, on which this hysteric's clenched claw will no longer pound on the map of the world, this day will be a day for the deepest sighs of relief and of salvation for many millions. On all sides people will sink into each other's arms with tears of joy and celebrate with the clinking of glasses their liberation from this plague, from oppression by this infernal rogue. For whomever this should be the case, whose birth is both his own and the whole world's misery, he ought, if then he must indeed *exist*, at the very least not *speak* of himself.

In the course of his cheerful address, Herr Hitler called for a rally around his character when he said "some or other Herr" might indeed come along and attempt to separate the German people from him, their Führer. Whoever would make such an attempt, however, must not know the German people. By now, the character of the German people is known everywhere, and Herr Hitler tells us nothing new with his statement that, for the time being, any such attempt would be futile. The German people are not equipped with the political astuteness and critical shrewdness of the Italians, who show an unmistakable aversion to fighting for their Duce,[7] because they believe that while one can perhaps put up with villainy, one may not at the same time also be an idiot. The German people will still march for a considerable time upright and true—so long, namely, as they believe what they are told, that they will be destroyed if they do not win Hitler's war. As soon as they recognize this as a gross lie, as soon as they become aware that Hitler and his gang constitute the single obstacle to a just peace and a happier community of nations, one eager to include them, they will, without any coaxing, let Hitler be off to where he belongs.

March 1941

German Listeners!
Up until now, what I have had to say to you from afar was passed on to you by the mouths of others. This time you are hearing my own voice.[8]

It is the voice of a friend, a German voice, the voice of a Germany that has shown and will show the world a different face than the ghastly

---

7 The fascist dictator Benito Mussolini's (1883–1945) title, meaning "Führer" in Italian. Mann is alluding to Italy's military failures in the early phase of the war, which triggered growing discontent among the population and ultimately led to Mussolini's removal from power in July 1943.

8 A BBC employee, Carl Brinitzer (1907–1974), recorded the first four of Mann's addresses. At the author's request, the BBC switched to broadcasting audio that Mann himself recorded at the NBC studio in Los Angeles.

Medusa mask that Hitlerism has stamped on it.[9] It is a *warning* voice—to warn you is the only service that a German like me can render for you today; and I fulfill this grave and heartfelt responsibility, even though I know that there is no warning that can be issued to you that has not long been familiar to you, that had not long been active in your own fundamentally undeceivable awareness and conscience. To warn you means: to reinforce your dark suspicions; it means: to assure you that these sinister suspicions are *true*, that they are only too justified—and this assurance must be given to you; for only in the awakening of your feeling that you are going down terribly false paths lies the hope that you might still perhaps be able to abandon these paths.

These, in the ultimate and deepest sense of the word, *bad* people who lead you know well that you still feel nauseous about all of the victories, that you mistrust the deception of these victories, and that you are horrified by the impossible, impracticable slaveholder-role that they impose on you. They know that you long for peace, for a civilized coexistence with the other peoples of the world, for the end of the nightmarishly unpredictable misadventure of Hitler's war, and for this reason they seek with all their might to reap morale-capital from every success that their crimes yield, successes which are nothing more than new hopeless crimes—as just now with the subjugation of Bulgaria.[10] "The power of the idea and of weapons," your press necessarily boasts, "is poised to sweep away the last resistance against the new order."—That is to say, of weapons alone; for what is the idea? The idea is violence and malice, and it is far from the case that the last resistance against them and their insufferable defilement of humanity were broken by their universal triumph. The resistance is alive and well, stands forthright, is powerful, tenacious, and indomitable. Its name is Great Britain;[11] and Great Britain is a world in itself. America is another; and in ever-increasing measure America's tremendous resources will be at the disposal of the British in their struggle for freedom—simply because this country is now fully aware that the struggle that Great Britain is waging is also *its own*. Have you heard that the so-called Lend-Lease Bill,[12] the statute providing for the most comprehen-

---

9   In Greek mythology, Medusa was a beguiling beauty who was transformed into a monster with snake hair by the goddess Pallas Athena. Whoever looks at her turns to stone.

10   Bulgaria initially remained neutral but was forced to join the Tripartite Pact as an additional signatory on March 1, 1941, thus avoiding occupation by the Wehrmacht.

11   After Britain's declaration of war on Germany on September 3, 1939, Mann revised his critical position toward British foreign policy and appealed for US support for the threatened country.

12   Mann juxtaposes the US-American Lend-Lease Act of March 11, 1941 with the German "Law to Remedy the Distress of the People and the Reich," more commonly known as the "Enabling Act" ("Ermächtigungsgesetz") of March 23, 1933,

sive aid to Great Britain, has now also been approved in the Senate of the United States by a large majority? You are at war not only with the British Empire, in reality, you are at war even today with America, and one does not need to tell you, you feel it yourselves, that your situation is becoming more frightening and more impossible from day to day. What is to become of you? If you are defeated, then all of the spirits of vengeance in the world are out to get you for what you have done to people, to peoples. If you are victorious, Great Britain collapses, you win the war of the continents too, you defeat the West and the East—does any one of you believe that that would be a sustainable victory that would establish order, tolerable for you and the others, a victory with which one could live? Can a people really endure as the henchman of all others, with police armies everywhere on a conquered Earth that must labor for the master race, the race of violence? Is that really a spiritual possibility for any people and in particular for you Germans? You can take as dim and as skeptical a view of history and humankind as you will; but that the world would acknowledge the ultimate triumph of evil, that the world would tolerate being reduced to nothing but a Gestapo cellar, to nothing but a concentration camp, in which you Germans serve as the SA sentries, not even the greatest pessimist can believe that.[13]

Your Führers denounce Great Britain's resistance, the support that America provides, as a "prolongation of the war." They demand "peace."[14] They, who drip with the blood of their own people and of other peoples, dare to take this word in their mouths. Peace—by peace they mean: submission, the legalization of their crimes, the acceptance of that which is humanly intolerable. But that is not possible. With a Hitler there is no peace, because he is by his very nature incapable of peace, and because, coming from his mouth, this word is a filthy, pathological lie—as has been every word that he ever produced or spoke. As long as Hitler and his arsonist regime exist, you Germans will have no peace, not ever, not under any circumstances. It will always have to go on and on, as now, with the inconsolable acts of violence, if only to ward off the spirits of retribution, if only to prevent the gigantic and ever-growing hatred from swallowing you whole.

To warn you, Germans, means to confirm to you your own dire intuitions. More, I cannot do.

---

characterizing the former as a true act of enablement and the latter as an act of disenfranchisement. For the Lend-Lease Act, see the annotation for the address of December 1940. The "Ermächtigungsgesetz" authorized the Chancellor to enact laws without the consent of the Reichstag, Reichsrat, or Reich President.

  13 The Sturmabteilung or SA (Assault Division, 1921–1945) was a paramilitary branch of the Nazi party.

  14 Mann refers to Hitler's extortionate peace offerings in, for example, his Reichstag speeches of October 6, 1939, after the subjugation of Poland, and July 19, 1940, after the subjugation of France.

April 1941

German Listeners!
Of course, I am aware that today is a bad time to talk to you. Reports of victory rain down on you like the firebombs of the tormentors of humankind who rule over you rain down on London,[15] and set your minds—at least those of the weak, the stupid, and the crude—in a state of flaming rapture that is immune to any admonition. Visions pass before your drunken eyes that inspire horror and disgust in anyone who still has a sense of human honor: the idiotic and repugnant sight of swastika-bearing flags flying over Mount Olympus.[16] Soon it will fly from the Acropolis—it is unavoidable.[17] Prudently, at any rate, you were given to understand that this time the terrain did not favor the grand innovation that is the blitzkrieg;[18] quick results, as achieved on the Western Front, were probably not to be expected.[19] A superfluous precaution. It all goes much faster than you were permitted to hope and faster than some of you feared. The German war machine, a technological monstrosity, works with overwhelming precision and speed. Heroism can be of no help against it—mercilessly, in mechanical triumph, it tramples the faith, the confidence in the law, the freedom of so many nations that I have now lost count.

Do your breasts swell with pride? Pride for what? There is only one Greek to face six or seven of you. That they even dare, that they block the narrow path of freedom with their bodies, is what is astonishing—not that you are victorious. Are you really comfortable in the role that the play of history has thrust upon you—when now the representative

---

15   After the successful Western campaign against Belgium, the Netherlands, and France in 1940, the Wehrmacht invaded Greece and Yugoslavia at the beginning of April 1941 in support of its Italian allies, with the Greek troops in particular putting up fierce resistance. Since July 1940, the German Luftwaffe had bombed southern England in preparation for a planned invasion with the operation name "Seelöwe" (Sea Lion). After failing to establish air supremacy in the Battle of Britain, Hitler redirected his conquest plans towards the Soviet Union, which was invaded on June 22, 1941. Nevertheless, the German Luftwaffe continued to launch massive attacks on British cities until May 1941.

16   In mid-April 1941, the German army had advanced via Serbia to Mount Olympus, the mythological home of the Greek gods.

17   As Mann predicted, on April 27, 1941, the Wehrmacht marched into Athens and hoisted the swastika flag on the Acropolis. Just a few days later, however, it was taken down again at night by two resistance fighters.

18   The blitzkrieg was an offensive tactic used extensively by the German Wehrmacht in the Second World War, in which air, ground, and naval forces interoperated to achieve rapid war success. Since motorized vehicles were increasingly used for this tactic, its effectiveness in the rough terrain of Greece was limited.

19   The campaign on the Western Front spanned only from May 10 to June 22, 1940.

struggle of humanity that was Thermopylae repeats itself in the very same place? Again, it is the Greeks—and who are you then?[20]

Your tyrants have beat it into you that freedom is nothing more than an obsolete trifle. Believe me, freedom is as ever—unaltered by all the bluster of philosophasters and all the moods of intellectual history, and will forever remain just what it was 2,000 years ago and more: the light and the spirit of the occident; and the love, the glory of history will belong to those who died for it, not to those who drove it into the dirt with tanks.

Would you renounce love and admiration, if only you could enjoy the triumph that replaces all else? May at least the better people among you recall that there is a false and empty form of triumph, an invalid and ruinous triumph, in contrast to the true and genuine one, a triumph that is achieved through service to humankind and that humankind honors. You give too much credence to superficial and tangible triumph, to violence, to war. When a people like the Germans for seven years denies itself every thought but those of war and preparations for war; when a people casts everything overboard that could stand in the way of this one thought: freedom, truth, humanity, pleasure in life; when a people establishes a total state of war and musters all of its abilities for the purpose of preparing itself morally and physically for war—for good measure, in a world that is *not* prepared for war, that despises it, no longer believes in it, has morally arrived at a peaceable disposition—how could it be, if finally that war were brought about, that it not result in some semblance of a great moment in history and of world conquest? But there is no hocus-pocus about it; there is nothing surprising about it, and certainly nothing admirable. It is unavoidable. And, on top of all of this, this triumph is devoid of all validity and is nothing but blood-stained rhodomontade.

I say to you at the moment of your most egregious arrogance—or possibly not yet your most egregious—that it will not be accepted, will not be tolerated. Don't believe that all that is at stake here is to achieve iron-clad facts, before which humankind will in the end bow down. Humankind will not bow down, because it is incapable of doing so. You may regard humankind as cynically and as bitterly-dubiously as you will—there is, amid all the wretchedness, undeniably and inextinguishably, a divine spark in the human being, the spark of reason and of kindness. Humankind is incapable of tolerating the ultimate triumph of evil, of lies and violence—humankind is simply incapable of living like that. The world that would result from Hitler's victory would be not only a

20 The three-day Battle of Thermopylae of 480 BCE was fought between Achaemenid Persian Empire under Xerxes I and an alliance of Greek city-states led by Leonidas I of Sparta, in which some 7,000 Greeks held off between 120,000 and 300,000 Persians for a week before being overrun.

world of universal slavery, but also a world of absolute cynicism, a world where belief in that which is good, that which is higher in human beings is impossible, a world thoroughly belonging to evil, subservient to evil. That cannot be, that will not be tolerated. The revolt of humanity against a Hitler-world of ultimate despair of reason and of kindness, this revolt is the most certain of all certainties: it will be a fundamental revolt, before which "iron-clad facts" will crumble like tinder.

The desperate revolt of humanity against Germanness—must it come to that? People of Germany, how much more you have to fear in the victory of your Führers than in their defeat.

May 1941

German Listeners!
The President of the United States has spoken.[21] World affairs now bear the stamp of his historic speech.[22] It is the speech of a statesman, of the finest, clearest, and probably the wisest that the world has today, not the speech of a fanatic possessed by insipid and malevolent instincts. That which I have assured you again and again in the addresses through which I have sought to reach your ears: namely, that the Hitler-peace—a world order of enslavement and of cynicism, this design of a sinister and diseased mind—will not be tolerated, not accepted, not suffered, that humankind will not bow down before it; this speech validated all of this in the gravest and most abiding terms. The President has declared a State of Unlimited National Emergency; that means that he has marshaled the great democracy that he leads to warlike self-discipline and unity against the foreign enemy, who is the enemy of all benevolent people, and, irrevocably, he has announced that a peace with Hitler, a so-called negotiated peace with the present rulers of Germany, will never be negotiated, because it would amount to nothing other than the victory of evil and wickedness, to the death of freedom and human dignity.[23]

---

21 Mann is referring to Roosevelt's speech of May 27, 1941 on the enactment of emergency legislation, part of a series of radio broadcasts known as the "fireside chats." The President's straightforward manner and refusal to sugarcoat the facts greatly contributed to his growing popularity in the States.

22 Roosevelt's speech can be considered historic insofar as, in it, he endorses the United States government's decision to provide support and unlimited assistance to all countries defending their freedom against aggressors, even though the USA had not yet officially entered the war.

23 Roosevelt speaks of the "so-called negotiated peace" and explains what this means: "Germany would literally parcel out the world—hoisting the swastika itself over vast territories and populations, and setting up puppet governments of its own choosing, wholly subject to the will and the policy of a conqueror." He then asks whether anyone could be so incredibly naïve and oblivious in the face of Hitler's breach of promise as to believe the "honeyed words" of negotiated peace.

What you suspected, you yourselves now know. You will have no peace—never, as long as you fight for the criminal clan that infantilizes you today. Year after year, the desolate misadventure in which these wretches have ensnared you will continue, endlessly, boundlessly. You tell yourselves, no matter what they may try to make you believe, that Hitler's final victory has receded farther into the distance than ever before, because America is throwing the entire weight of its power, its enormous resources onto the scales of freedom and of a better future for humankind. To be sure, you could also tell yourselves that Germany, thanks to the formidable fighting machine that it has constructed over many long years, and thanks to the positions that it has been able to wrest away from an ill-prepared and divided world, will not in turn be forced to capitulate for a long time yet. Your lords and masters will not be at a loss for excuses and resources for further fallacious triumphs, will continue to heap misdeed upon misdeed; they will continue to have you play the gruesome role among peoples of those run amok; they will make you more and more into something that you do not at all want to be. What lies ahead may be an entire era of mutual military destruction, in which there is no doubt that the unfortunate continent that has fallen into Hitler's clutches will suffer the most gravely. All of this because your Führers want, indeed must, impose upon the world a system for their own preservation, a system that the world cannot accept for any price, not even the highest.

But President Roosevelt, on behalf of America and the Anglo-Saxon world, not only repudiated a peace that is beneath human dignity—one Hitler wants and has no choice but to want—but he also categorically rejected the concept of peace that took hold in the years between Versailles[24] and the outbreak of the Third Reich. He declared unequivocally that no state of global affairs should come again in which the seed of a Hitler can flourish and bloom into new catastrophes. Your opponents do not wish to return to the old world, and it is a lie when you are told that they seek only to safeguard and uphold the prerogatives of privileged peoples and classes. Hitler's revolution is nothing but deception; he is no revolutionary but a mere looter and the exploiter of a global crisis that ought to lead humanity to a new and loftier stage in its social development and maturity. Justice and freedom, to each the

24 Mann refers to the years between 1919 and 1933, in which "the seeds of Hitler" were sown. The Treaty of Versailles that ended the First World War was negotiated by the victorious powers, the United States, France, and Great Britain, and proclaimed on June 28, 1919. In it, Germany was held solely responsible for the outbreak of war and sentenced to severe punitive measures: territorial cessions, reparation payments, arms restrictions, and more. The treaty was predominantly perceived in Germany as a dictated peace and proved to be a significant motivating factor in the rise of Hitler.

same opportunity to share in the resources of the world, these must be the foundations of the coming peace, and the future belongs to a community of free peoples, free, but responsible for their community and prepared to sacrifice a superannuated primacy of national sovereignty for the sake of this responsibility. No one can even think of wanting to realize this new order of nations with the exclusion of Germany. Every word of their propaganda that fills your ears with warnings about the ostensible annihilation of the German people being planned by your enemies is intended solely to bind you to the bloody undertaking—is nothing but lies and subterfuge. Think about it, Germans: the only obstacle to a just peace for all is Hitler and his dream of world domination. Keep this thought in your hearts and in your minds and let it ripen for your salvation and for the salvation of the world!

June 1941

German Listeners!
Your government and your press have a very curious way of informing you about the events that concern you the most. They announced the closure of the American consulates in Germany to the German public with the clarification that this was not an act of retaliation against the US for freezing German credit, but that the measure was taken because the US consuls were engaged in espionage on behalf of Great Britain. In the process, what they mercifully withheld from you was that before this, originally and spontaneously, the government of the United States had shut down the German consulates and deported their staff—first, because for a long time these agencies had in fact been nothing more than breeding grounds for espionage and sabotage,[25] and second, because the American people as a whole wish to make their position toward the present German regime clearer and clearer through their government. The guardians of public opinion in Germany were keen to present these events in reverse order. When you learned of America's actions against the German consulates, you were supposed to believe that it was an act of mere retribution. The opposite is the case; and I thought it worth the effort to share that with you.[26]

I thought it was worth the effort, because on a daily basis sand is thrown into your eyes regarding the deep and all but universal disgust that the people of America harbor toward the character and deeds of your current rulers, and because the United States has not only long

---

25 The German Reich financed a considerable network of agents, which was controlled by George Sylvester Viereck (1884–1962), and whose influence reached as far as Congress.

26 On June 14, 1941, the US government froze all German assets in the USA and ordered the closure of German consulates. As a result, the American consulates in Germany were successively closed, which the National Socialists sought to justify with accusations of espionage.

been at war morally, but already de facto finds itself in an actual war with Germany.[27] Since the foolish Herr Lindbergh[28] happens to be the best-known American in Germany, you are fed excerpts from his speeches, in which he calls for negotiated peace with Hitler, to be read as though they represented the voice of America. They do not. In the American democracy, there is freedom of speech, and the courage of dissent is respected. If Colonel Appeaser distributes 17,000 complimentary tickets, then he gets 20,000 applauding listeners[29]—this is not so impressive when one considers the size of this land, and neither the speech nor the thundering applause can prove much. The true voice of America is that of President Roosevelt, whose reelection[30] by the American people as commander in chief of the nation for the coming years was in all likelihood the decisive event of this war.

I am certain that the message Roosevelt sent to Congress a few days ago, after the nefarious sinking of the ship *Robin Moor*,[31] and then—instead of any diplomatic note—sent to the German government, has been withheld from you. They will present his message to you, like Churchill's most recent speech,[32] though they hardly differ in tone, as the utterings of a madman—and yet it is humanity itself who speaks through it.

---

27 This was not the case until December 11, 1941, when Germany declared war on the US after Pearl Harbor. The US was already morally and de facto at war following the ratification of the Lend-Lease Agreement in March 1941, which guaranteed massive military and economic aid to the beleaguered UK.

28 In May 1927, the pilot Charles Lindbergh (1902–1974) made the first non-stop flight across the Atlantic and became an international celebrity as a result. Lindbergh was an avowed antisemite. Before the war, he met with high-ranking Nazi officials such as Luftwaffe Reichsmarschall Hermann Göring (1893–1946) on behalf of the US government, and used his enormous popularity to promote American isolationism. He also served as the figurehead of the "America First" movement and the "America First Committee," a political pressure group formed in 1940.

29 Lindbergh argued that the US could not win a war against Germany and therefore should not take part in the war.

30 On November 5, 1940, Roosevelt became the only presidential candidate in US history to be elected for a third term in office (and even a fourth in 1944).

31 Despite being marked as a cargo ship, the American freighter *Robin Moor* was sunk by a German submarine in the South Atlantic on May 21, 1941. In a speech to Congress on June 20, 1941, Roosevelt interpreted the incident as an act of provocation and intimidation with the aim of enforcing a policy of "non-resistance to German plans for universal conquest" and assured that "the United States will neither be intimidated nor acquiesce in the plans for world domination which the present leaders of Germany may have."

32 Mann refers to Churchill's speech of June 22, 1941 on the occasion of the German invasion of the Soviet Union.

The president said verbatim: "The total disregard shown for the most elementary principles of international law and of humanity brands the sinking of the *Robin Moor* as the act of an international outlaw [...] Our Government believes that freedom from cruelty and inhuman treatment is a natural right. It is not a grace to be given or withheld at the will of those temporarily in a position to exert force over defenseless people. [...] The present leaders of the German Reich have not hesitated to commit acts of cruelty and many other forms of terror against the innocent and the helpless in other countries. Our Government here can only conclude that by committing such despicable acts of terror against helpless and innocent men, women, and children, the government of the German Reich hopes to intimidate the United States and other Nations into a course of non-resistance to German plans for world conquest—a conquest based upon lawlessness and terror on land and piracy on the sea. [...] The Government of the German Reich may however be assured that the United States will neither be intimidated nor will it acquiesce in the plans for world domination which the present leaders of Germany may have."[33]

So spoke President Roosevelt. In the meantime, Hitler has declared war on Russia,[34] so that now, remarkably, Germany is opposed by all of the three superpowers that exist beside itself, namely Great Britain, Russia, and America. All right, a new series of motorized horrors in the name of glory awaits. It may hasten fate in a happy sense—but it is more likely, sadly, that it will prolong the war for an unforeseeable period and delay the creation of a humane order on Earth for many years. That cannot be quite what the German people long for in their hearts. Nonetheless, this character, covered in blood and infamy, who is the *only embodiment of Bolshevism* on the planet in the most obscene sense of the word, introduces himself to the world anew as Saint George who slew the dragon,[35] and as the guardian of occidental values. I know the face that the world will make. I would like to see yours, German listeners.

---

33   Franklin D. Roosevelt's "Message to Congress on the Sinking of the Robin Moor" of June 20, 1941 appeared in newspapers the same day as "U.S. WON'T BE INTIMIDATED." See for example *The Oakland Tribune*, vol. 134, no. 171, June 20, 1941, pg. 14.

34   On June 22, 1941, the German Wehrmacht began its invasion of the Soviet Union under the code name Operation Barbarossa. Germany officially declared war on the Soviet Union on the same day.

35   St. George is a Christian saint who was executed during the persecution of Christians under the Roman Emperor Diocletian (284–305). In medieval legend, he is also depicted as a dragon slayer who liberates the people oppressed by an evil dragon and converts them to the Christian faith.

July 1941

German Listeners!

The alliance of Great Britain with the Russian people will not have failed to make an impression on you,[36] in particular the agreement that neither of the two countries is willing to enter into a peace treaty without the other. The United States belongs to this alliance. The Americans, too, consider Russia their ally; they, too, have declared unambiguously and irrevocably that they will never consent to the kind of peace treaty that Hitler seeks. Today, the boogeyman knows that his attempt to win over the world for his concept of "order" by playing the savior of civilization from Bolshevism has failed piteously. Not even a dog would believe him in this role—with the exception of a few dogs and quislings in Europe,[37] whose business it is to believe him. Needless to say, he is not a savior—not from anything. He is the enemy of humankind, he alone, and the world must be saved from *him*. The German people must know, it cannot be repeated to them enough, that it will never achieve peace, never achieve quiet, under the current regime. This war will go on year after year until such time that the individual Hitler, his ghoulish garniture, and his entire system have been exterminated from the face of the Earth. This is how it must be. This and nothing else. A peace agreement with this swindler, who has proven himself again and again incapable of upholding a treaty, who is so dumb that he knows nothing of faith and loyalty, nothing of justice and goodness, but understands only lies and violence, is impossible; the world cannot live with him and he cannot live with it. Can you imagine this evil and peaceless fool one day being crowned as the prince of peace and savior of the millennium of a world placated by his victorious sword, molded by his faulty ideas? It is utter nonsense, Germans. It cannot be. Consider that the colossal majority of humankind lives in uncompromising hostility to the ambitions of Hitler and his henchmen, the ambitions of the so-called Axis Powers. Add up the peoples of Russia and China and the British Empire and America—that *is* all but the whole of humankind! How should this colossal weight not sooner or later cause the scale to sink, a scale additionally laden with the secret wishes and hopes of all the oppressed, plundered, abused peoples of Europe!

---

36 The "Anglo-Soviet Agreement" was signed in Moscow on July 12, 1941. In it, Great Britain and the Soviet Union made a commitment to mutual support for the duration of the war and vowed not to negotiate a separate peace.

37 During the Second World War, "quisling" was a common synonym for collaborator and traitor, named after the Norwegian fascist leader Vidkun Quisling (1887–1945), who was subordinate to the German Reichskommisssar as Prime Minister after the occupation of Norway. Quisling was charged with war crimes after the war, and convicted and executed on October 24, 1945.

I know well that after these eight numbing years you are hardly even capable of thinking of Germany without National Socialism. But is it easier for you to imagine its perpetuation through the ultimate victory that he wants to make you believe in? Is this boundlessly corrupt, lawless, pathologically nefarious regime under which you live and fight something fit for eternity? Just remember its origins, the means with which it came to power, the sadism with which it exerted this authority, the moral destruction that it spread, the crimes that it committed first in Germany then everywhere it carried its war machine! Look at the gallery of its supporters, this Ribbentrop,[38] Himmler,[39] Streicher,[40] Ley,[41] this Goebbels,[42] a wide, unhinged mouth of lies, the ill-inspired Führer himself and his fat, preening Grand-, Arch-, and Imperial Marshal[43] of the greater German Empire! What a menagerie! This is supposed to triumph, to remain in place, to endure, to place its foot on the neck of the world? This is supposed to be the answer to the questions of our age, indeed, to the question of humankind itself, the problem of humanity, and is supposed to determine life on Earth for a thousand years? Who can believe such a thing? All of it bears the stamp of an nightmarishly bizarre interlude, a through-and-through diseased, abnormal, and fantastical occurrence, bears unmistakably the stamp of a reckless misadventure and a bad dream on its forehead—a dream from which thank heaven there is and must be an awakening, if Germany is ever to regain a natural and unperverted relationship to the world, to humankind. "Germany, awaken!"[44] With that call you were once enticed to enter the ruinous, rapturous dream of National Socialism. He who calls to you today has higher hopes for you: "Awaken, Germany! Awaken to reality, to sound reason, to yourself, to the world of freedom and justice that is waiting for you!"

38 Joachim von Ribbentrop (1893–1946) was Foreign Minister in the Third Reich; he was tried, convicted, and executed as a war criminal in Nuremberg.

39 Heinrich Himmler (1900–1945) was "Reichsführer–SS"; he committed suicide after the war on May 23, 1945.

40 Julius Streicher (1885–1946) was the publisher of the antisemitic hate sheet *Der Stürmer* and Gauleiter of Franconia; he was charged with crimes against humanity, convicted, and executed.

41 Robert Ley (1890–1945) was head of the German Labor Front; he committed suicide after his indictment as a war criminal on October 14, 1945.

42 Joseph Goebbels (1897–1945) was Reich Minister for Public Enlightenment and Propaganda; he committed suicide in Hitler's bunker on May 1, 1945.

43 Hermann Göring was Reich Governor of Prussia and head of the Luftwaffe; he committed suicide on October 15, 1946 after being convicted of war crimes.

44 Refrain from the antisemitic poem "Sturm" (Storm) by rightwing publicist Dietrich Eckart (1862–1923), which became a popular slogan in SA and NSDAP propaganda.

August 1941

German Listeners!

All over the world, a debate is taking place regarding whether it is possible to distinguish between the German people and the powers that rule them today, and whether Germany is even capable of integrating itself in good conscience into the new, socially improved order of nations, founded on peace and justice, that must emerge from this war.[45] If I am confronted with these questions, then I answer as follows:

I admit that what we call National Socialism has deep roots in German life.[46] It is the virulent degenerate form of ideas that always carried the seed of murderous corruption in them, but that indeed were in no way foreign to the old, the good, Germany of culture and refinement. These ideas lived there on elegant footing, they were called "Romanticism" and had many enchanting qualities to offer the world. One can surely say that these ideas have gone to the dogs, and that they were destined to go to the dogs, since they had to result in Hitler. Together with Germany's outstanding adaptability to the technical age they form today an explosive combination that threatens all of civilization. Yes, the history of German nationalism and racism, from which National Socialism issues forth, is a long, sinister history; it stretches back a long way, it is at first interesting, and then becomes increasingly mean-spirited and more ghastly. But, to confuse this history with German intellectual history itself and thereby to conflate them is crass pessimism and would be a mistake that could endanger future peace. I am, I respond to the stranger, credulous and patriotic enough to trust that the Germany that they love, the Germany of Dürer and Bach and Goethe and Beethoven, will in the end prove longer-winded historically. This other Germany will soon run out of breath—very soon: one must not misunderstand its present snorting as a sign of long-winded stamina. It has run its course or is about to run its course, to truly run itself into its demise and death, namely through the "Third Reich," which, as the unmasking of an idea through its very implementation, represents something unsurpassable and absolutely deadly. — *Precisely herein lies all hope*. It lies in the fact that National Socialism, this political fulfillment

---

45 In January 1941, the British diplomat and aesthete Robert Vansittart (1881–1957) published a series of radio broadcasts under the title *Black Record: Germans Past and Present*. The brochure triggered debate mainly among German emigrants. It regarded the question of whether there was one or two Germanys: a bad one or a good and bad one.

46 Thomas Mann once again addressed the question raised by Vansittart about the character of the Germans immediately after the war on a grand scale in his Washington lecture "Germany and the Germans," in which Mann traces the roots of National Socialism beyond Romanticism to the late Middle Ages.

of ideas that have been rumbling for at least a century and a half among the German people and the German intelligentsia, is something most extreme and, physically and morally, something completely extravagant, an experiment in ultimate immorality and brutality that cannot be surpassed and cannot be repeated. Throwing all humanity overboard; running amok against everything that binds and civilizes; the desperate rape of all values and spiritual possessions that the Germans otherwise also held close to their hearts, and no less than anyone else; the creation of the total-war state in the service of the race myth and world domination—more they cannot do, further they cannot go. If this experiment fails—and fail it *shall*, since humankind cannot tolerate the final triumph of pure evil—then German nationalism, the most dangerous form that has ever existed, because it is engineered mysticism itself, will literally burn itself out, and Germany will be compelled—let us rather say: Germany will be allowed to pursue an entirely different course. The world needs Germany, but Germany also needs the world, and since it could not make the world "German," Germany will have to absorb the world into itself as it has always been wont to do with love and sympathy. It will consider itself obliged to revive traditions that have today been trod deep into the dust, but that are no less patriotic than those whose ruinousness has become so obvious. These traditions will make it easy for Germany to unite with a world in which freedom and justice are realized to the extent that they can be for humankind in this hour of its life.

That is one consideration. The other is that Germany will never have been *happier*—and this in principle is already sensed today—than as a member of a depoliticized world union made peaceful through freedom and through the abolition of nation-state highhandedness. Germany was literally born for such a world, for if ever power politics were a curse and a corrosive abomination for a people, this they were for the fundamentally unpolitical German people. A mischievous Frenchman once said that if the German wanted to appear graceful, he would jump out of the window. And that is just what he does, and does so with even wilder determination, when he wants to appear political. Power politics, for the German that means *dehumanization*: Hitlerism, this hideous leap from the window proves it. It is the convulsive overcorrection of a lacking that the Germans were never proud enough to take pride in.

The end of nation-state power politics—for no nation will it mean such salvation, such a promotion of its best, its strongest, and most noble attributes, as for the German nation, and precisely in *this world*—which the German nation now seeks to prevent in a deluded struggle—these great attributes will be able to flourish happily.

(Special Broadcast)
August 1941

German Listeners!
The greatest moral blessing that can be afforded the German people is to count them among the oppressed peoples. For what judgment of Germany could be rendered, and what hopes for the future could one harbor for Germany if the misdeeds being committed under its current regime were acts of free will and clear conscience? You, who surreptitiously listen to the voice of freedom from afar, evidently consider yourselves to be members of an oppressed people,[47] and the very fact that you are listening is in itself an act of spiritual resistance against Hitler's reign of terror and an act of spiritual sabotage against the bloody and dubious misadventure into which he has plunged you Germans. In Russia, the youth of Germany bleed to death by the millions; your rulers themselves admit that this campaign alone will drag on into the winter, and meanwhile, the nearly inexhaustible forces of the opposition continue to grow in a world that wanted peace, thought only of peace, and that at first almost helplessly faced the war machine that Germany had built over seven years. A fearsome fate will befall Germany if the war continues, for one or even two more years, and it will continue, because not even you yourselves believe any longer that you will triumph over the majority of humanity that opposes Hitler's plans. Germans, let it not come to such a bitter end! You yourselves should shake off the wicked, unspeakably degrading rulers in whose hands a sinister snare has ensured your downfall, you ought to prove what the world still tries so hard to believe, that National Socialism and Germany are not one and the same. If you walk with Hitler through thick and thin until the end, then you call forth a vengeance that everybody who means well with Germany dreads. Look how the oppressed peoples of Europe defend themselves against the same enemy that also oppresses you. Do you want to be more pitiful, more spineless, more cowardly than the others? Consider that it is your hands that provide the tools for enslaving the world, and that Hitler cannot continue his war without your help. Deny him your hands and cooperate no more! It will make a tremendous difference for the future, whether you Germans yourselves eliminate the man of terror, this Hitler, or whether outsiders will have to do it; only if you free yourselves will you earn the right to take part in the free and just order of nations to come.

---

47 That the German people were oppressed by Hitler and the National Socialists was the conviction of the majority of German exiles, above all dramatist Bertolt Brecht (1898–1956). Mann's view is somewhat more complex. For a more detailed analysis of their views, see Hans Rudolf Vaget, *Thomas Mann, der Amerikaner: Leben und Werk im amerikanischen Exil, 1938–1952* (Frankfurt am Main: S. Fischer, 2011), 427–33. Subsequent citations as *Thomas Mann, the American* with page number(s).

September 1941

German Listeners!
In his marvelous *History of the Thirty Years' War*, Schiller relates how the enemies of the gallant Gustav Adolf intentionally disseminated the most appalling rumors about his gruesome conduct in war, which also could not entirely be dispelled by the splendid examples of philanthropy that the king gave. *"They feared,"* Schiller says, *"suffering from others a treatment that they themselves had meted out in a similar situation—as they were perfectly aware."*[48]—Is that not the very essence of the reason why the German people believe that they must fight this boundless and ultimately unwinnable war to the bitter end, why they must bear endless tortures and follow their desperate Führers farther and farther to God knows what end? The German people are afraid that, if they were to desert their warlords, they would suffer precisely *that* which they know the Nazis would inflict on *others* if they were to prove victorious: *annihilation*. Goebbels's propaganda shouts it in their ears daily: You must be victorious or you will be annihilated. You have only the choice between all-encompassing war and perdition.

But first, you Germans should accept the idea that a leadership that brings its people to the abyss of this alternative—that they must either conquer the world or be annihilated—is a leadership of evil marauders. And second, the idea of eradicating peoples and exterminating races is a Nazi idea—there is no place for it in the minds of democracies. What should and must be eradicated in order to protect humankind from the most sickening form of slavery to ever disgrace the face of the Earth, is the Nazi regime, is Hitler and his henchmen, but not the German people. To expect intentions of annihilation of any kind, economic, political, or even direct physical destruction of the German people by Great Britain—where in the midst of war perhaps the most important social revolution in its history is taking place[49]—or by Franklin Roosevelt's America, is flagrant nonsense. These nations and their politicians know that the world is in a state of crisis that—though it is being perverted into an anachronistic plunder-raid of conquest and enslavement by Hitler—should in truth lead humankind to a higher level of social maturity and autonomy. They wish nothing more ardently than to *win over* Germany, which is indispensable for an order of nations perfected in freedom, for precisely this new order, born of the spirit of a rejuvenated democracy. Indeed, the main significance of the Atlantic Summit between Churchill and Roosevelt lies in the

---

48 Friedrich Schiller, *Geschichte des dreißigjährigen Kriegs*, Drittes Buch. *Schillers Werke. Nationalausgabe*, vol. 18, ed. Harl-Heinz Hahn (Weimar: Hermann Böhlau, 1976), 193.

49 Possibly an allusion to the introduction of a more socially fair income tax on April 7, 1941.

fact that America assumes *co-responsibility* for the coming peace[50]—and who can believe that a peace agreement concluded in Washington would bear any sense of similarity to the peace that the Nazis would dictate?

To be sure, what *they* have always loved to do, is to create fait accomplis. And the most irreversible of deeds done will always be annihilation. Hitler's infamous Chief of Criminal Police Himmler has stated openly that he intends to physically and utterly annihilate the Czech nation, if the Czechs do not submit to the yoke of the master race without resistance, and everything that is being undertaken in the conquered territories, in all of these hellish general governates and protectorates, is deliberately aimed at the biological and moral degradation, the spiritual—and by no means not always only spiritual—castration of the peoples. The Nazis know why they allow their victims at most an elementary education, and everywhere seize the first opportunity to close the universities. Institutions of higher education and research are breeding grounds of human pride and a spirit of freedom; they breed those individuals who could become leaders of the people against their oppressors—the master-race politics of the Nazis, a politics of unprecedented infamy, which they will not tolerate. We have these masters' response to the Czechs' appeal to be permitted to reopen the University of Prague. "If we lose the war," so it reads, "you will reopen your university. If we win, then you do not need a university."—You do not need one—that means: you will forever be a dull, ignorant, intellectually and morally neutered herd of slaves, not even *perceiving* your fate, and instead vegetating in a pathetic condition of contentment. That is what the master race intends for the servile peoples of the New Order; for no trace of sympathy, of respect for the existence of the other, the honor of the other, no trace of fellow-feeling to be found in these disgraceful brains to whom fate—which must be reversed, *will* be reversed—has dealt so much power to do evil.

I speak not of the "irrefutable facts" that they manufactured against Poles and Jews. These facts belong to the reasons why it will certainly be no pleasure to be German after this war. But I cannot get past one statement by an influential Nazi official, which was directed at France. "Out of Paris," so it goes, "we will make the amusement park, out of France in general the bordello and the vegetable garden of German-Europe."—Could there be a more brazen vulgarity? It is true that, in the year 1940, France was in poor moral condition. Its bourgeoisie was diseased with fascism, its generals and a number of its respected political figures were

---

50 In August 1941—after the start of the Russian campaign and before Pearl Harbor—Churchill and Roosevelt met on a ship off Newfoundland and signed the so-called Atlantic Charter, in which the "common principles" of a postwar order were laid down, including the renunciation of territorial gains and the right of all peoples to self-determination. After the Lend-Lease Act, this was the second declaration of solidarity between the USA and Great Britain.

traitorous enemies of the people, the Third Republic was corrupt and on the brink of collapse—its defeat came easy. But the idiotic conceit that a nation with the historical dignity of France is theirs to dispose of freely, as displayed in this announcement and as will in fact occur, if Hitler triumphs—this illiterate conceit, oblivious to any grasp of what this is and will remain, in spite of all: *Frankreich*—is an abominable injustice that cries out to heaven for satisfaction. The guiding spirit of Europe will not allow a New Order that is founded on such brutality.

Hitler has on occasion been compared with Napoleon—a tasteless juxtaposition in my eyes; for the Corsican was a demigod in comparison with the bloody coward that you Germans have for a while held to be a great man; and the universal domination with which the Son of the Revolution then threatened the world was a trifle, indeed, it would have been a tyrannical blessing in comparison with the filthy terror that Hitler would establish. But hear this verse from "Epimenides' Awakening," in which Goethe, after Napoleon's downfall, presciently doomed the Hitler-misadventure:

> "Woe unto him who, insolent
> And heeding ill advice,
> That what the Corsican once did
> Now as a German tries.
> May he feel soon, may he feel late,
> Be it eternal right:
> He and his kind 'spite force and pain
> Should end in bitter plight!"[51]

October 1941

German Listeners!
The new order in Europe drips with blood.[52] I cannot describe to you the revulsion aroused in this country by General Stülpnagel's hostage slaughter.[53] It goes without saying that it was a ludicrous lie that the

---

51 Sophie (1921–1943) and Hans Scholl (1918–1943) also cite Goethe's poem *Des Epimenides Erwachen: Letzte Strophe* (Epimenides' Awakening: last stanza, 1815) in the first "Weiße Rose Flyer" of June/July 1942, in which they channel Goethe's vision of the fall of Napoleon Bonaparte in order to invoke the inevitability of Hitler's demise.

52 In his speech in the Berlin Sportpalast on January 30, 1941, Hitler announced the goal of a "great reorganization of Europe," in which Germany would rule over Europe. See Max Domarus, *Hitler: Speeches and Proclamations 1932–1945: The Chronicle of a Dictatorship*, 4 vols. (Wauconda, IL: Bolchazy-Carducci Publishers, 2004), here VI, 2366. Subsequent citations as "Domarus" with volume and page number(s).

53 General Otto von Stülpnagel (1878–1948) was appointed Military Commander in France on October 25, 1941. A few days prior, French resistance

murderers of the German occupation officers in France were incited to their desperate acts by Russia and Great Britain. That is about as true as that only Jews and communists resist the so-called collaboration with the German oppressors. The eyes of the French people have been opened to how they have been deceived, betrayed, and what kind of an enemy they have been delivered to. The assassins are neither communists nor Jews, nor were they hired by Great Britain or Russia; they are simply young, hot-blooded patriots, who can no longer watch idly the atrocious humiliation and the draining of their country's blood, the choreographed genocide that Hitler commits against France, and who resort to extra-legal means in order to send the world a signal that the soul of France lives on, even if this life only consists of rage and helpless despair. They have far more justification for their violent deeds than this Schlageter had in his time for the murderous act of sabotage that made him a national hero.[54] Schlageter was a hero and martyr, the French assassins however are cowardly, paid cutthroats. That is the logic of German nationalism—a dishonorable logic absent of any sense of fairness. It demands that for *one* German life, one hundred, two hundred French pay with their blood—so much more noble, more precious is the blood of the German master race than the blood of other peoples. And upon this ridiculous megalomania, this godless pretension, they want to establish a new order!

The President of the United States captured the general opinion with his statement that the German hostage murders in France are the crimes of people who know deep in their hearts that they cannot win.[55] In truth, the entire Nazi war bears this stamp of hopelessness. Violence always contains an element of despair—despair is in fact the dominant element in violence, and even the career of a Napoleon was at bottom *one* long battle of despair, the outcome of which was certain to every knowledgeable person and quite in secret to himself as well. Does any one of

---

fighters, mainly communists who had mobilized after the German attack on the Soviet Union on June 22, 1941, attempted to assassinate several members of the German field command. In response, forty-eight hostages were shot on the orders of Stülpnagel. Ordered by Hitler to execute one hundred hostages for every German soldier, Stülpnagel had a further fifty hostages shot. Stülpnagel resigned from the position on February 15, 1942 in protest of the inordinate number of hostage shootings.

54 Albert Leo Schlageter (1894–1923) was executed on May 26, 1923 for acts of post-First World War sabotage against French occupational forces, becoming a martyr in Germany with broad non-partisan appeal.

55 Thomas Mann makes a timely reference to Roosevelt's radio address of October 27, 1941 on the German submarine war in the Atlantic. In this speech, Roosevelt responds in particular to the attack on the American destroyer USS *Kearny*, as well as to German plans for conquest: "The forward march of Hitler and of Hitlerism can be stopped—and it will be stopped."

you believe that the fate of the unfortunate creature that calls himself the Führer of Germany will be any different than that of all the other brutes of history? His victories, these mechanical, lackluster, inglorious, stillborn victories—they make no human heart beat harder, no one respects them or believes in them, even the German people look upon them without pride, without enthusiasm, only with horror at the currents of blood that they are now costing in Russia, and with a nagging sense of worry that is only too justified, for these victories will lead to nothing but ruin and misery. The Nazis and the graying cadettes that serve them as generals believe that the world ultimately will see reason and yield to the unavoidable, that is, to their rule. That is a mistake. There are things that must be avoided and that humankind will know how to avoid, even if the Nazis continue to seek to prove their unavoidability through so many victories. Hitler's victory will be avoided, on this I give you my word. His fate has been decided—only he does not yet know it, though perhaps at times his twisted brain somehow senses the inevitable. He may conquer Moscow, may conquer the Caucasus, deliver fait accomplis as much as he wants—these facts are irrelevant, they will not be recognized, not be tolerated, and the war will continue—how many years, no one can say, but what is certain is that no peace will be made with the Nazi Regime, that there will be no peace for Germany, as long as Germans follow Hitler. Peace will be made with Germany—with a Germany whose people and government are ready to integrate themselves into a world order that is within the power of and agreeable to humankind, a world order with the same rights and the same responsibilities for all.

November 1941

German Listeners!

He who speaks to you again today, has had the good fortune during his now already long life to make some contributions to the intellectual prestige of Germany. For this, I am thankful, but I have no right to boast of it, for it was providence and was not my intention. No artist creates their works intending to increase the fame of their nation and their people. The source of productivity is individual conscience, and even if the sympathy that it arouses benefits the nation by whose language and tradition it is borne, there is still too much arbitrariness at work for it to justify any claim to gratitude. You Germans cannot thank me for my work today, not even if you wanted to, and so be it! It was not done for your sake, but out of most personal necessity. But there is something that was truly done for your sake, a matter of social and not of private conscience and with each day my conviction grows that the time will come, a time growing ever closer, when you will thank me for it and hold it in higher esteem than my story books: namely, that I warned you, before it was too late, of the despicable powers in whose yoke you are helplessly harnessed today, and which lead you through a thousand evil deeds into unfathomable ruin. I knew them, I knew that nothing but catastrophes and misery for Germany and for Europe could come of their unspeakably wicked character, while the majority of you, in a state of blindness that is no doubt incomprehensible to you now, saw them as the bringers of order, beauty, and national dignity. Must this not bring to mind Goethe's saying about the "obedient German nation, which only feels fully exalted when all its dignity has been squandered"?[56] I also knew you, you good Germans, and knew your fallibility in recognizing your true honor and dignity, and back then in October 1930, overcoming my natural inclination, I climbed into the political arena and delivered the speech in the Beethoven Hall in Berlin,[57] one interrupted already then by the obnoxious bellowing of the Nazi boys.[58] As some among you probably still remember, I called the speech "Appeal to Reason," although it was in truth an appeal to all that is better in Germanness—and it serves today, as fruitless as it was, to quiet my conscience more meaningfully than everything that I was able to accomplish through my more serendipitous accomplishments as an artist.

I sought with my meager influence to impede what had to come and what did arrive some years ago: the war—the blame for which your dishonest Führers lay on the Jews and the British and the Freemasons and God knows who else, while at the same time to every perceptive person there was no doubt about the matter of blame from the moment that these Führers came to power and began to build the machine with which they intended to crush freedom and justice. And what sort of war is it to which you shackle yourselves—an incalculable, destructive, hopeless misadventure, a quagmire of blood and crime into which Germany is in danger of descending. How do things look on your end? Do you think that

---

56 The distich appeared in Book 5 of the so-called "Zahme Xenien" (mild host gifts)—as opposed to the genuinely hostile Xenien, a collaborative collection of attacks composed by Goethe and Schiller against their ostensibly mediocre artistic and critical contemporaries.

57 On October 17, 1930, in the Beethoven Hall of the old Philharmonic in Berlin, Thomas Mann delivered his most important political speech of admonition and warning, "German Address: An Appeal to Reason" ("Deutsche Ansprache. Ein Appell an die Vernunft"). In it, Mann implored the bourgeois camp not to be taken in by Hitler and instead to vote for the Social Democrats.

58 Joseph Goebbels, the NSDAP Gauleiter of Berlin, had ordered twenty SA men dressed in rented tuxedos to disrupt the Nobel Prize winner's lecture. In his address, Mann characterized Nazism as a "tidal wave of eccentric barbarism." The following day, Goebbels noted in his diary: "Our people spat on the head of Thomas Mann, who shamelessly insulted us in a lecture entitled 'Appeal to Reason.' 'Barbarians.'" Joseph Goebbels, *Die Tagebücher von Joseph Goebbels: Sämtliche Fragmente. Teil 1: Aufzeichnungen 1923–1941*, ed. Elke Fröhlich, vol. 2.1 (Munich: K. G. Saur, 2005), 264.

we on the outside are not as familiar with the facts as you are? Barbarism and misery run rampant. Your young men, as young as eighteen, sixteen, are sacrificed unscrupulously to the Moloch of war by the hundreds of thousands, by the millions—there is not one home in Germany that hasn't a husband, son, or brother to mourn. The collapse has begun. In Russia, there are not enough doctors, nurses, medicines. In German infirmaries and hospitals, the seriously wounded are gassed to death together with the old, the frail, the mentally ill[59]—two thousand out of three thousand, as one German doctor in a single hospital related. That is what the regime is doing that roars in protest when Roosevelt accuses it of wanting to obliterate Christianity and all religion, and that pretends to wage a crusade of Christian morality against Bolshevism—that Bolshevism of which it is itself nothing but a watered-down perversion. The Christian counterpart to the mass gassings are the "Mating Days,"[60] where furloughed soldiers are ordered to engage in bestial hour-long marriages with BDM girls in order to produce bastards of the state for the next war.[61] Can a people, a next generation, sink any lower? Anathema and blasphemy of humanity, wherever you look. Long ago, one Johann Gottfried Herder lovingly collected folk songs of every nation.[62] That was Germany in its goodness and greatness. Today it knows nothing but the murder of nations and races, imbecilic destruction. Three hundred thousand Serbs have been murdered, not even in battle, but after the battle with this country, by you Germans on the orders of the profligate scoundrels who govern you. The unspeakable things that have happened and continue to happen in Russia and with the Poles and Jews, you know of them; you would, however, prefer not to know out of justifiable fear of the equally unspeakable hatred, mushrooming into a colossus, that must one day—when all of your forces, human and machine, languish—come crashing down on your heads. Yes, terror at this day has taken over, and your Führers take advantage of it. They, who seduced you to all of these iniquities, say to you: Now you have committed them, now you are chained to us forever, now you must endure until the bitter end, or else Hell will descend upon you. Hell, Germans, descended upon you when these Führers descended upon

59 A reference to the euthanasia program that had been in place since 1939.

60 Part of the "Lebensborn e.V." (literally: "Fountain of Youth") initiative, created in 1935 by Heinrich Himmler for the purpose of breeding racially superior children. Thomas Mann's house—"Poschi"—was one of the first houses used by the Munich-based Lebensborn association, from 1937 to 1939.

61 The Bund Deutscher Mädchen/Mädel (League of German Girls) was the only female youth organization in Germany and the counterpart to the male group, the Hitler Youth.

62 Johann Gottfried Herder's (1744–1803) *Volkslieder* (Folk Songs) appeared in 1778/1779.

you. To Hell with them and all of their henchmen! Then you can still be saved, then peace and freedom will come to you.

(Special Broadcast)
December 24, 1941

And Christmas again, German listeners, war-Christmas again, for the third time and not for the last—oh, not for the last time by far. Your rulers now appear to think it is wisest to admit at least this, that a long and difficult war lies before you, bringing bloody Christmases year after year. The international situation, they say, dictates that this be so—the international situation that they created. For once, you can believe what they say, and as for what they are not saying, you can guess: that there will be no peace through victory at the end of your war, because Germany's victory would mean no peace at all, and humankind must and shall prevent the kind of peace that your rulers have in mind.

War-Christmas again, one of many to come—and wretched grounds for celebration. Do you not wish that the festival no longer existed at all, and that you no longer needed to prepare its celebration meagerly, not have to remember each other with gifts that lay bare the disintegration of all the trappings of life, not to mention the state of mind in which they are given and received? How do you feel, Germans, during the festival of peace, the festival of the birth of light, the festival of the arrival from above of mercy born to humankind? Do I guess correctly that you are wrought up with shame and infinite longing; longing for innocence—from complicity in the maddening guilt in which you inextricably flounder; shame, burning shame before the loving spirit of this festival? Look around at what you have done! In Greece, two hundred people die of hunger each day[63]—that is only a single example of the misery that cries out to heaven for justice: the deaths of nations, the human desecration, the agonies of the body and soul all around you, for which your corruptibility, your unforgivable obedience are to blame. What should become of Europe, what should become of you yourselves in the course of this "long and difficult" war, which they announce to you with all false forthrightness? If despair began to creep into your souls, that would be good, Germans; it would be the beginning of goodness. Despair is good, it is better than cowardly braggadocio. From despair, so long as it is deep enough, comes exaltation, new hope, the reincarnation of light. Behold, the Christmas star that humankind follows burns and shines even through

---

63 Greece had been attacked on April 6, 1941 in the course of the Balkan campaign; from May 1, 1941, large parts of Greece, including Crete, were occupied by the German military administration, while the remaining parts of the country were controlled by the Italian military.

the thick and bloody fog of these times. It is the star of peace, of fellowship, and of justice.

December 1941

German Listeners!
How did you like the order of the day in which Hitler dismissed his defeated generals in Russia, and, guided by the "voices" he hears, named himself Supreme Commanding Officer in all theaters of the German war of world conquest?[64] Here, in the US, the document has been met with that combination of disgust, horror, and laughter evoked by every expression of life from this poorly wrought individual.[65] Fear, pomposity, maudlin self-aggrandizement, the usual measure and even the exorbitance of lies, the threat of new calls for sacrifice, new weapons, new slaughter, the pitiful pleas to "his" soldiers, for whom he promises to do everything conceivable, and who should do their utmost for him—for *him*, mind you—all this howls and bellows from this decree in the voice that we have come to know, and which has become so excruciatingly familiar to the world, the voice of a rabid attack dog.

Intermittently, he speaks French—as the conqueror of Gaul he believes he owes that much at least, even if his command of French fails him at times.[66] The "raison d'etre," he says, requires that all authority be vested in one hand. And by "raison d'etre" he ostensibly means the right to life of the German Volk, their *freedom*, that is the point of the struggle; for by "freedom" he understands their most dishonorable kind of enslavement as a means of plunging the entire world into dishonorable enslavement.

Exhausted from his criminal acts and transported to Berchtesgaden for recuperation,[67] in the invigorating mountain air the fiend soon regained faith in his mission—he quickly made a full recovery to his former insanity. At every turn, his decree refers to intuitions, inner voices, calls from within; his therapists were evidently unable to prevent this.

---

64 On December 19, 1941, after the failure of the German advance on Moscow, Hitler dismissed General Field Marshals Walther von Brauchitsch (1881–1948) and Fedor von Bock (1880–1945) and assumed supreme command of all military operations himself. The goals of the Russian campaign included expelling the Slavs beyond the Urals and colonizing Russia as part of the so-called General Plan East, indicating that Hitler's broader aim was world conquest.

65 Not long after Hitler declared war against the United States on December 11, 1941, the US-American media reported the removal of the army commanders.

66 Mann draws attention to Hitler's imprecise use of language: here, by "raison d'être" Hitler means the reason or justification for the dismissal of the army leaders.

67 Hitler's country residence "Berghof" on the Obersalzberg near Berchtesgaden.

Since the Maid of Orleans there has been nothing so romantic[68]—only *she*, not Napoleon, Caesar, or Frederick the Great compares to this mystical hero, even if one must regret the injustice done here to the entirely respectable young woman.

Most of all he wants to deceive himself and his poor soldiers into believing that he always knew how things would turn out. Ever since he began preparing Germany's defense—"defense," he calls it!—he would have us believe that he foresaw the desperate situation into which he has brought Germany, the world-engulfing war that he ignited. The blind marauder, who is driven from one unforeseen crime to the next by his accursed star, claims to have known at the time he started it all that he would one day pit the three great powers of the world—Great Britain, Russia, and the United States—against him and his disgraceful regime. Here a wretch makes himself seem guiltier than he is—and then he comforts himself by remembering Japan, the agile comrade-in-arms,[69] whom he will soon likely crown as the Aryans of the North, and who, with *their* surprise attack on the Pacific outposts of America,[70] conveniently turned the tides of Hitler's War anew.

That's what he says to his soldiers. However, what his voices should say to him is that America's insouciance was the insouciance that comes from a tremendous feeling of power, and that it was probably rather unwise of his yellow brothers-in-arms to wake the lion so rudely. Actually, America has hardly even lifted its somewhat lethargic paw, and it will surely still learn to participate in the radical war that it at first did not understand. In coming years, before the catastrophe comes crashing down on Führer Hitler's head, we will often hear the cry, wailing ever more pathetically, with which he now endeavors to justify himself: "All I ever wanted was Germany's greatness!" And whom does he ultimately call as protector and witness of his edict? God, the almighty. The *most godless of all creatures* who stands in no other relation to God, the Lord, than as *a scourge of God*, has no compunction about coopting the name of the one to whom millions of his tortured victims cry out. Leave *that* name to *us*, scoundrel, to cry from the depths of our hearts: God in heaven, smite him!

---

68   Joan of Arc (ca. 1412–1431) invoked supernatural powers such as visions and the voice of God to explain her actions on behalf of France in its fight with England in the Hundred Years' War.

69   In the Tripartite Pact signed on September 27, 1940, Germany, Italy, and Japan committed to mutual political, economic, and military support.

70   The day after the December 7, 1941 Japanese attack on the American Pacific Fleet at Pearl Harbor in Hawaii, Congress authorized the United States' declaration of war on Japan.

1942

January 1942

German Listeners!
The news sounds unbelievable, but my source is good.[1] In numerous Dutch-Jewish families, so I have been told, in Amsterdam and other cities, profound mourning reigns for sons who have died a gruesome death. Four hundred young Dutch Jews were brought to Germany to serve as objects of research on poison gas.[2] The deadly efficiency of this chivalric and thoroughly German means of warfare, a true Siegfried weapon,[3] has been demonstrated on the young subhumans. They are dead—having died for the "New Order" and the master race's ingenuity in waging war.[4] At least they were good enough for that. After all, they were Jews.

I said: the story sounds unbelievable, and all over the world many will be simply unwilling to believe it. Powerful vestiges of that unwillingness to believe, by which we refugees from Germany have been so bitterly plagued all these years: of unwillingness to believe in the true nature of National Socialism, to consider it even *humanly possible*, are still to be found everywhere, even today: the inclination—not to say: the tendency, to see such stories as horrific fairy tales remains widespread, much to the enemy's advantage. They are, however, not mere stories, they are *history*. The Nazis consciously make history through all of their misdeeds, and the experimental gassing of four hundred young Jews is a conscious and demonstrative historic act, an instructive and exemplary expression of the

---

1   Apparently a memorandum from the BBC Monitoring Service, which was able to access information from the British Secret Intelligence Service. See the introduction.

2   The number of victims cited here soon proved too conservative; see the June 1942 broadcast.

3   In Richard Wagner's (1813–1883) *Der Ring des Nibelungen* (*The Ring of the Nibelung*, 1869–1876), Siegfried slays the dragon and shatters Wotan's spear, and thus the old order, using his sword "Nothung." The sarcastic allusion refers to the looming genocide of the Jews of Europe, which was anything but "chivalrous."

4   In his speech to the Reichstag of October 6, 1939, after the defeat of Poland, Hitler spoke of a "new order of ethnographic relations" in Europe, which initially meant expulsion and resettlement. However, the term soon came to signify Nazi rule in Europe.

essential character and ideology of the National Socialist revolution, which cannot be understood unless one conceives of the willingness to commit immoral acts as a revolutionary achievement. In this retrogressive—by thousands of years—willingness lies the very essence of the National Socialist revolution: it has not brought about anything else and it never will. One must not forget that this war began not in 1939, but in 1933, with the abolition of human rights. "Human rights have been abolished," Dr. Goebbels then declared at the Berliner Sportpalast,[5] and ten thousand poor, foolish devils roared with pathetic-nonsensical approval. It was a historic proclamation, the principal foundation for all that Nazi Germany today inflicts on the peoples of the world, including its own people: the declaration of a revolutionary achievement that will mean the *abolition* of all of humankind's moral achievements over the millennia—not only the achievements of the French Revolution, but also the moderating and moralizing effects of Christianity, its refinement of human conscience. The content, the new teachings and deeds, the theory and praxis of the National Socialist revolution is bestialism—that alone: and the product of this revolution is the Europe of today: a half-exterminated land of hunger and pestilence, that, if Hitler's war continues for a few more years, will be nothing more than a meeting place for wolves.

Trying to imagine the coexistence of the German people with other peoples after this war is terribly difficult and a matter of constant disconcerting worry. There have always been wars, and, in their course, the nations that fought them have always inflicted a great deal of misery on each other. Thanks to the short memories of human beings, the misery tended to be very quickly forgotten once peace was concluded. This time it is different. What Germany is doing, what sorrow, misery, despair, ruin, what moral and physical destruction it is currently inflicting on humankind while practicing the revolutionary philosophy of bestialism on such a scale,[6] is so abominable, so hopelessly unforgettable, that it is impossible to envision how our people are supposed to be able to live as equals among equals among the fellow peoples of the Earth. The longer the war goes on, the more hopelessly this people entangles itself in guilt, and the sole reason the war continues to this day is because to you Germans it appears to be too late to stop; because you feel that too much has happened for you to be able to go back; because

---

5   Built in 1910 and seating up to 14,000, the "Sport Palace" was the largest multi-purpose indoor arena in Berlin until its demolition in 1973. Today, it is best known for the rallies and speeches held during the Nazi period.

6   As is evident in his emphatic uses of the term, Mann regarded the relapse of civilization into bestialism as an essential feature of the theory and practice of the "National Socialist revolution."

you are gripped with horror at the thought of the liquidation, the reckoning, the atonement. You must win, you think, so that the revolution of bestialism can extend across the whole world and so that under its banner a dark compact between you and the rest of the world is possible. But that cannot happen. You see it with your own eyes that the world is determined to do its utmost to avert the fate of stooping to confront you at the depth of bestialism, and the power of your despair is no match for the will of three quarters of humankind.

There is no need for you to *triumph*, for you cannot. You need to *purify* yourselves. The atonement that you struggle to avoid must be your own work, the work of the German nation, of which your soon demoralized and exhausted army is one part. That atonement must come from within—for only revenge and punishment can come from without, but not purification. I always contradict those who recommend a compulsory reeducation of the German Nation from without for the period following the collapse of Hitlerdom.[7] Any reeducation, I answer them, is the responsibility of the German nation itself, must be its responsibility alone. Those of you for whom my name still means something certainly know that I am no revolutionary or man of the barricades, by nature certainly not one to incite bloody deeds. However, this much I do know about the laws of the moral world and have sufficient reverence for them to declare to you with assurance: A purification, rectification, and liberation must and will occur in Germany, so fundamentally and with such determination that it will be commensurate with evil deeds, the like of which the world had never seen before. This purification must, I say, and will occur so that the great German nation can look humanity in the eye again and freely extend its hand in search of reconciliation.

February 1942

German Listeners!
The need to cloak bestialism with legality is a familiar peculiarity of Nazism.[8] Thus, the maltreatment and butchering of Russian prisoners of war, for which the Soviet government has repeatedly issued formal charges, is supported by a previously unheard-of military doctrine entirely made up for the purpose of justifying such actions. Namely, enemy army groups that are—from the German perspective—surrounded, boxed in, cut off, are already considered to be prisoners, and if they do not surrender their weapons, then their resistance is no longer an act of combat,

---

7   Already during the war, the topic of reeducation had become the focus of debates about Germany after Hitler. Mann distances himself here from the advocates of forced education, like British diplomat Robert Vansittart and German-Swiss author and historian Emil Ludwig (1881–1948).

8   See annotations for the address of January 1942.

but one of insurrection, through which they forfeit the legal protections for prisoners of war. —What has become of the code of honor for German soldiers? In the past, an enemy soldier who had bravely defended himself to the utmost, was considered worthy of respect in the soldier's mind. Today he is declared contemptible. By what right? That is something nobody can figure out who does not first understand the insane logic of National Socialism as practiced already before their "seizure of power."[9] In essence, National Socialism holds that one may not resist it at all. To wage war against it when it takes over somewhere is in and of itself criminal: the nations must submit to it peacefully and voluntarily instead of forcing National Socialism itself into a war of self-defense through blasphemous rebellion. — It is an unprecedented, appalling phenomenon. The crime itself takes root on Earth as that which is untouchable, as a power blessed by God and history, so that raising a hand against it is a sacrilege worthy of death. The human spirit goes cold and silent in the face of such an apocalyptic effrontery.

The human spirit, however, will hardly surrender. The news that the Russian soldier receives about the fates of his comrades in German camps are said to have intensified his great aversion to sharing this fate: even if the German high command regards him as surrounded, he will not surrender so easily—for the same reasons, neither will those nations that are still trapped in unlawful wars with Nazi Germany surrender so easily. They have been informed about the outrageous activities of the German master race in the subjugated territories of Europe, through photographs, for example, that have reached us from Poland and which illustrate a misery, a violation of all that is human, for which there are no words: the bloated and starved corpses of Polish children, the thousands upon thousands of bodies of Jews who perished in the Warsaw ghetto from typhus, cholera, and consumption, piled together for the mass graves. The united nations know what dangers await them if he wins: they know what they themselves are in his eyes, in the eyes of Nazi Germany: vermin, human trash, inferior races, destined for slavery—destined to serve the bright and chosen royal race of the Germans, once they have been sufficiently ravaged, morally and physically: their pride, their virility broken, morally and biologically reduced such that they can never again pose a danger to the absolute dictatorship of the German noble barbarians. They see just how this happens with their own eyes from the example set in Poland. The Governor-General, a former hack lawyer known as Frank II,[10] has expressly declared: Poland is the model of how victorious

---

9   The quotation marks indicate that Mann sees "seizure" as a propaganda term. Hitler did not seize power; it was transferred to him as a result of risky political calculation.

10   After the end of hostilities in September 1939, parts of Poland (Reichsgau Wartheland; Danzig-West Prussia) were de facto annexed by Germany. On

Nazism intends to rule all over the world. Most notably, the country was methodically robbed of its potential intellectual and political leaders[11]: intellectuals, doctors, lawyers, university instructors, the affluent, and the highborn were murdered or tortured to death in concentration camps. Next came the common people. Eighty-five thousand were executed by the conqueror-race, a million and a half sent to Germany for hard labor, the women, the young girls consigned to prostitution through official channels. The rest of the population lives in devastating and stupefying, beggarly conditions.

Degradation, emasculation, extermination—that is all that Nazi Germany intends for the fellow nations of the Earth. In France the methods were only modified slightly to make them more subtle—but does not the captivity of French prisoners of war, the isolation of these one and a half or two million young men from natural life serve the same end of biological reduction?

Yes, Nazism knows how to convince the world of the absolute necessity of its elimination. The free nations, as repulsive as war is to them, as little prepared as they were for it, will fight on, year after year if necessary, and they will summon the last of their energies—though it will not come to that very soon—in order to rid the world of this plague of murderous arrogance. And the German people, upon whose shoulders their Führers amass a burden of guilt that makes one shudder? Do they alone have no concept of what is absolutely necessary, that without a doubt, precisely because it is necessary, will also be accomplished? Do they not begin to curse the teaching that idiotic scoundrels drilled into them of their chosen, noble blood that justifies any iniquity? Do they not long to be a people with which the others can live, so that the cry: "One must destroy the Nazis!" does not become even more emphatically the cry "One must destroy the Germans!"? How will a people with whom no other can coexist be able, itself, to live? How can a people participate in the spiritual and intellectual life of humankind, in the shared culture of humankind? After this war, what face will all that is German present to a human and humane society? German Listeners! As long as our people cannot make

---

October 12, 1939, the central and southern parts of the country were declared the "Generalgouvernement," with Krakow as its capital. Hans Frank (1900–1946) was appointed "Governor General"; in 1946, he was executed in Nuremberg as a war criminal.

11   The attack on Poland was essentially a war of extermination with the aim of decimating the Polish population, insofar as it was not used for slave labor, and robbing it of its leaders in order to suffocate any danger of a resistance movement. In the course of this "AB" action ("Außerordentliche Befriedung"; emergency pacification), around 30,000 intellectuals, professors, teachers, and priests were systematically rounded up and murdered by police task forces and Wehrmacht units.

peace with the belief that they are a people like any other, with their merits and equally significant flaws, they will be in danger of suffering the nightmarish fate of a global pariah. Only by virtue of their commitment to their humanity will they return to the place that is proper to them, in the community of nations.

March 1942

German Listeners!
Recently, I told you: "As long as the German people cannot admit that they are a people like any other, with their merits and their equally significant flaws and shortcomings, they will not find their place in a free and equal society of nations and will face the sinister fate of a global pariah, which will only lead to further criminal acts."[12] I am convinced that most Germans long for nothing more today than peace and freedom, sensible integration and collaboration. But this is not what that one character has in mind, that one whom a great people—once called to dignity and admiration in the realm of freedom—still allows to call himself their Führer. In his last speech[13]—and it is entirely possible that it was one of his last—in his last speech—if something like that can be called a speech—delivered on the occasion of the so-called Heroes Day of Remembrance in the Berlin Arsenal[14]—he indeed spoke of the "long, blessed years of peace that will follow this struggle," without going into detail about what any form of peace that had his blessing would look like, and without considering in his impoverished, bloodthirsty brain that, given the state in which he will leave Europe, the generational genocide that he himself brought about, there can be no talk of a blessed peace for a long time to come. But once again he barked emphatically about the fundamental uniqueness of the German people, the irreconcilability of its ideas and wishes with the most natural wishes and hopes of the rest of humankind: namely just as he was speaking of the United States and President Roosevelt, whom he indeed regards as his personal enemy and rival. Incidentally, it ought to be noted that his obsession with constantly comparing and measuring himself against Roosevelt (as though an itinerant marauder like him could even be placed in comparison with a real statesman like Roosevelt,[15] who is truly committed to the future of humanity), is a sight as absurd as it is revolting. The sentence from his chatter that I refer to is the following: "It is no concern of ours," he says "in what kind of a world the President

12 Although Mann uses quotation marks here, this is not a quote but a paraphrase. See the conclusion to the address of February 1942.
13 Mann is referring to Hitler's speech of March 15, 1942.
14 See Domarus VI, 2596–2600.
15 Mann had met Roosevelt during two visits to the White House (June 29, 1935; January 12–14, 1941) and admired him more than any other statesman. Vaget, *Thomas Mann, the American*, 67–149.

of the United States wishes to live. However, if he intends to reorganize Germany or Europe according to his own wishes, if he wants to create a world that is foreign and detestable to us, then we can only assure him that—."[16] Now, it is clear what he assures us of here. What we ask ourselves is only how and why it is that the beneficial outcomes President Roosevelt has described as the ultimate goals of this war unleashed by Hitler should be foreign and detestable to the German people and indeed all Europeans.

The president has promised the people four freedoms[17]: freedom of speech and of religion; freedom from want and from fear. But that is precisely what the peoples of Europe, including the Germans, are demanding from the bottoms of their tormented souls. The German people is not constituted so peculiarly, is no such monstrosity that it would prefer to live in a world of strangled speech, of religious persecution, and of want and fear. Anyone who claims such a thing is an illiterate chatterbox, who once heard something about the profound Germans, who do not aspire to happiness, but rather to a heroic existence. That is some beautiful heroic existence that he has given to you Germans, and that he hopes to continue to give you! It is an existence fit for a dog, and you will not be able to escape from it until you have rid yourselves of this catastrophe of a Führer.

I call it a wretched aristocratism, a pariah's privilege, to find detestable what everyone longs for, what everyone needs, and what the essential hope is of that true revolution that spreads across the Earth and in comparison to which Hitler's revolution is only a miserable cock-and-bull story. The peoples want to be free, free within a greater equality, freed from the fear of international brigandism and sharing equally in the enjoyment of this Earth's bounty. Does Hitler have any idea of the profound upheaval that is being brought about in the social life of the Anglo-American countries, of the rejuvenation and perfection of the democracy that is at stake, of the struggle by visionary people for a new balance of freedom and equality, justice and responsibility, the individual and the collective? Does he even know what democracy is when he condemns it in his stale propaganda? That Russia and the West now fight on the same side against him, the enemy of humankind, is only the most visible sign

---

16 Mann summarizes and paraphrases. His German citation of Hitler reads as follows: "Es geht uns nichts an," sagte er, "in welcher Art von Welt der Präsident der Vereinigten Staaten zu leben wünscht. Aber wenn er beabsichtigt, Deutschland oder Europa nach seinen Wünschen neu zu ordnen, wenn er hier eine uns fremde und verabscheuenswürdige Welt schaffen will, so können wir ihm nur versichern—." See Domarus IV, 2599.

17 In his address to the American people on January 6, 1941, Roosevelt refers to the four freedoms: freedom of speech, freedom of worship, freedom from want, and freedom from fear.

of the essential truth that socialism and democracy have long ceased to be opposites, that their values strive toward synthesis and that this is the revolution that will be victorious over the morass of lies and violence that he calls a revolution.

This era of suffering and the ruin of so many is at the same time an era of inclusive hope. Humankind can emerge from this catastrophe one great step ahead in civil cultivation and maturity. Possibilities come into focus that until only recently nobody would have dared to envision: the organization of a society of peoples, the administration of the Earth for the good of all, peace, freedom, and security.[18] The arbitrariness of the nation-state must be discarded, and yet the nation will live on. Germany will live, in pride *and* humility, a unique people, and a people like all others.[19]

(Special Broadcast)
April 1942

This is the first anniversary of the devastation of Coventry by Göring's airmen[20]—one of the most ghastly achievements through which Hitler-Germany taught the world what total war is and how one wages it.

It started in Spain,[21] where the engineers of death, this indoctrinated National Socialist race with their empty, bestial faces, rehearsed for this war. What great sport, where there is no resistance whatsoever, to buzz down ready and eager from above on fleeing masses of civilians. The

---

18   In Washington on January 1, 1942, the "Big Four" nations (the US, the USSR, Great Britain, and China) waging war against the Axis powers signed the "Declaration by United Nations," and the next day, twenty-two other nations signed the document too. They pledged to fight together against the Axis powers according to the principles of the Atlantic Charter and not to seek a separate peace. The declaration represents an important step toward the founding of the United Nations.

19   That Germany was called upon to play an exceptional and dominant role in the world was a pillar of National Socialist and "völkisch" ideology. The laconic ring to the phrase "a people like all" is reminiscent of the final words in Gurnemanz's story of Titurel's death in Act 3 of Richard Wagner's opera *Parsifal*: "Er starb,—ein Mensch wie alle" (He died—a human being like all others).

20   The worst damage occurred on the night of November 14–15, 1940, when, at the direction of Göring, Luftwaffe squadrons with a total of 515 aircraft carried out "Unternehmen Mondscheinsonate" (Operation Moonlight Sonata). Over 500 people lost their lives and over 1,000 were injured in the attack. Mann's statement that Coventry Day, April 8, 1942, marked the anniversary of Coventry's destruction is based on a misunderstanding. The BBC used Coventry Day to mark one year since the bombing in Coventry resumed.

21   During the Spanish Civil War, Germany provided military assistance to the fascist putschists under General Francisco Franco (1892–1975). On April 26, 1937, the "Condor Legion" bombed the town of Guernica near Bilbao.

commemoration of the massacres in Poland is similarly unforgettable,[22] a glorious chapter as such accomplishments are known, and Rotterdam,[23] where thirty-thousand people met their ends in twenty minutes, thanks to a bravery that is difficult to distinguish from moral mental derangement.

The noble von Ribbentrop hid his face and wept:[24] This isn't what we wanted! Those were the good days when there was only weeping about harm inflicted upon others. The time is coming—and is already here[25]—in which Germany will also have to weep about what it has suffered. And this touching narrative will get out of control just as the world, which wanted to know nothing of such service to humanity and wasn't prepared for it, steps up to its task of defense and assumes the role of the apprentice who surpasses the master.

Did Germany believe that it would never have to pay for the atrocities that its initiation of barbarism allowed it to commit? It has barely begun to pay—not on the other side of the Channel nor in Russia. And what the Royal Air Force has wrought to date in Cologne, Düsseldorf, Essen, Hamburg and other cities is only a beginning. Hitler boasts that his empire is ready to fight a ten-year, even a twenty-year-long war. I imagine that, for your part, you Germans are thinking that after only a fragment of that time not a single brick would be left standing on another in Germany.

During the most recent British raid over Hitlerland, old Lübeck had to suffer.[26] That is my concern. That is my hometown. The attacks were intended for the port of Travemünde, the military industrial facilities there, but there were fires in the city, and it is no pleasure to me to think that the Marienkirche, the glorious Renaissance city hall or the office of the shipping company should have suffered damage. However, when I think of Coventry, I have no objections to make against the tenet that everything must be paid for.

There will be more Lübeckers, more Hamburgers, Cologners, and Düsseldorfers, who have no objection to this, and when they hear the thunder of the Royal Air Force planes overhead, will wish them every

22   See annotations for the address of February 1942.

23   The major port city of Rotterdam was bombed on May 14, 1940. The bombing completely destroyed parts of the city and killed over 800 people.

24   Joachim von Ribbentrop was Reichsminister of Foreign Affairs from 1938. No source for this story has been identified. Mann's description of Ribbentrop as a "nobleman" is to be understood ironically: Ribbentrop had made a fortune in the liquor trade. He acquired his aristocratic title by allowing himself to be formally adopted by a noblewoman in return for a pension. He was executed as a war criminal in 1946.

25   See John 16:32.

26   The attack on Lübeck, Mann's hometown, was the most ambitious campaign in the war against Germany up to that point. Over 200 bombers were involved. The historic part of the city burned and over 300 people lost their lives.

success. It might even be possible that my own sense of justice in particular would be put to a unique test by such a bombardment.

Swedish papers report—and American papers have questioned me about it—that my grandparent's house, the so-called Buddenbrook House on Mengstraße,[27] is supposed to have been destroyed during the raid. I don't know if the news is true. For many who are not from the city, because of the novel written in my youth, the name Lübeck is associated with the idea of this house, and it readily comes to mind when bombs fall on Lübeck. For locals, however, it has long since ceased to be called the Buddenbrook House. The Nazis, disgruntled that foreigners constantly ask about it, have redubbed it the Wullenweber House.[28] The stupid lowlifes don't even know that a house that bears the stamp of the eighteenth century on its Rococo gable could not reasonably have anything to do with the reckless mayor of the sixteenth century. Jürgen Wullenweber inflicted a lot of damage on his city in the war with Denmark. And the people of Lübeck did with him what the Germans will perhaps do someday with those who led them into this war. They executed him. It should be said of the inhabitants of the house, after whom the house was renamed in order to erase my name, that they have always only done good for the city. And in my own way I have even followed their example. Following an example in one's own way, that is tradition. The old town house, which, it is said, now lies in ruins, was to me the symbol of the tradition from which I come, but such ruins do not scare those who live not only out of sympathy for the past, but also sympathy for the future. The downfall of an age need not be the downfall of the individual rooted in it, who outgrew it, and who portrayed it to you. Hitler's Germany has neither tradition nor future. It can only destroy.

May a Germany arise from its fall that can both remember and hope. One receptive to the experience of love for the past and for the future of humankind. In this way, in place of hatred, Germany will win the love of its fellow nations.

April 1942

German Listeners!
Germany, Japan, and pitiable Italy, in short, the Axis Powers, are the ones who pervert the social revolution currently reshaping the world in order to create vast empires. Only the democracies—which are accused of

---

27 The Manns' home at Mengstraße 4 was built in 1758. The family purchased the house in 1841, and it remained in their possession until 1891. Except for the façade and the cellar, the house was destroyed during the bombing of Lübeck on March 28–29, 1942.

28 Mann is misinformed. During the Third Reich, the house was renamed the "Brun-Warendorp-Haus," named after a fourteenth-century mayor of Lübeck who commanded the Hanseatic League's armed forces.

senescence, of morbid clinging to the old and the enervated—are sincere about the revolution and about a better, happier future. For Hitler's Germany and Japan on the other hand, the "New Order" is,[29] the hopes of peoples are nothing more than the means of propaganda to the ends of treachery, subversion, conquest, and oppression. If the social revolution has taken on the form of a bloody, ravaging, and still unforeseeable war—it is their fault: because it was they who contaminated the process of necessary change—a mutation of democracy that, in virtue of its inevitability, could have taken place peacefully—with their debasing ideas of nation and race, and reduced the revolution to a fraudulent contrivance of nationalistic superpower politics. At a moment in history when the increasing obsolescence of the national has become glaringly evident to everyone; when the merely national orientation fails to provide a solution to any problem, can no longer solve a single political, economic, intellectual, or moral problem; and when the necessity of dismantling and curtailing national sovereignties has become self-evident, they reveled in nationalism, they single-handedly provoked the nationalist war of conquest—this war for the homicidal idea of racial supremacy and the enslavement of peoples by some chosen master bloodline.

This will have been pointless. Nothing is more idle or criminal than the war of the imperialist governments, which the democratic nations sought to escape for so long, and wage so reluctantly and only out of necessity—which does not mean that they will not win it. The actual and true revolution will gain the upperhand over war as pillage. The results of all bloodshed will be revolutionary results, not those of war. The people, if not also their governments, can sense this—as is evident from their comportment in the face of the victories that their Führers serve up to them. It is a completely joyless and completely distrustful comportment. The Germans look upon Japan's victories with poorly disguised resentment. They get nothing from them, and it's beginning to appear to them as though they are actually shouldering the costs of Japan's conquests with their own goods and blood.[30] Conversely, they have long faced their own victories with an apathy that clearly demonstrates that they consider them to be pointless and ruinous. They have subdued nine nations, but they are not proud of it. The collapse of France filled them with joy—not because they enjoyed the sight of war, but rather because they believed that it would be the end of the war. But since then? When, at the movies, they saw German troops marching into Russian cities, a profound silence

29   See annotations for the addresses of October 1941 and January 1942.

30   The Japanese Empire, which had been expanding since the end of the nineteenth century, used the Second World War as a pretense to establish the Greater East Asia Co-Prosperity Sphere by conquering British Hong Kong, British Malaya, French Indochina, the Philippines, and other territories.

occupied the theater. When the screen showed Göring's airmen dropping bombs on London, one heard no applause, but rather sighs. Those were not just sighs of anxiety at the coming retaliation: no, this complete lack of enthusiasm about victory is an expression of intrinsic knowledge that Germany's military victories are false victories and bloody plunder-raids, a lot of rubbish that leads to nothing, because conquests are futile before that which is truly historic: revolution.

Germany came no closer to a revolution in the year 1933 than it ever had before. *Russia* had a true revolution,[31] and, to the astonished admiration of the entire world, their faith in that revolution has carried them through their defensive struggle against the Nazi invasion. In the Anglo-American countries, revolutions are taking place in the midst of war, revolutions that reduce all the fascist propaganda-bleating about plutocracy and capitalist calcification to childish taunting. Is it Roosevelt who wants to return to the nineteenth century? Is Churchill a Manchester Man?[32] It was the two of them together who wrote the Atlantic Charter,[33] a revolutionary document that established the principles of peace and proclaimed a "New Order," a social order of justice and the fulfillment of the right to peace and security for all, compared to which Hitler's version of the concept is nothing but an imbecilic abomination.

Democracy does not look backward, it looks forward. It is in the process of renewing itself socially. For democracy, revolution is no pretense for conquest, plundering and subjugation, but rather the cause itself is the end, the cause of humanity. If tomorrow the mischief of war were to end, if you Germans were to chase off your plundering mob, the Nazis, and offer freedom to the world—then the work could begin, the work on the "New Order" for which all nations long.

You say that you can't? The terror is too great, the Gestapo state too insurmountable?[34] We have to cling to the war in order to put off the horrors of defeat? Then it must be repeated to you: A people who *wants* to be free *is* in that very instant free. If the people went out onto

---

31 The Bolshevik Revolution in Russia of 1917.

32 In other words, a representative of the outdated theory of free trade and unrestricted economic liberalism that emerged in Manchester during the mid-nineteenth century.

33 The Atlantic Charter of 1941 was a joint declaration of US-British goals for the world after the end of the Second World War, including free trade, self-determination, disarmament, and collective security. See the annotations on the address of September 1941.

34 The Secret State Police, or Gestapo, created by Göring in 1933 and subordinate to Heinrich Himmler—the commander of the Schutzstaffel (SS) from 1934—had the task of silencing critics and opponents of the Nazi regime. The Gestapo operated outside the law and spread terror and death in the European territories occupied by Germany.

the streets of the German cities and cried in unison: "Down with war and with the defilement of the nations, down with Hitler and all Hitler-trash—freedom, justice, and peace for us and for everyone!"—the Nazis would recognize that they have lost: they would shoot, naturally, but a regime of reckless marauders that has to shoot at its people is doomed, and surely a German uprising would not cost as much of your blood as currently flows in Russia.

Germans, the free nations still have hope for you, right to the very end they will have hope for you. America most of all, which knows no hate against the German people, entertains this hope: for, in order to make amends for the sins committed against it by an imbecilic berserker, they would much rather send ships delivering provisions to the tortured continent than darken the European heavens with squadrons of planes delivering devastation.

May 1942

German Listeners!
Encounters with the essential and characteristic are always pleasing. For this reason, a statement by Nazi Propaganda Minister Goebbels was indeed received with distinct psychological satisfaction by the world. It reads: "In the event of defeat, we will all be hanged with the same rope."[35]

This is of course not true, since the extermination of the German people is neither feasible nor desirable, and no sensible person is contemplating it. But it is an expression of uplifting authenticity, a snippet of gangster slang, revealing of the kind of self-understanding that brought it forth, the word of a condemned gallow's bird who is fully aware what he and his ring of accomplices have coming to them when it all falls apart, who also already sees that it will in fact all fall apart, and now seeks to diffuse his fate as widely as possible, who now cannot emphasize enough the nation's shared liability for everything that has happened and cries out to you, squawking: "Don't just abandon us now! You chose to consort with us, tolerated us, went along with everything. Once you say A, you have to say B, then you have to recite the entire alphabet of crimes to the very end, and maybe you'll get off with a black eye. If you desert us, if you refuse to play along any more—then the same rope awaits us all."

The rope is waiting for him, for him and the whole regiment of scoundrels whose mouth of lies he was, first and foremost for that indescribable creature who for nine disastrous years has been permitted to call himself the Führer of Germany. If this rope is a metaphor, then it is an accidentally well-chosen metaphor, for the rope is the instrument of dishonorable execution, and one can only hope that the German people will not relinquish this instrument to foreigners, but rather themselves put

---

35 The source of the quote has not been identified.

to death the criminal coterie that has ruined and abused it like no other people has been ruined and abused. This is the first thing and the least that the world expects of the German people, as a sign that, after a long aberration, it is intent on leading a new, decent life.

A people is always capable of such a new start, particularly a people with the adaptability of the Germans. However, no one claims that it will be an easy and comfortable new start. Nobody intends to lull you Germans into the false belief that human society will—after the deluge of offenses that they had to tolerate from you—welcome you with open arms from one day to the next as a member in good standing, as soon as it pleases you to give them a sign of willingness. That person would do wrong who painted such a picture for you. The sentimental savages among you should not be permitted to scream again that you have been lured with enticing promises that have not been kept. The more clever and just among you know quite precisely how things stood. They know that your leaders at the time scorned and rejected Wilson's Fourteen Point Plan as long as there was a spark of hope for victory left in them.[36] It was only when they ran out of breath that Wilson's plan[37]—for which no one was prepared at the time, least of all we Germans—would be invoked as a kind of safeguard,[38] to justify their well-worn talk of "national restoration."[39]

---

36 On January 8, 1918, President Woodrow Wilson (1856–1924) presented a Fourteen Points peace plan to the American Congress, which was to serve as a guideline for the peace negotiations and the postwar order. The most important points concerned Germany: the evacuation of Belgium and Russia; the return of Alsace-Lorraine to France; self-determination of the peoples in the Austro-Hungarian dual monarchy; the creation of the independent states of Poland, Romania, Serbia, Montenegro, and Turkey; as well as the League of Nations. See "President Wilson's Message to Congress," January 8, 1918, Records of the United States Senate, Record Group 46, National Archives. For Mann's own initially skeptical assessment of President Wilson and his Fourteen Points peace plan, see Mann's diaries, 1918–1921.

37 On October 3, 1918, Reich Chancellor Prince Max von Baden (1867–1929) submitted a request to President Wilson for an armistice according to the terms of his Fourteen Points, but only after the failed spring offensive of 1918 when the military situation had become hopeless and at the urging of Field Marshal Erich Ludendorff (1865–1937) and the Supreme Army Command.

38 In the original German, Mann uses the term "Palladium," referring to the sacred shied of Pallas Athena, the patron goddess and protector of Athens.

39 Mann's use of the term "Nationale Wiedererstarkung" appears to be a dismissive reference to the Nazi narrative in which the allegedly empty promises of the Fourteen Points actually justified and legitimized their goal of national rejuvenation.

As a revolutionary plan for a new, social, and just order of nations that should result from this war, the eight points of the Atlantic Charter go much further than the Wilsonian list, and self-evidently they are also valid for Germany.[40] If anyone says to you that the world needs Germany and that everyone would be only too happy to see a Germany that had rejected violence, ugly self-exaltation, and homicidal mania honestly integrating itself into the "new order," that is no pretense intended to enervate you. But they would be lying if they said to you that this will be accomplished overnight. Too much has happened, humankind has suffered too much; the corruptibility, ease of intoxication, and political immaturity of the German people have brought about too many atrocities for it to reasonably expect a swift restoration of trust. Transgressions of morality demand atonement, and Germany has dedicated itself to transgressions of morality that truly cry out to heaven. The despicable orgy to which Germany's educated class surrendered itself—when in 1933 the lowest in the country rose to its highest ranks, and National Socialism introduced its rule—is unforgettable. Believing that it was this riff-raff's calling to restore national dignity and honor; failing to see that from the very first day their dominion spelled war, catastrophe, the abyss, and nothing else; reveling with studied perversity in the shabbiest pathology and wanton criminality like a barbarian basking in the glow of a successful raid—it is unallowable to lack intuition to such a degree, such a frenzy of miscalculation is punishable, and nothing could make the Germans look worse than self-pity in defeat, after they themselves exacted such atrocities as had never before been seen in history.

Honor and equal rights will have to wait. Germany has denied and trampled freedom and equality for too long for the Germans to demand them for themselves on the first day of capitulation. An extended quarantine of caution and surveillance will be unavoidable. Germany will have to be helped financially, but military power will necessarily be denied to a nation that for the longest time could only envision its union with the world in the form of world conquest and subjugation. The internal political organization of Germany will be left to the Germans themselves, whereby the task of the German people, and the most indispensable guaranty of their future trustworthiness will be that they bring themselves to undertake an ideological cleansing of society, one that needs

---

40 Articles 4 and 6 of the Atlantic Charter are relevant here. In Article 4, the USA and Great Britain pledge to "further the enjoyment by all States, great or small, victor or vanquished, of access, on equal terms, to the trade and to the raw materials of the world which are needed for their economic prosperity." Article 6: "After the final destruction of the Nazi tyranny, they hope to see established a peace which will afford to all nations the means of dwelling in safety within their own boundaries, and which will afford assurance that all the men in all lands may live out their lives in freedom from fear and want."

to be thorough and must not be limited to wiping out the pestilence of Nazism. It must extend to the entire class of people who instrumentalized Nazism in the service of their hunger for power and possessions, and who must never again be in any position to make Germanness the scourge of the human race.[41]

June 1942

German Listeners!

In one of my earlier broadcasts, I was guilty of a regrettable reduction of the truth.[42] I was speaking about the disgraceful crimes of the Nazis and mentioned that four hundred young Dutch people of Jewish descent had been transported to Germany to be murdered with poison gas. I now hear through indirect channels from Holland that my account turned out to be too low by nearly half.[43] It was in fact close to eight hundred individuals who were arrested, taken to Mauthausen, and gassed to death there.[44] In the meantime, the precise number has been published by the Dutch government, but since I do not suppose that this report has made it to your ears, I do well to pass on to you this information, which I received privately. It demonstrates that Nazi dehumanization always surpasses what is reported and what is ascribed to it: there is never any risk of exaggeration; assuming the worst always falls short of the truth by half.

And is not the bestial mass murder of Mauthausen just one unremarkable detail in the greater scheme of this state of dehumanization? Does it not become lost in the sea of abominable atrocities that spans the entire tortured dominion of Hitler's wickedness? Since the violent death of Heydrich,[45] the most *natural* death that a bloodhound like he can die,

---

41   Mann means primarily representatives of heavy industry such as Fritz Thyssen (1873–1951), Hugo Stinnes (1870–1924), and the descendants of Friedrich Krupp (1854–1902). See the address of July 1942.

42   See annotations for the address of January 1942.

43   Apparently, Thomas Mann had received copies of one Thea Dispeker's (1902–2000) correspondence with her sister-in-law Grete Weil, née Dispeker (1906–1999) in Holland. Grete, a professional photographer and later author, was married to Edgar Weil (1908–1941), a Germanist of Jewish descent, who had gone into exile in Holland after losing his position as dramaturge at the Munich Kammerspiele in 1933. After the occupation of the Netherlands, he was arrested on June 11, 1941 and transported to the Mauthausen concentration camp near Linz, Austria, where he was murdered on September 17, 1941.

44   Opened in August 1938 near Linz on the Danube, Mauthausen was the first concentration camp built in Austria after the Anschluss. In the summer of 1941, the camp began murdering prisoners from all over Europe in gas chambers and mobile gas chambers on trucks. See the address of January 1942.

45   SS-Obergruppenführer (lieutenant general) Reinhard Tristan Heydrich (1904–1942) was known as "the Butcher of Prague." He held several high-ranking positions: founder (as of 1931) then director (as of 1933) of the

the terror rages on more diseased and self-indulgent than ever. It is grotesque, and the mixture of brutality and howling self-pity that has always been a hallmark of Nazism overwhelms one with repulsion. That the assassination and the escape of the assassins could hardly have succeeded without a nod of approval and assistance from the Nazis goes without saying. Corruption is a swamp with no bottom: there is simply nothing that is beyond it. But has any person of Heydrich's ilk ever ended any differently? Is not the death that he met the most natural consequence in the world, a common occupational hazard and a cold matter of probability, the fulfillment of which cannot surprise any being endowed with logic, let alone leave them distraught. Wherever this two-bit murderer went, rivers of blood flowed. Everywhere, in Germany as well, he was known crudely as "the Hangman." His name was a signature under death sentences, nothing more. He rapidly issued thirty-four of them before he went from Prague to Paris, for a short but effective visit that yielded 153 murdered hostages. That happened even before he occupied Hradčany as protector,[46] and there he subjected the Czech people to a form of protection that will blemish the German name for one hundred years. Now then, he has been murdered. And how do the Nazis receive this news? They fall into convulsions. They literally behave as though the most incomprehensible iniquity had occurred, the pinnacle of humanity profaned, the crown, the palladium stolen. Every flicker of logical decency is foreign to them, even the faintest sense of justice eludes them, they possess not even a glimmer of reason. Their voices fail them when they scream for retribution. And then they get down to business. The grief-stricken Führer, who lost a manly-beloved murderer, gives his directives, concocted during slumberless nights. Butchery and gunfire break out, a rampage against defenselessness and innocence, quite in accordance with Nazi tastes. Thousands must die, men and women. An entire village that is supposed to have provided sanctuary to the culprits, Lidiče, is

---

Sicherheitsdienst (Security Service), head of the Gestapo (as of 1934) and the Criminal Investigation Unit (as of 1936), director of Himmler's Reichssicherheitshauptamt (Reich Security Central Office, as of 1939), and finally interim Deputy Reich Protector for Bohemia and Moravia in Prague (from 1941). Heydrich was wounded in an assassination attempt on May 27, 1942 by two agents of the Czechoslovak exile government in London and died on June 4, 1942. The success of the Czech resistance inspired exiles and informed, e.g., Fritz Lang's 1943 film *Hangmen Also Die,* featuring a score by Hanns Eisler (1898–1962) and a screenplay to which Bertolt Brecht contributed.

46 Hradčany is the district surrounding Prague Castle, former seat of the kings of Bohemia and presidents of Czechoslovakia, in what is now the Czech Republic.

exterminated and bulldozed.[47] The population of Prague that is left alive must line the streets while the funeral cortege of the saint passes by. At home, he is provided with a grandiose state funeral, and another master butcher says of him before the grave that he was a pure soul and a human being with immense feeling for humanity.[48]

All of this is insane. It is the insanity that a confused world has allowed to become absolute, and that now has the power of indiscriminate desecration of language, of the healthy sense of reason, of human decency. To insanity, power is everything; and, in order to run amok, insanity requires power unconditionally. No rational being is dependent on and craves power like insanity itself does. Nobody needs power to be able to tell the truth. But to be able to say: Heydrich was a noble human being,[49] that requires power—the absolute power to dictate what is truth and what is nonsense. And no rational person does everything that they happen to have the power to do. The Nazi on the other hand looks around to see if there is someone there who might interrupt them, inhibit them, punish them. If no one is there, if the avenger is too far away, then they act.

Philosophers of history have called power itself evil. I do not believe that.[50] Only the degenerate see power as an opportunity to do evil without punishment.[51] May this war give power to those in whose heads reason, in whose hearts sympathy resides and for whom power is a means to a good end.

---

47 Lidiče is a small village north-west of Prague. The occupying forces intended to make an example of the town, allegedly because it had harbored the assassins.

48 An official ceremony took place in the Reich Chancellery on June 9, 1942, at which Himmler and Hitler gave speeches.

49 A "noble" from the perspective of Nazi ideology. Heydrich came from a musical family, was well-educated, and was an exemplary Nazi in both spirit and "Nordic" appearance.

50 *Geschichtsphilosophie* was a movement beginning in the late eighteenth century (Herder, Kant, Schiller) that sought to understand the present and envision the future based on patterns demonstrated throughout history. See, e.g. Jacob Burckhardt (1818–1897) in *Weltgeschichtliche Betrachtungen* (World-Historical Considerations, 1905): "Und nun ist die Macht an sich böse, gleichviel, wer sie ausübe" (And so it is that power is evil in itself, no matter who exercises it).

51 The alleged "Entartung" (degeneracy) of their opponents was a prominent concept in Nazi racial and cultural policy, as demonstrated in the Nazi use of the phrase "entartete Kunst" (degenerate art) to denigrate modern art that they claimed insulted German culture. Here, Mann turns the adjective "degenerate" against its advocates.

July 1942

German Listeners!

I know well that one need not warn you against overconfidence, now that Hitler is once again on a winning streak and has conquered Rostov, the city on the Don that he had already conquered once before.[52] It is known to all that things like this do not inspire overconfidence in you, that the radio fanfares with which they are announced to you disgust you,[53] that you are not the least bit glad about them. There is no victory high among you to dampen: one must comfort you. We on the outside are not the ones who require comfort when the war situation looks as it does right now. If you only knew how confident we are in our purpose, which is only a start and a prerequisite for everything else, that is, the purpose of Hitler's downfall. His fate is sealed. Just believe, and have no fear.[54] It is a global necessity, wholly unavoidable, and will be accomplished one way or another: the fact that this is guaranteed simply makes the wretch's victory a mere bloody absurdity.

You are distraught and despondent. You think to yourselves: what if he triumphs after all? And what if we never get rid of him? And the world is supposed to become German in the desperate way that we are German now? —Take heart! Talk of Hitler's victory is words devoid of meaning: there is no such thing, it exists nowhere in the realm of the acceptable, the permissible, the conceivable. It will be prevented—much more, he himself will always prevent it, the wretched scoundrel, by virtue of what he is, of his very nature, of the impossibility of his hopelessly defective disposition, which enables him to think, to want, and to do only that which is wrong, deceitful, rejected for its depravity sight unseen. One speaks of the devil deceived.[55] But the Devil does not come to be deceived, he *is* deceived, of his own accord and from the outset. This brainless Beelzebub will not accompany Faust's soul, the soul of humankind, to hell, he will go down *alone*.

---

52 Having been captured on November 21, 1941 and liberated by Red Army units in December, the Russian city Rostov-on-Don once again fell under German control after heavy fighting from July 19 to 24, 1942.

53 With the beginning of the Russian campaign, the special reports of the Großdeutscher Rundfunk were introduced with fanfares from Franz Liszt's (1811–1886) symphonic poem *Les Préludes* (1854).

54 A common expression of divine consolidation in both the Old and New Testaments (e.g., Luke 12:5).

55 Tales about deceiving the devil have been a staple of burlesque farce since the Middle Ages.

I say: Take heart! Do you think that he only needs to gain the Caucasus to be able to re-oil his steamroller of world conquest?[56] And if he does gain it, and the Russians are pushed back to the Urals—where next? But of course: onward. It can only continue, ever deeper into night, madness, and death: there is no end for *him*, there is only *his* end.

The Russians will not make peace—surely none of you believes they will. The Nazi revolution of lies has run up against a real and true revolution, one from whose determination to clean house you might be able to profit, you Germans, when your hour comes. And this Russian revolution is linked by its long-term, clear-willed treatises, unique in the history of humankind, with Anglo-American democracy,[57] which—now awakened to obligations to social duty—is likewise engaged in a process of revolutionary rejuvenation, allied with it in a struggle that Hitler, with his devil's dung of a "New Order," can never survive. The subjugated, plundered, martyred, half-exterminated peoples of Europe look to this alliance, in which the hatred of the shameless oppressor—still impotent and yet time and again unleashing itself in desperate individual acts—rages and ferments unceasingly, and who are only waiting for the moment when they can cast off in terrible revolt the most loathsome yoke that ever was forced upon any people. That is what Germans like you await. Ought one not ask you when you will finally expel the infernal pimp who does all of this to you and who remade the German countenance as a Medusa grimace? When you will give up and capitulate to reason? There is no point in pushing or questioning you like that, we all understand, because you cannot. It is not like 1918 when Germany collapsed. A body politic like yours, harnessed and splinted with iron, does not collapse, but rather stands up gruesomely, even when everything beneath the iron is already rotten.

Do I have to tell you how rotten it already looks under the armor that holds you upright? You know it better than we do, and I believe that nobody can be as terrified of you as you have become terrified of yourselves. But the hobbled ghost that you are quickly becoming will have to collapse at some point, and that will be the moment of your rebirth as a human and humane people. Were there not already last winter mass executions of mutinous troops? There will soon be more and ever more of them. The strike of the senselessly bled-out People's Army[58]—according to all probability, that will be the form of both your fall and your ascension.

56 Rostov was strategically important for the Army Group South's advance toward the Caucasus Mountains and the Russian oil fields.

57 Mann refers here foremost to the revolutionary social legislation of the New Deal in Roosevelt's first term of office (1933–1937), but also to similar efforts in Great Britain, which resulted in the "Beveridge Report" (1942), which in turn created the basis for national social insurance and free universal healthcare implemented after the war. Mann welcomed these social democratic reforms as the awakening of Western democracies to their "obligations to social duty."

58 Volksheer is a generic German term for people's army or state militia.

The end is coming, Germans, believe me and take heart! At this very moment, I say, even when things once again appear to point to success and victory and conquest. The end is in sight—not for you, not for Germany. Talk of the so-called annihilation of Germany is empty words, a non-existent absurdity just as empty as talk of Hitler's victory. But the end is coming, and there will be an end, and soon at that; the end of the disgraceful system of the state of plunder, murder, and lies of National Socialism. —

Hitler's philosophical garbage and disrepute and the deeds of garbage and disrepute that flowed from them will come to an end. They will reckon, reckon devastatingly, with his fat cats, his movers and shakers and helpers, attendants and beneficiaries, his generals, diplomats, and Gestapo-hyenas. They will reckon, reckon devastatingly, with his intellectual trailblazers, shield bearers, and the journalists and philosophasters, who licked up his spittle, the geopoliticians,[59] war-geographers, professors of warfare and race will be reckoned with, too. Germany will be purged of everything that had anything in the slightest to do with the filth of Hitlerism and that made it *possible*.

And a freedom will be established in Germany and in the world that believes in itself, that respects itself, that knows how to defend itself, and that does not privilege the deed, but rather first the thought behind it, in that cultivation of ideas where human beings bond with God.

August 1942

German Listeners!
The Greek myths tell of a king, Midas, who turned everything he touched into gold.[60] We are learning today that there is a touch that instantly turns everything, even the most noble of things, into dreck: it is National Socialism upon which this disgusting gift was bestowed. All the ideas of the age, born of the ardor for intellect and a better future, of the wish for a more perfect social existence, everything that is good and well-intended, National Socialism usurps, steals, bends, twists, corrupts, and pollutes, endows it with repulsive deformities, the stench of repulsion and hell—everything it touches—and it touches everything—in its hands perforce becomes excrement and filth. I said it early on and I say it again: the element of *defilement* is the most striking and most characteristic in this

---

59 For example, Karl Haushofer (1869–1946), who taught at the University of Munich and whose book *Bausteine zur Geopolitik* (*Foundations of Geopolitics*, 1928) informed Hitler and the Nazis' ideas about expansion and conquest.

60 In legend, Midas was the king of Phrygia in Asia Minor. His story is told by Ovid in the 11th book of *Metamorphoses* (ca. 8 CE). Midas is granted the fulfillment of a wish by Dionysus as a reward for a good deed. Midas's wish that everything he touches will turn to gold soon proves to be foolish, because it also affects, among other things, his food.

ghastly phenomenon.[61] It has defiled every idea that the world's best held sacred and made of them something that no decent person wants anything to do with. The idea of *socialism* for example, as it recently showed itself to us once again in its truth and purity in the world-famous speech on the "Century of the Common Man" by the Vice President of the United States, Henry A. Wallace[62]—what will become of it when the Hitler pack takes it into their mouth and practices it? Humiliation and disenfranchisement, darkness, mass apathy and languor, in short: slavery. The idea of *revolution* itself, which even in its crassest manifestations has always been associated with the noble-minded aspirations of humankind, the longing for greater freedom, greater justice, and greater happiness on Earth—as a National Socialist revolution it is theft, plundering, genocide, dissolute disavowal of the achievements of millennia, fantastic regression into the bestial. The idea of *peace*, to mention it as well, have we not loved it and believed in it? Did we not feel that peace was the order of the day, and that war was only a wanton evasion and a flight from responsibility like that of truant children before the great challenges that now confront humanity, and that they could only be accomplished in peace and through peace? Now, even National Socialism says "peace," demands "peacetime." But what does it mean by that? The coerced submission to evil, the self-abdication of the human being—that is what is meant: and it has made out of the most convinced pacifist a supporter of the war,[63] of the unavoidable war against *National Socialism*. — Was not *patriotism* something beautiful, something natural, and something good—love for one's heritage, culture, the language of the people from whom one descended—a love that lent itself so well to sympathy and admiration for human diversity, the intellectual charms and cultural contributions

---

61 Defilement (*Verhunzung*) is a key term in, for example, Mann's 1938 essay "Bruder Hitler" ("That Man is my Brother," published in English in 1939).

62 On May 8, 1942, Vice President Henry A. Wallace (1888–1965) delivered his speech, "The Price of Free World Victory," later renamed "The Century of the Common Man," to the International Free World Association, a left-liberal and antifascist organization founded in 1941. The speech's significance lies in its outline of an alternative to the powerful press czar Henry R. Luce's ideas about a post-war world order, which he presented prior to America's entry into the war in a far-reaching essay entitled "The American Century" (*Life*, January 17, 1941). Wallace rejected the imperialist spirit of the "American Century" and prophesied a "Century of the Common Man" characterized by the pursuit of social justice. Mann supported Wallace when he ran against Harry Truman and Thomas Dewey in the 1948 presidential election as the nominee of the Progressive Party, because he considered Wallace to be Roosevelt's more legitimate political heir.

63 Mann himself was no staunch pacifist even before Hitler turned him into a militant antifascist. As early as 1922, in "On the German Republic," he declared: "I am not a pacifist."

of other nationalities? What has the reverse-Midas, National Socialism, created from the gold of patriotism? Indeed, dreck, self-evidently. From patriotism it has created idiotic boasting, apoplectic racial arrogance, manic-murderous self-idolization, hatred, violence, and nonsense. And it wants to build the "New Order,"[64] to build Europe, upon perfected infamy, upon the most insane degeneracy of German nationalism.

Europe! National Socialism is indeed about to despoil even the idea of "Europe" for us: yes, more than any other, this idea has fallen victim to National Socialist defilement. "Europe wants to become one," Nietzsche once wrote. "We good Europeans," is his phrase, as is the coinage "European microstate mentality," which would need to come to an end.[65] The concept "Europe" was dear to us, something natural to our thoughts and desires. It was the opposite of provincial insularity, of narrow-minded egoism, of nationalistic crudeness and illiteracy; it stood for freedom, openness, intellect, and benevolence. "Europe," this meant a niveau, a cultural standard: a book, a work of art was good if it was known throughout Europe: you were only a good German, an exceptional German, if you were a European. National Socialism followed suit. It too speaks of "Europe"—but in the same way it invokes "revolution," or "peace," or "fatherland." It is not Germany that should become European, but rather Europe that should become German. Amid the desperate resistance of the peoples, wading in blood, surrounded by misery and curses, numb to a hatred such as no people on Earth has ever had to bear, it is fast at work transforming Europe into a nullified, neutered, spiritually diminished tool of monopolistic Germany, sparsely populated by exploited slave races, a German "protectorate" in the most contemptible sense of the word. In the protectorate "Czechoslovakia,"[66] the universities and almost all of the secondary schools have been closed, libraries and laboratories looted. It is not permitted for Czech history to be taught in schools, but German class and classes in Nazi ideology and German history are held for sixteen hours a week. The Czech language is being killed off: it is banned in administrative bodies, courthouses, for the drawing up of laws. Everywhere, a war of annihilation rages on against the populations whose territories were flattened by the steamroller of conquest. In the annexed territory called "Warthegau,"[67] Poland will likely cease to

64 See the annotations for the address of October 1941.
65 In Part 8 of *Beyond Good and Evil* (*Jenseits von Gut und Böse*, 1886), on "Peoples and Fatherlands," Nietzsche speaks of the "most unambiguous signs [...] that Europe wants to become one" ("unzweideutigsten Anzeichen [...], daß *Europa Eins werden will*"), but also notes that those signs are being "arbitrarily and mendaciously reinterpreted" ("willkürlich und lügenhaft umgedeutet").
66 Mann refers here to Bohemia and Moravia.
67 Warthegau was an administrative unit established by the Nazis in Poland and existed from October 1939 until the territory was liberated in January 1945.

exist. Whoever cannot perform forced labor in the Balkans is simply left to starve. Greece is starving and dying out. Romania, Finland, and Hungary are bleeding to death on the battlefields, while Yugoslavians are massacred on the spot. The Dutch are being "relocated." There, as everywhere, the office of racial politics is collaborating harmoniously and effectively with the Gestapo's murder squads. The population of France is likely to and will shrink to twenty million. In Paris they "encourage" the nightlife. The Nazis have never conceived of "Paris" as anything but "nightlife." It is a gorilla-like conception, and the conceptions that the Nazi has of Europe as a whole, how he thinks of it, how he regards and loves it, can be extrapolated from the answer that a German officer of the general staff gave to the Mexican military attaché in Berlin in response to the question: What indeed would the Nazis do to solve the problems of revolt and hunger in Europe? "All of Europe may starve," the German says, "if only our Wehrmacht is sufficiently provided for. We are determined to exterminate the entire civilian population rather than to capitulate." A man's word, the word of a good German-European. Was it perhaps uttered right as the "European Writers' Conference"[68] convened by Goebbels met in Weimar, under the chairmanship of poor Hans Carossa[69] and with the participation of all kinds of quisling scribes[70] and yes-men collaborators from north, south, east, and west?

A macabre farce like this Writers' Conference, that is Hitler-Europe through and through—the vile perversion and contamination of a great idea that had long since been poised for realization. It will be realized, however, God willing, not in the disreputable style of Nazism. A general

68 At the "European Poets' Meeting" in Weimar in October 1941, on Goebbels's prompting, the European Writers' Association (Europäische Schriftsteller-Vereinigung or ESV) was founded as a fascist alternative to the London-based PEN International, from which Germany had already withdrawn in 1933.

69 The poet and author of short prose Hans Carossa (1878–1956), a doctor by profession in Lower Bavaria, acted as chairman at the "European Poets' Meeting" in Weimar in October 1941 and was elected president of the ESV. After the war, Carossa sent Mann his autobiography *Ungleiche Welten* (Different Worlds, 1951), in which Mann's radio speeches are described as "mutwillige Florettstiche" (malicious stabs with a (fencing) foil), prompting Mann to admit that he had done Carossa an injustice, having then not known the coercion that compelled him into this role.

70 Authors from fifteen countries took part in the Weimar Poets' Meetings in 1941 and 1942, with France (Robert Brasillach, 1909–1945; Pierre Drieu La Rochelle, 1893–1945; and others) and Italy (Emilio Cecchi, 1884–1966; Antonio Baldini, 1889–1962; and others) particularly well represented. See Hans Rudolf Vaget, "Leiden an Deutschland – Hoffnung Europa: Thomas Mann und die europäische Bewußtseinsbildung," in *Die Goethezeit. Werke – Wirkung – Wechselbeziehungen: Eine Festschrift für Wilfried Malsch*, ed. Jeffrey L. High (Göttingen: Verlag von Schwerin, 2001), 383–401, 395.

project of intellectual restoration will have to begin when Hitler has been defeated—it must already begin now, so that he will be defeated. The ideas of socialism, revolution, peace, and patriotism will have to be restored from their defilement by the gorilla-Midas. Above all, the idea of 'Europe'—which was, at its core and in the hearts of the finest, the idea of freedom, national honor, compassion, and human and humane cooperation—must be restored to its original meaning.

September 27, 1942

German Listeners!
One would like to know how you think in private of the conduct of those who act on your behalf in the world, for example, in the case of the Jewish atrocities in Europe[71]—how you as human beings feel about it, one would like to ask you. You continue to stand by Hitler's war and tolerate the utmost out of fear of what defeat would bring: fear of the vengeance of the abused nations of Europe against everything that is German. Yet, from the Jews of all people, such revenge is not to be expected. They are the most vulnerable, the most averse to violence and bloodshed of all of your victims. Even today they are not your enemies; you are only theirs. You won't succeed in making the hatred mutual. Jews are almost always pro-German, and when your situation becomes dire, as it probably is— they of all people, unemotional and wise from the ages as they are, will advise against retribution in kind—they will, perhaps, be your only friends and advocates in the world. They have been stripped of their power, their rights, their property, brought to their knees in humiliation—was that not enough? What sort of human beings, what sort of monsters are these who can never have enough of the defilement, for whom every misery that they inflicted on the Jews was always just another incentive to thrust them into even more profound, even more ruthless misery? In the beginning there was some semblance of restraint and reason in the treatment of these vestiges of antiquity, who nonetheless had assimilated, everywhere, to modern national life. The Jews, so it went, ought to be segregated from their hosts, to be barred from administrative office and influence, to live as tolerated guests, but be permitted to devote themselves, undisturbed, to their own creed, their own culture. Those days are long gone. At every step, the sadism continues to surpass itself. Now they have become set on annihilation, the maniacal resolution to completely exterminate the

---

71 According to his diary entry of September 17, 1942, Mann read a report by Polish-Jewish-American labor leader Jacob Pat (1890–1966) in *The New Leader* of September 12, 1942, "Nazis Gas 11,000 Jews in Warsaw District, But Ghetto Spirit of Revolt is Undaunted."

Jewish community of Europe.[72] "It is our goal," Goebbels said in a radio address, "to exterminate the Jews. Whether we are victorious or suffer defeat, we must and will achieve this goal. Should the German armies be forced to retreat, they will be sure to wipe the last Jew from the face of the Earth on their way back."[73]

No creature endowed with the power of reason can put themselves in the mindset of these putrefied brains. One asks oneself, to what end? Why? Who is served by this? Will anybody have it better, if the Jews are exterminated? Did the heretical fabulist finally convince himself that the war was instigated by "world Jewry," that it is a Jewish war being fought for and against the Jews? Does he believe that "world Jewry" will give up on the war against the Nazis in horror, when they find out that the fall of the Nazis would bring about the fall of the last Jew in Europe? Gundolf's half-baked apostle has come to the realization that defeat is now well-nigh possible.[74] But the Nazis will not descend to hell alone, they will take the Jews with them. They cannot exist without Jews. It is a profoundly felt fellowship of fate. I certainly believe that the waves of German armies returning home will have other things on their minds than pogroms. But until they are defeated, they take the eradication of the Jews insanely seriously. The ghetto in Warsaw, where five hundred thousand Jews from Poland, Austria, Czechoslovakia, and Germany have been crushed together into two dozen wretched streets, is nothing but a pit of hunger, pestilence, and death, which reeks of the rising stench of corpses. In *one* year, the most recent one, sixty-five thousand human beings perished there. According to information from the Polish government-in-exile,[75] all told, already seven hundred thousand Jews were murdered or tortured to death by the Gestapo, seventy thousand of them from the vicinity of Minsk in Poland alone.[76]

---

72 The fact that complete extermination of the European Jews was indeed already official policy can be seen from the secret minutes of the Wannsee Conference of January 20, 1942, which, at this writing, Mann could not have known, though he was clearly convinced that this was so.

73 Mann's German original reads: "'Es ist unser Ziel' hat Goebbels in einer Radio-Rede gesagt, 'die Juden auszurotten. Ob wir siegen oder geschlagen werden, wir müssen und werden dieses Ziel erreichen. Sollten die deutschen Heere zum Rückzug gezwungen werden, so werden sie auf ihrem Wege den letzten Juden von der Erde vertilgen.'" The source of the quote has not been identified.

74 German poet Friedrich Gundolf (1880–1931) belonged to the Stefan George circle of poets and thinkers and taught German literary history at the University of Heidelberg, where Goebbels had been one of his students.

75 After the German invasion of Poland on October 1, 1939, a Polish government-in-exile under the leadership of General Wladislaw Sikorski (1881–1943) was set up in London, which published its first sensational report at the end of 1942: *The Mass Execution of Jews in German Occupied Poland*.

76 Minsk, the capital of Belarus, was then under German occupation.

Do you Germans know this? And how do you feel about it? Recently, in unoccupied France, three thousand and six hundred Jews were removed from a number of concentration camps and transported by freight train to the East.[77] Before the death train could embark, three hundred people committed suicide. Only children aged five and older were allowed to stay with their parents; the younger ones were left to their fates. This caused a great deal of bad blood among the French people. And what about your blood, Germans?

In Paris, within only a few days, sixteen thousand Jews were rounded up, loaded into cattle wagons, and deported.[78] Where to? The German locomotive conductor knows this,[79] the one all of Switzerland is talking about. He fled there because on multiple occasions he'd had to drive trains full of Jews out to the middle of the line, where the cars were stopped, hermetically sealed, and filled with gas. He was not able to stand it anymore. However, his experiences are by no means out of the ordinary. There also exists an accurate and authentic report regarding the killing of no fewer than eleven thousand Polish Jews with poison gas.[80] They were brought to a particular field of execution in Konin in the Warsaw District, put into air-tight, sealed wagons and transformed into corpses within a quarter of an hour. We have the detailed description of the entire series of events, the screams and the prayers of the victims and the jolly laughter of the SS-Hottentots who orchestrated all the fun.[81]—And here you Germans are, surprised and even indignant that the civilized world is conferring on the method of reeducation with which to make human beings out of the generations of Germans whose brains have been molded by National Socialism, that is out of malformed killers lacking even the slightest concept of morality.

77 The Vichy regime took over control of the various internment camps in southwest France (Gurs, Rivesaltes, etc.) in 1940 after adopting a policy of cooperation with Germany.

78 In August 1940, the German occupying forces opened a reception camp in Drancy, a suburb of Paris. From there, French Jews were transported to concentration and death camps in Germany and Poland.

79 The source for this episode is a letter from author and translator Rudolf Jakob Humm (1895–1977), who wrote to Mann on August 12, 1942: "In Basel, there is talk of a German engine driver who fled because he was driving trains carrying Jews, which stop on the open track and then are filled with gas. He couldn't stand it any longer."

80 See the annotation above regarding the report of the Polish government-in-exile.

81 The manuscript reads "S-cannibals," which Mann changed to "SS-Hottentots," "Hottentot" having originally been a derogatory Dutch term for the Khoikhoi peoples of South Africa and Namibia.

Address to Americans of German Descent[82]
October 15, 1942

German-Americans,

I am grateful to the organizers of this event for presenting me with the opportunity to say a few words to you—as one of your own, so to speak; for it will not be long until I myself will become an American citizen, an American of German descent, like you.[83]

That is no easy position to be in today, an American with a German background, from the German tradition—today, when America is at war with Germany: namely, with a Germany that after seven years of preparation has invaded, subjugated, and enslaved its European neighbors, and, if it succeeds in holding on to its plunder, in turning its misdeeds into undisputed facts, to inevitably, be it directly or indirectly, rob even America of its freedom—the freedom that your forbears sought when they left the old continent and became citizens of the United States.

This attempt to make themselves the slave master and sheriff of the world is being undertaken by a Germany unknown to you, undertaken under the spell of a party government that bears no resemblance whatsoever to the government of any decent people, but whose personnel from top to bottom is assembled of nothing but reckless criminal marauders capable of every form of inhumanity. What you have heard and read about the immeasurable cruelty with which they mishandle the peoples of Europe, how they suck them dry, humiliate them, trample them underfoot, is no propaganda, no terrifying fairy tale—it is impossible to exaggerate when describing the depravity of these people, and if anything that has been said of them strikes you as beyond belief, you may rest assured that it falls short of the truth by half.

It would be a grave misapprehension to confuse the heinously seduced and disfigured Germany of today with that country that you envision when you reminisce about the homeland of your ancestors, with the Germany whose songs they sang to you and whose language many of you have preserved, a country of hospitality, of trustworthiness, and of a profound disposition. Today, the world is faced with an entirely different Germany, a fanatical *verächter und vernichter*—enemy and exterminator of all that is just, all freedom, all that is good; a Germany that persecutes the Christian faith, and whose celebration of Christmas beneath the Christmas tree has therefore become an absurdity and a calumny; a Germany without love, without compassion, filled only with raging

---

82   The address was delivered in German on the station WHOM for the "German-American Loyalty Hour." Here, Mann appears to be addressing German-Americans beyond his target audience, who identify as German-Americans but no longer speak German at home.

83   Mann became a naturalized US citizen on June 23, 1944.

self-aggrandizement, with a racial delusion of grandeur that drives it to force itself on the world as tyrannical oppressor.

I do not hold it against you that this Nazi Germany has nothing to do with the Germany that you remember and to which you remain faithful, because I do not doubt in the least your dedication to the country where you now claim citizenship. You are far too comfortable with its free institutions, with the protection of the law it offers you, for you to be capable of wishing for its defeat, which would be no more and no less than the defeat of humankind.

But it would indeed be a disaster if your sentiments in this war were divided in the slightest; if you were to think in private: "Germany is Germany, whatever its government may be. We retain our devotion, its victories are our pride, and even if we do not wish for the downfall of American freedom, it is too much to ask of us that we should wish for the annihilation of Germany." — Nobody is asking that of you. The annihilation of Germany is an empty phrase that Goebbels' propaganda bellows out in order to make the German people believe that they must march through thick and thin with the Nazis until the bitter end. Nobody wants to annihilate Germany, nobody can even think of doing such a thing. What must be annihilated, if the human standard of civilized behavior should be rescued from the plunge into blood, violence, and defilement, is the evil demon who presently reigns over Germany and by whose rule millions of Germans in the Reich also suffer unto despair. He must be annihilated so that Germany, which has strayed from itself, might be restored to its former self again, and so that you too, German-Americans, could love it again with a clear conscience.

No, the hyphen between "German" and "American" cannot come to mean any spiritual schism, any parting of sentiments, any conflict in the duties of loyalty. I say this to you as a German who left the land of his birth and the Europe that has been raped by this land, in order to be able to finish his life's work on free soil. This life's work, for whatever else it is worth, has been determined entirely by European, by German tradition. One of my books, the story of a burgherly Hanseatic family, had the good fortune to be loved by millions of Germans and to become a fixture in German home libraries.[84] After the war had already begun, I wrote a book about the greatest German author, about Goethe,[85] that the Germans are currently not allowed to read, which, however, one day, when they are once again free people, will find its way into their homes. It means something profound, dear friends, that I left Germany, that I could

---

84 Mann is referring to his 1901 debut novel *Buddenbrooks*, cited by the Nobel committee as the principle work for which they awarded him the Nobel Prize in 1929.

85 Mann is referring to his 1939 novel *Lotte in Weimar*.

no longer live there. Nothing, no change of government, no political turn, no revolution could have driven a person like me out of Germany—nothing on Earth would have been able to bring about my departure, but only this one thing, only that, which calls itself National Socialism, only Hitler and his band of outlaws. For this is no politics and no state and no form of society, this is the wickedness of hell, and the war against it is the sacred self-defense of humankind against the definitively diabolical.

If you, with your American concepts of human dignity and freedom of thought, were dropped into Germany today, you would be shot tomorrow for anti-national sentiments and lack of faith in ultimate victory. That happens every day there. Hundreds of Germans, simple and educated people alike, have been executed because they somehow let it slip that they hold Hitler's war to be madness. But those who think this way without saying so out loud number not in the hundreds, but in the thousands upon thousands, and I believe that there are even generals among them. Do you want to be more "German" than those Germans over there, who know better, and believe that one has to be a Nazi just because today Germany is under Nazi rule? No, you are not committing this most trivial disloyalty to the country of your origin if you invest all your wishes and energies in America's victory and in that of the United Nations. For it is also on Germany's behalf that this victory will be won.

October 24, 1942

German Listeners!

The European Youth Congress, which was recently drummed up in Vienna by those standard bearers and "white knights" of occidental culture, the Nazis,[86] was originally conceived as a victory celebration that was supposed to be held after the conquest of Stalingrad.[87] That plan suffered a misfire. But, as a response to President Roosevelt's address to the world's youth,[88] the ingenious event could still serve some purpose. Young delegations from all occupied and allied nations of the continent were coerced to appear in order to enact the creation of a European youth

---

86 The assembly of the "Europäischer Jugend-Kongress" (European Youth Congress) took place in Vienna from September 13 to 19, 1942. It was attended by representatives of fascist youth organizations from thirteen countries, who came together to form the "Europäischer Jugendverband" (League of European Youth).

87 The purpose of the conquest of Stalingrad (now Volgograd), a strategically important industrial city on the Volga, was to gain access to the Russian oil fields. The Russian army successfully defended the city at great cost to themselves as well as to the German army, ensuring the failure of the Nazis' campaign in Russia and marking a turning point in the war.

88 Mann is referring to Roosevelt's "Address to the International Student Assembly" delivered on September 3, 1942.

organization—under the direction of Baldur von Schirach,[89] a hack-rhymester baby-fat boy of advanced age who has always been a German youth leader by the grace of Hitler and who has now ascended to the rank of European youth leader. The speech that he delivered there surpassed most of the imbecilic effrontery ever emitted from a Nazi's mouth. What becomes of the word "Europe" on his lips; how it sounds when bloody vulgarians invoke Praxiteles, Michelangelo, Rembrandt, and Dürer, lay claim to these names for themselves and preen about draped in the glory of the continent that they have trampled, plundered, martyred, and desecrated; to this the world was treated yet again—to bursts of utterly disgusted laughter. The middle-aged golden boy played his part so well that it was a joy to behold. "Where are your Praxiteles and Rembrandt?" he barked at America. "Where do you find the nerve to raise your weapons against the divine inspirations of European genius in the name of your barren continent?" Right, that is exactly what is happening. America and the United Nations are doing battle against Praxiteles and Rembrandt, and out of jealousy no less. They want to steal the treasures of Europe's museums in an illegitimate imitation of the Nazi fat cats.[90] But they will see. He, Baldur, and his allied and subjugated youths are the inheritors of Europe's sacred, fertile cultural soil, and they will know how to defend it against General Motors and General Electric. While it is true that Germany also has General Göring and General I. G. Farben and General Siemens-Schuckert, they are noble blossoms nourished by the culture-rich soil of Europe. It is true that we Nazis have just smashed to pieces everything in the Gogol Museum and in the Yasnaya Polyana Museum and in the Tchaikovsky Museum,[91] too; but it would be a mistake to therefore doubt our heartfelt reverence for culture. It is true that even before our

---

89 Baldur von Schirach (1907–1974) was a Gauleiter (leader of an occupied administrative subdivision) and the Reich Governor of Vienna at the time; from 1933 he served as the NSDAP Reichsleiter for Youth Education and Reichsführer of the Hitler Youth. Schirach belonged to Hitler's inner circle and was sentenced to twenty years in prison for crimes against humanity at the Nuremberg War Crimes Trials.

90 After the occupation of France, Göring acquired around 700 works of art, most of which were looted Jewish property that he incorporated into the "Hermann Göring Art Collection" at his country residence "Karinhall."

91 Mann is presumably referring to the house where author Nikolai Gogol (1809–1852) was born in Velyki Sorochyntsi, Ukraine. The actual Gogol Museum is located in Moscow. "Yasnaya Polyana" was author Leo Tolstoy's (1828–1910) country estate, 200 km southwest of Moscow. Composer Pyotr Ilyich Tchaikovsky's (1840–1893) country house lay in Klin, 85 km northwest of Moscow, where he spent the final year of his life. The German occupiers speedily removed the furniture and memorabilia, and used the first floor as a garage for motorcycles and the upper floor as sleeping quarters.

time most of the living breathing masterworks of European culture, arts, and sciences had gotten away and fled for the shores of Great Britain and America. Nonetheless, Praxiteles and Rembrandt belong to us, they are prestige-patrons of the Europe brought together by Hitler and of Nazi culture. It is true that all of Europe lies low in convulsions of desperate resistance against the form of unification that we bring, but only because the bolshevist-capitalist-imperialist enemy alliance incites them to do so. The alliance finds itself fossilized in piteously outdated concepts of national sovereignty; we have brought about the most transformative social revolution in the history of the world, the revolution in which everybody has no choice but to sacrifice their sovereignty, everybody but Germany. The revolution in which the most absurd German nationalism and racial megalomania usurps the name "Europe" and establishes a monopolistic system of plunder so shameless as to be unprecedented in the entire history of imperialism.

German listeners, the discovery of Europe by the Nazis is not only a perverted but even more so a rather delayed discovery. These murderous provincialists started preaching about Europe the moment these ideas themselves had already begun to acquire a distinctly provincial stench. I believe that he whom the youth leader Schirach calls "the sick man in the White House," Roosevelt, understands the times and the world better than Schirach when he says: "The old term, 'Western Civilization,' no longer applies. World events and the common needs of all humanity are joining the culture of Asia with the culture of Europe and both of the Americas to form, for the first time, a world civilization."[92]

November 29, 1942

German Listeners!
Of all the lies of the monster who will for a short time yet be allowed to call himself the Führer of Germany, the most outrageous was always the "European" lie, the theft of the idea of "Europe,"[93] the shameless misrepresentation of his buccaneering raids and crimes as acts of unification inspired by the European spirit. To pass off the enslavement, humiliation, and emasculation of the European nations under the yoke of Nazism as unification was a grotesque falsification of the European idea, one that only tortured us because of the danger that weak minds and hearts among you over there might succumb and mistake the falsification for the idea itself, mistake the ugly face of falsehood for the truth.

This danger has vanished, the lie of the "New Order" itself has been scattered to the wind through the harrowing event that Vichy Radio first

---

92 See Roosevelt's "Broadcast to International Student Assembly" of September 3, 1942.
93 See annotations for the address of August 1942.

made known to the world: the sinking of the French fleet in Toulon by its crew and commandants.[94] Rather than allowing these ships to fall into Nazi hands, the French sailors buried their love and their pride in the ocean and did not spare their own lives in the process[95]—a tragically resolute deed, a deed that history will bear witness to always in honor of deeply humiliated France, and a deed that belies Hitler's "New Order" before the whole world[96]—the whole world, even you Germans—in order to expose its bankruptcy.

For us, this bankruptcy had been a long time in the making. We knew from the very start that the Nazis' accursed band of tormentors would be the last on Earth capable of bringing about any sort of new order, any kind of peace among the peoples, any cooperation among nations. But many needed to learn the hard way—simply because they had not yet experienced it firsthand—what this so-called National Socialism really is. This, firsthand experience, appears to be absolutely necessary in order to fathom National Socialism: for the simple reason that without direct and tangible experience, human nature is incapable of believing such a degree of shameless malevolence and simian depth of degradation. Because the social world is absorbed in a painful crisis of development that is creating much confusion everywhere, there were and possibly are today still people everywhere who think: "In the end, this Hitler is really the man to bring us order, security, peace; ultimately the best thing is to submit to him." Have you Germans not also thought this yourselves? And then one only has to experience it! One has to march through the hells of hatred, misery, abysmal despair over all that is humanly absolutely unendurable and that Nazi rule foments in order to learn its lessons, in order to understand that there is one thing in the world compared to which everything, really everything else in the world, is preferable, namely National Socialism.

The Norwegians, who, in their naivete, waved from their windows with their handkerchiefs to the German troops as they marched in, now know; all of the conquered peoples of Europe know, and the unfortunate, gallant French people, toward whom the great ape at first maintained certain courtesies, know it with all terrible certainty. But a gorilla is a gorilla, and how things stand with the gorilla's popularity can be seen in the monstrous episode in Toulon, which, far beyond its military significance,

---

94 After the Allied forces landed in French North Africa—in Casablanca, Oran, and Algiers—on November 8, 1942, the Wehrmacht occupied "France libre," which was controlled by the Vichy regime. This meant that the French fleet anchored in Toulon and its advanced technology was in danger of falling into German and Italian hands and being used against the Allies. To preempt this, the French scuttled seventy-seven of their own warships on November 27.

95 During the scuttling of the fleet, twelve members of the French navy were killed and twenty-six wounded.

96 See annotations for the address of October 1941.

is an unprecedented unmasking of the Nazi's European swindle. After two years of attempted cooperation, a desperate France is once again at war with Germany:[97] both in the mother country and in the colonies—these are the facts of the matter, and they are instructive. For they demonstrate that a victorious Nazi Germany could never, ever bring peace to the world. All of the cleverer people outside and inside of Germany always knew, and now even the ignorant ones grasp it, that a Nazi victory would be a more dreadful misfortune for Germany than the defeat into which a fanatical idiot is now leading it. Such a victory would be unbearable and unsustainable. Its certain and short-term consequence would be everything Nazi propaganda threatens you with if you were to lay down your weapons and no longer defend a miserable band of criminals: it would be the annihilation of the German people, their expulsion from human society.

December 27, 1942

German Listeners!

In the process of being translated into English, Hitler's speeches undergo a substantial distortion that works in their favor;[98] but the linguistic cleansing can do nothing to alter their spirit; it remains nightmarishly intact, and for this reason I almost always read the English versions very closely—not for my enjoyment, but rather in order to see what it looks like in the mind of a modern conqueror and how deep the human spirit can sink.

These two concepts, conquest and depravity, are of course one and the same. The phenomenon that we are witnessing as we experience Hitler, is the process of decay, the hopeless gone-to-the-dogs state of the conqueror. It is the final, pitifully belated manifestation of the conqueror archetype, robbed of every noble trait and singularly repulsive. This is what he looks like today. His squalid depravity is proof that he has become obsolete. After Hitler, there will be no more conquerors. He has degraded the craft to such an extent that humankind will wash its hands of it once and for all.

Now then, I remember how our Genghis Khan, in one of his most recent speeches, was unable to conceal his exasperation about the unjust assessment of victory and defeat in this, his war of conquest. He harbors the dark suspicion—and cannot comprehend how this is possible—that the losses of his enemies appear to the human eye to be shrouded in an aureola of glory, while his victories remain lusterless, gloomy, unappreciated, and nobody can really be bothered with them. "Our modest successes,"

---

97 In other words, despite the armistice of June 22, 1940, France was once again in a state of war.

98 In 1942, Norman H. Baynes published *The Speeches of Adolf Hitler, April 1922–August 1939*, English translations of select passages arranged according to their subject matter.

he says with imbecilic bitterness, "needless to say, in no way compare with whatever it is that our enemies consider to be a victory. When we gain a thousand kilometers, when we advance to the Don River and Stalingrad, which we will soon take, then that is nothing. It is also nothing when we stand at the foot of the Caucasus Mountains, open up grain-rich Ukraine for German Europe, bring home the coal of the Don basin, claim seventy percent of all the iron in Russia. But Namsos in Norway[99] and Dieppe[100] and, in particular, the retreat of the British from Dunkirk,[101] these are glorious deeds, unforgettable, immortal achievements, this is what these military idiots celebrate as their victories!"[102]

He is right, victories they are not. Churchill beat him to the point by soberly declaring immediately after Dunkirk that wars are never won by retreats. But the ruffian's sneering lack of appreciation for the dignity of stalwart bearing in defeat, the lack of humane compassion and admiration, conditioned, after so many years of grooming, by the inevitable initial triumphs of his conquest machine, this lowly lack of understanding, utterly foreign to any high-mindedness, is singularly characteristic—and will remain his congenital predestination, even if, now that his advantage is wearing thin and the page is about to turn, he attempts to imitate his enemies and begins to acquire an appreciation of defeat.

After a series of successful stratagems employed by the British Eighth Army in North Africa, Rommel, a shameless Nazi gang leader, has been dealt a devastating defeat.[103] This was the prelude to events that you

---

99 Namsos is a warm-water port on the North Sea in Norway, of strategic importance at the time for the transportation of Swedish iron ore to Germany. In April 1940, Namsos saw fierce combat between Germany and the British and French forces. The fighting ended when the Allied troops were evacuated from the ravaged town by the British navy to the British naval base at Scapa Flow.

100 Dieppe, France, is a port city on the English Channel. British and Canadian forces attempted to land there on August 19, 1942, but suffered heavy losses and were ultimately repelled.

101 After the Battle of France, the British Expeditionary Forces (BEF) as well as Dutch and French forces found themselves surrounded on three sides. The BEF retreated to the area around the port of Dunkirk on the English Channel. Because Hitler had given the order to halt the Wehrmacht's advance for three days, the BEF was able to evade capture. In a well-organized rescue operation involving all available ships, including some private ones, almost 340,000 Allied troops were brought to safety in Great Britain between May 26 and June 4, 1940.

102 Mann both summarizes and paraphrases Hitler's speech of September 30, 1942, on the opening of the Kriegswinterhilfswerk (the winter relief campaign), held in the Berlin Sportpalast. See Max Domarus, *Hitler: Speeches and Proclamations, 1932–1945: The Chronicle of a Dictatorship*, 4 vols. (Wauconda, IL: Bolchazy-Carducci Publishers, 2004), IV, 2673.

103 From February 1941 to October 1942, Field Marshal Erwin Rommel (1891–1944) commanded the "Africa Corps," which had been sent to North Africa to rescue the Italian units in Tunisia and elsewhere. There, his surprising

know about. The Goebbels press will now have to portray the retreat of the defeated general toward Tripoli with the battered remains of his army to the German public as an uplifting stroke of genius, more glorious than any victory, an accomplishment of sheer epic resourcefulness, and lay claim to all the sympathetic recognition and avid attention of history for this unkind twist of fate suffered in the service of Hitler.

Dearest newswriters, that is not going to work.[104] There is no way to sweeten the bitter German defeats. Hitler's cause is entirely dependent on raw success, pure and simple. If that fails to materialize, if success ever turns to failure, then there is nothing left of his cause, and then nothing but disgrace and hellish laughter will be its reward, by no means will it be anything to write home about. You will never have a Dunkirk to celebrate. The defeat of a Nazi general is as brutish and as unattractive as his victories were; humankind turns its eyes away from it, and no song will ever commemorate it.

---

maneuvers earned him the popular nickname "Desert Fox." Rommel's mission to advance to the Suez Canal failed in the Second Battle of El-Alamein. In 1944, the investigation into the 20 July Plot to assassinate Hitler showed that Rommel had been in communication with the conspirators. The Gestapo offered him a choice between suicide and execution; he chose suicide.

104 Mann is addressing the journalists of the German press.

1943

January 15, 1943

German Listeners!
A somber anniversary needs to be marked: ten years of National Socialism. What have they brought the German people? There is only one answer that tells it all: the war, this war, the way it stands today and the way it will end for the German people. Hitler's war, in which your sons bleed to death by the millions, and which will leave the continent—including Germany—a wasteland. When you are asked what was accomplished during this decade, you can trace everything back to the war. From the start, everything pointed toward this war, everything steered toward its realization. Everything else, whatever lying name it was given, beginning with the lying name of the movement itself, all of it was nothing but a rehearsal and systematic restructuring toward the ineludible and ruinous misadventure of this war, which your Führer, of course, had imagined very differently than how it looks now. A desperate struggle, in which Germany feels compelled to heap one unpardonable atrocity onto another, and the physical and moral fallout of which it will have to bear for who knows how long.

All of the so-called benefits that the regime is supposed to have reaped for Germany show their true face in the light of this accomplishment. Their absurdity is thereby revealed even to those who, in their utter wretchedness, ever saw anything else in them but deceit, madness, and infamy. One hears that Hitler liberated Germany from joblessness. Yes—by building up the military. National Socialism—that means solving social questions with war. One hears that he united Germany like never before and, in creating a German *ethnic community*,[1] implemented Socialism. This *Volksgemeinschaft* was the dictatorship of the mob, an abominable partisan terrorism that gave rise to a moral devastation, a human perdition, a desecration of conscience, a destruction of the most natural, solemn bonds as no people has ever experienced before and which was founded on anything but the goodness in human beings. Today, this *Volksgemeinschaft* is in such a state that seven hundred

---

1   Mann's original term is *Volksgemeinschaft*.

thousand heavily armed members of the Praetorian Guard[2] must fend off not only the people, thirsting for peace, but also the half-extinguished militia army.

And socialism? It is the self-enrichment of the fat cats, the transformation of the Nazi Party into a colossal economic enterprise, as bloated as Göring himself. Further, Socialism is embodied in the delightful institution "Strength through Joy,"[3] that is in shipping disenfranchised herds of laborers to scenic locations. But did National Socialism not cleanse the nation of republican corruption and restore Germany from disgrace and shame to its former respectable standing in the world, to its former honor? There is not a child left in Germany who does not know that the few, minor moral blunders of the Republic, inflated through asinine trials,[4] are the very embodiment of harmlessness when compared with the high-heavens stench of corruption under Nazi rule.

And then there is German honor. Broken is the dignity of science, every sense of justice trampled into the ground, Germany's sovereign judges made servants of party interest, Germany's word of honor reduced to a mockery by contract violations piled high and oaths of honor torn to shreds, by the vile conception of politics as a sphere of absolute cynicism; Germany's name made the epitome of all terror, every form of wanton predation and plunder, disgraceful cruelty, merciless violence, so that the world's memories of how the German spirit bestowed on humankind so many gifts that were good, great, and worthy are in danger of drowning in a sea of hatred, the surging waves of which you are now barely able to dam with a desperate exertion of might, with "Strength through Fear," to prevent them from sucking you under. This is German honor restored. This is the record of ten years of National Socialism. And I am thankful that I have been granted no more than these mere five or six minutes to set it straight. History will be more thorough.

---

2   Mann is comparing Julius Caesar's bodyguards with the Gestapo and other security agencies.

3   The "NS Gemeinschaft Kraft durch Freude" was an organization set up by the NSDAP in 1933. They used state-sponsored vacations, boat trips, etc. to introduce people to the material comforts that the Nazi dictatorship would make possible. It was affiliated with the Reich Labor Service; both were headed by Robert Ley, who was responsible for organizing slave labor during the war. Ley hanged himself in a prison bathroom in Nuremberg in 1945.

4   Mann was one of the most tireless critics of the conservative German justice system during the Weimar Republic, repeatedly speaking out in protest against, e.g., the death penalty, the criminalization of homosexuality, and the persecution of socialists and communists.

January 24, 1943

German Listeners!
The Nazis are beginning to dedicate some thought to their demise. At this moment, they are at work painting the end in glowing colors, both for themselves and for us all.

The idea of their return to obscurity can hardly be new to them. At the beginning of their reign, they must have strongly suspected that the civilized world would understand just what kind of a threat the Nazis posed to them, would understand that this was no government, but a murderous mob of lowlifes, and that the civilized world would soon put their undertakings to an abrupt end through common action. At the time, they probably would not have made much of a fuss and would not have thought it was anything like the end of the world. Back then, they still felt like the little people, like the brazenly adventurous economic knights of their day that they were, and would hardly have been surprised if their undertaking had amounted to nothing more than a glorified Kapp Putsch.[5] In the meantime, they have run wild like weeds so that it is astonishing, not least of all to themselves. And how they have been conditioned to see themselves in the meantime, what they believe they are now entitled to, that is evident in the descriptions that they give in advance of their downfall, which are carefully calculated to make our blood curdle.

At first, they send Great Britain and its allies cryptic warnings not to make life impossible for them, since otherwise things will happen that no one could possibly conceive. "You children of civilization," Goebbels says more or less, "have no fantasy for horror and still cannot imagine what we are capable of. You simply have no idea, and we won't spoil it for you either, but if our hand is forced, our response will defy all credibility. Be on your guard, cooperate with us, and make peace, so that we can get out of this war that we, God knows, are on a course to lose. It is better not to drive people like us to despair—otherwise you are in for a rude awakening."

There is probably nothing to be done about it; we will have to see reason and let them have Europe and Africa as plunder. It is difficult to get along with contemporaries such as these. If they triumph, they will subject the world to an abomination, the likes of which has never been. And if they are defeated, they will nonetheless, at the last minute, perpetrate

---

5   The coup d'état led by Wolfgang Kapp (1858–1922), Walther von Lüttwitz (1859–1942), Erich Ludendorff, and others, lasted from March 13 to 17, 1920, and was the first right-wing attempt to bring down the Weimar Republic. The government fled to Dresden and Stuttgart. The coup failed when the government called for a general strike, which workers largely followed.

something monstrous in its atrociousness. They threaten to blow the entire house to pieces. Goebbels says so literally in "Reich":[6]

"If ever the day should come when we have to depart; if we should ever be forced to make our exit from the stage of history, then we will slam the door behind us with such force that the planet will quake and all humankind stand aghast in horror."

Now it's true that I believe that the sound of that door crashing closed will be drowned out by a tremendous chorus of boos from the auditorium of the world, because nothing as abysmally dreadful as the performance of this bloody, low-rent touring company has ever been staged. But what are these apocalyptic delinquents thinking, that they believe their demise must be a twilight of gods? An unfortunate confluence of external and internal contingencies dealt into their hands the power to commit damnable mischief in and beyond Germany for ten years; and now they want to strike up Kleistian tones and declare that a reign like theirs can only be buried with a bloodbath that would blot out the sun—the fools![7]

Freedom and human dignity must not perish, the United Nations must not stand down from their objective of shattering the Nazi-scourge and putting an end to German nationalism and delusions of racial superiority altogether. That will happen, even if the Nazis howl that they will do terrible things if anybody gets too close. The free nations must not be moved by their extortive warnings and threats. But you Germans should heed them! You German workers and German soldiers! Germany has changed in the extreme and so has the world's opinion of the German people, who have allowed such outrageous crimes to be committed in their name without ever rising up in outrage.

The Nazis do not care about Germany in the least. What they do care about is saving their own skins. Do you want to allow them free reign to the bitter end, allow them to bring about ruin for yourselves, for Germany? Would you not rather restrain these lunatics before they can outdo all of their heinous acts, until, in the final hour, the barrel bursts, forever rendering impossible a merciful peace, one guided by the spirit of rapprochement?

Goebbels has given fair warning. The warning is for you, people of Germany!

6   Mann's source is unknown. The original German reads: "Wenn je der Tag kommen sollte, wo wir gehen müssen; wenn wir eines Tages gezwungen sein sollten, von der historischen Szene abzutreten, dann werden wir die Tür hinter uns zuschmettern, daß der Erdkreis erbeben und die Menschheit starr dastehen soll vor Entsetzen."

7   In his anti-Napoleonic essay "What is at Stake in this War?" (1809), Heinrich von Kleist (1777–1811) described the struggle against Bonaparte in similar terms, writing of German civilization that it can only "be buried with blood, before which the sun will darken." As Mann points out repeatedly in his addresses, Hitler's war was not a war of self-defense (as was the struggle Kleist describes), but quite the opposite.

February 23, 1943

German Listeners!
One day, history will be divided on what was more despicable, the Nazi's deeds or their words. History will also have difficulty deciding when this riff-raff insulted humankind more: when it lied or when it told the truth. Namely in one mouth in particular, even truth becomes a lie, a tool of deception—and certainly one cannot lie in a more despicable manner than with the truth. Goebbels and his minions have recently gushed about their love of truth. The unreserved honesty with which they informed the German people of the disaster in Russia,[8] which, mind you, belongs to the most devastating failures in all of military history, was unprecedented and overwhelming. Nothing about the nightmarish end of the occupation of Stalingrad was glossed over—except perhaps the omission of the fact that Hitler alone was personally responsible for this catastrophe.[9] On the radio, accompanying the news, they did not play the party anthem, the Horst-Wessel-Lied, which perhaps would have touched a nerve, but rather "I Had a Comrade."[10] They proclaimed four days of mourning across the Reich, grieving for the failure of the Nazi regime's attempted atrocities—a mockery of the real grieving into which the people have been plunged by the senseless destruction of ten thousands of its sons. Any indignation, despair, defiance that could be stirred is buried in mourning. Let us all mourn together, the Führer and his seduced captives, and sing "I Had a Comrade!"

The repulsive aftertaste left by this truthfulness stemmed from its intent. Its purpose was to pervert the fundamental patriotism of the people in order to rescue the regime, and to inspire them to a mobilization of the last remaining resources, a levée en masse—whereby its proponents were less interested in the dubious results of this last stand than in the accompanying distraction of emotions. Secondly, however, and conspicuously, the victories of the Russians, the defeats of the Nazis were presented so openly and honestly, and even possibly embellished in order to inspire

---

8   The Battle of Stalingrad raged from July 17, 1942 to February 2, 1943 and ended with the surrender of the 6th Army under Field Marshal Friedrich von Paulus (1890–1957). The military and civilian casualties on both sides are estimated at 2 million. Stalingrad marked the final turning point of the war in the East.

9   Hitler, who did not have much confidence in his army commanders, took control of the Russian campaign on December 19, 1941. He ordered Field Marshal Paulus, who wanted to abandon Stalingrad and break out of the encirclement, to fight "to the last bullet."

10 "Der gute Kamerad" (The Good Comrade) a.k.a. "Ich hatt' einen Kameraden" (I Had a Comrade) is a patriotic poem written by Ludwig Uhland (1787–1862) in 1809, during the Napoleonic invasions of the German states. As Mann points out repeatedly in his addresses, Hitler's war was not a war of self-defense, like the one Uhland described, but quite the opposite.

a sense of horror in the Anglo-American world at the "Red Menace," at the Bolshevik inundation of the European continent. The confused message that Hitler had read on the tenth anniversary of his seizure of power is full of extortionary warnings of this kind, full of rhetorical flights akin to that of Rudolf Hess over the English Channel,[11] undertaken in the unrelenting hope to recruit Great Britain and the United States to his side against "Central Asia," that is to say: Russia. East Asia, namely Japan, his ally, is very good, but "Central Asia," namely Russia, which he himself shamelessly and stupidly smothered in war, is the enemy of the entire world. He himself, Hitler, is the embodiment of Europe at its finest, most noble, most sensitive, most sophisticated; but the land of Pushkin, Gogol, and Tolstoy is a realm of Huns,[12] whose hordes are preparing to plunge Hitler's flourishing continent into "unfathomable barbarism."

It is a wretched scam, and it will prove futile. It suddenly befits the Nazis to play the proper socialites and have Göring deliver a hint of their intentions that is as thick as he himself is: "If need be, we will make peace with Gentlemen, but never with Soviets." Do they not yet know that they will have missed their chance to negotiate a peace treaty? That nobody will conclude peace with them, neither democracy nor socialism? That peace will only arrive once they have departed? —As for the Red Menace, in his address of November 6, 1941, Stalin said: "Our first goal is to liberate Russian soil and its inhabitants from the yoke of German Nazism. We do not and cannot harbor war objectives such as imposing our will and our form of government on the Slavic and other enslaved peoples of Europe." And through his messenger Maisky he made it clear:[13] "The Soviet Union defends every nation's right to independence and to the inviolability of its territory … and even their right to establish the social order and to choose the form of government that it considers prudent and necessary." But with regard to Germany he said: "A Hitler will come

---

11   Rudolf Hess (1894–1987), Hitler's deputy in the party leadership and former private secretary, flew to Scotland on May 10, 1941, on his own initiative, in a futile attempt to persuade Great Britain to make peace with Germany. In Germany, Hess was declared insane; the British arrested him as a prisoner of war. At the Nuremberg Trials, he was sentenced to life imprisonment; after more than forty years he committed suicide.

12   The Huns were a nomadic warrior people from Asia who plundered the Eastern and Western Roman Empire in the fourth and fifth centuries CE. Colloquially, the term refers to a barbarian enemy force. During the First World War, the Allies regarded the Germans as "Huns"; in the Second World War, the Germans regarded the Russians as "Huns."

13   Ivan Mikhailovich Maisky (1884–1975) was ambassador in London from 1932 to 1943.

and go, but the German people and the German state will remain."[14] He certainly wishes to punish the people who inflicted such limitless suffering on his country, but never has a threatening word against nor an expression of the will to annihilate the German people crossed his lips. Did Russia attack Germany, or was the opposite the case? The day is perhaps not far off when the German people will come to recognize a levelheaded friend in Russia.

March 28, 1943

German Listeners!
There is something wrong with the man who brought us the Second World War, the Führer of all Germans. That there is something wrong with him is hardly a new presumption, but more recently, it has become increasingly and uncannily inescapable to the observer. He delivered a speech in the Berlin Arsenal,[15] which, likely due to an order, drew absolutely no applause, and lasted no longer than fifteen minutes. That in itself is unsettling. He has otherwise never spoken for less than an hour and a half. Without fail, his prolific intellect always had so many excellent, wise, and constructive thoughts to convey to the German people and the rest of the world that any less time would not suffice. And now a scant quarter of an hour—scant, not only in terms of time, but in terms of the poverty of its content. Did he want to 'provide evidence,' as they now say in Germany instead of 'prove,' that mental defectiveness can be revealed just as well in fifteen minutes as in ninety? But that is not a sufficient explanation. The lack of enthusiasm with which the speech was delivered was palpable. One could tell that it had come into being because, after several months of depressive silence, a sign that the most supreme commander of the army was alive seemed absolutely necessary. And yet the speech did not provide sufficient proof of life. It bore witness to a depleted if not defeated temperament. There was no bellowing, no seething or screeching, nothing for the heart or the soul, none of the second-rate Austrian comedian's tricks. It was as boring as it was short, and the speaker seemed to speak without any personal interest, as though he were not reading his own words. The crisis in Russia had been overcome, he said, the German losses had been "relatively minor," and thanks to the total mobilization of forces that had been decreed, the

---

14 Stalin's sentence, "The experience of history says that Hitlers come and go, but the German people, the German state remains," was circulated in various versions, including on Russian leaflets, which suggests the slogan's primarily propagandistic meaning: that German soldiers ought to deliver themselves to the Red Army as prisoners.

15 The Berliner Arsenal, also known as the Zeughaus, is a former military warehouse which is now home to the Deutsches historisches Museum (German Historical Museum).

ultimate victory over the entire hostile judeo-pluto-communist world had been secured.[16] That was all he said, and purely objectively, there would be a great deal to be said against his account, not least concerning the assessment of German losses as relatively minor, for which our friend provided a figure that is indeed low when compared to reality. But it is not worth it. The distinct impression that nobody is listening to this person anymore, anyway, relieves one of the obligation to raise objections—and, does his surly concision, the mechanical torpor of his address not indicate that he shares this impression with us all? His condition is probably best described as acute disgruntlement, deep indignation—not only due to the bankruptcy of his intuitive powers regarding Russia, and because his ignominiously deposed generals once again are having to intervene in order to save whatever can be saved; but his despondency stems from the realization that he has gambled away everything, that he is being abandoned, that even his quislings abroad who staked their trust on him,[17] as well as the domestic traitors of the people are giving him up as a hopeless case, that whatever he goes on to say is meaningless, makes no sound, as if spoken into a vacuum. The war may still be long and difficult, but the world has already moved beyond Hitler and his war, and he knows it. The words that resonate and that people are listening to, because they address plans for the post war world, are coming from Great Britain, from Russia, from the United States and China. However this world might look—he and his regime no longer find any mention in the plans that are being drafted, and whatever he still attempts to say about the matter falls on indifferent ears and is shrugged off.

That is a great relief, since it was to humankind's great shame that it was forced to listen to this wretched intellect, this malformed soul for years. I have consulted an old newspaper from that harrowing time when, unbelievably, the regime consolidated its power in Germany.[18] It features a report on the party's convention in Nuremberg of 1934 at which

---

16   A key point of Nazi war propaganda describes the plutocracy in America as secretly no different from Bolshevism in Russia, since in the end, both are merely tools in the great Jewish conspiracy to achieve world domination.

17   See the annotation for the address of July 1941. The reference to "quislings abroad" primarily regards sympathizers in the Allied camp: the "Cliveden Set" (influential British pro-appeasement personalities who met at the country estate of Lady Nancy Astor (1879–1964) in Cliveden, Buckinghamshire); and Hitler's so-called "American friends."

18   Mann is referring to an undated newspaper clipping, probably from a Swiss newspaper: "Das Fest ist zu Ende" ("The Party is Over"), a report on the NSDAP's Reich Party Congress in Nuremberg of September 5–10, 1934, known as the "Triumph des Willens" ("Triumph of the Will"). The clipping is part of the collection of materials for a political essay entitled "Politicum" that Mann planned to but did not write.

the Führer himself gave twelve speeches, including the one they called at the time his 'great speech on culture.' Now then, the war is gruesome, but one must admit: it has the one benefit that it prevents Hitler from giving speeches on culture. In those days, his megalomania led him to offer the following to us, word for word: "Twenty years ago, the artistic depiction of the speed of a body was associated with the arrangement of the sharp end pointing forward and the bulge pointing backward. In twenty years, *reckoned from today*, aesthetic taste will conclude definitively that the reverse form of the droplet is identical to the idea of speed. The artist is therefore always ahead of both science and humankind in general in his inner understanding of such natural laws. It is his duty to direct his god-given intuition and insight born of a striving humanity toward the future rather than toward the past ..."[19] End quote! Back then, the world had no choice but to listen to such utter bullshit with a certain reverence. Maybe they smiled, both the Germans and the outside world, and thought that somebody could probably bluster on in an aesthetically clueless manner and yet nonetheless be a formidable statesman. Poor world, so full of hope! It neglected to consider the totality of his character. They repressed the intuition that should have guided their response, that the political ideology of this individual would be precisely the same bullshit as his cultural philosophy, only unfortunately not merely perpetrated in words but in the convulsing flesh and blood of the peoples.

Thank god, the drip no longer speaks about the aesthetics of the droplet, but instead only about pluto-bolshevism, and at that only for a spiritless fifteen minutes. National Socialism, however, identically to the idea of great speed, is biting the dust with its bulging end forward.

April 25, 1943

German Listeners!
Today I want to tell you about a book that is scheduled to be published this fall and that you, too, will read some day, only later than those peoples who can read whatever they want.[20] It is only a book of stories, but

---

19   Mann is referring to Hitler's speech of September 5, 1934, for the Reichsparteitag Kulturtagung held at the Nuremberg Apollotheater. *Adolf Hitler: Reden zur Kunst- und Kulturpolitik 1933–1939*, ed. and commentary Robert Eikmeyer, introduction by Boris Groys (Frankfurt am Main: Verlag Revolver, 2004).

20   Mann is referring to the 1944 volume, *The Ten Commandments: Ten Short Novels of Hitler's War Against the Moral Code*, which featured ten contributions by ten authors, one for each commandment. The book emerged from the war effort that affected all areas of culture and social life, which the United States was compelled to undertake after entering the war. Mann's contribution, the Moses novella "Das Gesetz" ("The Law," a.k.a. "The Tables of the Law") first appeared here as "Thou Shalt Have No Other God Before Me," *The Ten Commandments:*

an unusual one. There is great demand for the book all over the world. Publishers in five languages have already agreed to publish it, the translators are fast at work, and the film industry is watching with a keen eye.[21] The book will appear in English with Simon & Schuster both in New York and in London.[22] It will be published in French in Canada, in Spanish in South America, in Swedish in Stockholm, and in German there likewise. It is a collection of novellas—not by one author, but by ten, featuring such names as Sigrid Undset,[23] Jules Romains,[24] Franz Werfel,[25] the British author Rebecca West,[26] and the American Bromfield.[27] It has but *one subject*, and indeed a timely one: it is the *Ten Commandments*. Inventing freely yet in response to current events, the ten authors in this book reimagine the commandments that were given to humankind in ancient times as their fundamental moral law.[28] Or rather, they reimagine, point by point, the blasphemous *corruption* being inflicted upon this fundamental law of human decency by those powers against which a world still attached to religion and the concept of humanity chose, after a long period of hesitation, to take up arms. In other words: the book is about the war and what this war is about. Hence the demand.

Ten Short Novels of Hitler's War Against the Moral Code, ed. Armin L. Robinson, with a preface by Hermann Rauschning (New York: Simon and Schuster, 1943), 3–70. Mann also refers to the then-forthcoming German edition: Thomas Mann, *Das Gesetz: Erzählung* (Stockholm: Bermann Fischer, 1944).

21 Initially, Robinson tried to pitch the idea of a major episodic film adaptation of *The Ten Commandments* to Metro-Goldwyn-Mayer, without success. Lion Feuchtwanger (1884–1958), Carl Zuckmayer (1896–1977), and Alfred Polgar (1873–1955), who had been brought on for the film, were not involved in the book, presumably to give the project a more international flair by enabling more non-German authors to participate.

22 The publishing house Simon & Schuster, founded by Richard Simon (1899–1960) and Max Schuster (1897–1970) in New York in 1924, released the book in 1943.

23 The Norwegian author Sigrid Undset (1882–1949) won the Nobel Prize for literature in 1928. She fled Norway for the United States in 1940, where she was active in various antifascist organizations in Brooklyn, New York.

24 The French novelist Jules Romains (1885–1972) came to the United States in 1940, moving to Mexico City in 1941.

25 The Prague-born author Franz Werfel (1890–1945) came to the United States in 1940, where he achieved international success with his novel *The Song of Bernadette* (1941).

26 The British journalist, critic, and novelist Rebecca West (1892–1983) later reported for *The New Yorker* on the war crimes trials in Nuremberg.

27 The American novelist Louis Bromfield (1896–1956).

28 The four authors who have not been mentioned are Bruno Frank (1887–1945); John Erskine (1879–1951); André Maurois (1885–1967); Hendrik Willem van Loon (1882–1944).

The person speaking to you wrote the first piece that appears in this volume,[29] the introductory chapter. It is also a mere story, but it does not take place in the present, as do the others, but rather in ancient times: the story of Moses, the son of Amram; the naturally depicted story of the man who received the Decalogue, the concise moral law of humanity, and brought it down to humankind from Mount Horeb or Mount Sinai. Since the words with which he delivers the tablets of law to his people meld seamlessly with the framework of my broadcasts to you, German listeners, you will therefore have the opportunity to hear them before those readers who will get their hands on this timely storybook before you will.

"In the stone of the mountains," says Moses, "I engraved the ABC of human conduct, but no less shall it be graven in your flesh and blood, O Israel, so that everyone who breaks one of the ten commandments shall shrink within himself and before God, and it shall be cold about his heart because he overstepped God's bound. Well I know, and God, He too knows well that His commands will not be obeyed, but will be rebelled against over and over again. But everyone who breaks the laws shall from now on grow icy cold about the heart, because they are written in his flesh and blood and he knows the Word will avail.

But cursed be the man who stands up and says: 'They are good no longer.' Cursed be he who teaches you: 'Up and be free of them, lie, steal, and slay, whore, dishonor father and mother and deliver them to the knife, and you shall praise my name because I proclaim freedom to you.' Cursed be he who sets up a calf and says: 'There is your God. To its honor do all this, and lead a new harlot dance about it.'[30]

Your God will be very strong; on a golden chair will he sit and pass for the wisest because he knows the desires of the human heart are evil from youth onwards. But that will be all that he knows; and he who only knows that is as stupid as the night is black, and better it were for him had he never been born. For he knows not of the bond between God and man, which none can break, neither man nor God, for it is inviolate. Blood will flow in streams because of his black stupidity, so that the red pales from the cheek of mankind, but it can do no else but to fell the villain. And I will lift up My foot, saith the Lord, and tread him into the

---

29 George R. Marek (1902–1987) published the first English translation of "Das Gesetz" (The Law) under the title "Thou Shalt Have No Other Gods Before Me: A Story." This title is misleading in that Mann's story is by no means only about the first commandment; rather, it serves as an introduction to the theme of the Ten Commandments in the book as a whole, as much as it treats the first commandment on its own. The text printed above is Marek's, with minor emendations from the present translators.

30 See Exodus 32:19: "When Moses approached the camp and saw the calf and the dancing, his anger burned and he threw the tablets out of his hands, breaking them to pieces at the foot of the mountain" (New International Version).

mire—to the bottom of the Earth will I tread the blasphemer, a hundred and twelve fathoms deep, and man and beast shall make a detour around the spot where I trod him in, and the birds of the air high in their flight shall swerve that they fly not over it. And whosoever names his name shall spit towards the four quarters of the Earth, and wipe his mouth and say 'God save us all!' that the Earth may be again the Earth—a vale of troubles, but not a field of iniquity. Say Amen to that!"

And all the people said, Amen.

May 25, 1943

German Listeners!

When I was staying at the Baltic Sea in the summer of 1932,[31] I received a package from which,[32] when I opened it, black ash and charred paper fell out on me. The contents consisted of a burnt, only barely recognizable copy of a book that I had written, the novel *Buddenbrooks*—sent to me by its owner as a punishment for my public expression of horror at the steady ascension of the Nazi calamity.[33]

That was the personal prelude to the symbolic action produced in grand style by the Nazi regime throughout Germany a year later, on May 10, 1933: the ritual mass-burning of books written by liberal authors[34]—not only German, or Jewish authors, but also American, Czech, Austrian, French, and above all Russian authors; in a word, world literature went up in smoke on the funeral pyre—a desolate, woeful, and grotesquely ominous sport, of which, incidentally, many of the young people who participated happily took advantage in order to pilfer as many of the books that

---

31 Mann's final stay in his vacation home in Nidden on the Curonian Spit (now Lithuania) lasted from July 3 to September 3, 1932.

32 Mann describes the incident in his letter to Germanist Carl Helbling (1897–1966) of September 8, 1932.

33 In an article in the *Berliner Tageblatt* of August 8, 1932, Mann had denounced the Nazis' terrorist acts of violence and described Nazism as a "national disease," a conflation of "hysteria and muffled romanticism, whose megaphone Germanism is the caricature and mockery of everything German." The article could only be published in a watered-down form.

34 From March to June 1933, the Deutsche Studentenschaft (DSt; German Student Union) collaborated with the SA, the Hitler Youth, and the Nazi Party on book burnings. Pamphlets carrying the motto "Against the un-German spirit" justified the burnings as a reaction to the "shameless atrocities of Judaism abroad." The organizers of these events targeted critics of National Socialism, especially Jews and Marxists. While Heinrich and Klaus Mann's books were on the list, Thomas Mann's works were initially spared, apparently in the hope, nurtured by Goebbels, that the author could be persuaded to return to Germany. The most widely publicized campaign took place on May 10 in the square next to the State Opera in Berlin (now the Bebelplatz).

the Nazis transported as possible, so as to acquire enlightening readings in the most affordable way.

It is curious enough that among all of the iniquities that National Socialism has committed and that followed upon this one in such a long, bloody chain, this idiotic ritual made the greatest impression on the world and will likely live on in human memory longer than any other.[35] The Hitler regime is the regime of book burnings and this it will remain. The shock delivered to the European cultural conscience was severe, and its effects have continued to linger—while at the same time in Germany this act of drunken nationalism is probably already as good as banished from memory. Very soon after the humbug took place, a 'Society of Friends of the Burned Books' was created in London, headed by H. G. Wells.[36] It worked together with Parisian emigrant groups and provided the funds to establish a "German Freedom Library" in Paris. It opened on the first anniversary of the auto-da-fé, May 10, 1934, and since then, naturally has become one of the Gestapo's victims, along with its entire Anti-Nazi-Archive. But this date, May 10, remains indelibly etched in memory, at least for the Anglo-American peoples, and here in America the tenth anniversary of this particular May 10 has led to truly moving and, for us German refugees who fled Europe, deeply humiliating demonstrations. At 12 o'clock noon on this day, the flags were lowered to half-mast at the New York Public Library and at three-hundred of the most important public libraries across the country, and at all of these locations people gathered to listen to the addresses delivered by proponents of literature and science, who commemorated the Nazi atrocity and affirmed the inviolability of freedom of thought for all. The "Council of Books in Wartime" published a pamphlet containing a list of the most renowned of the burned and banned books, which was sent to thirty-thousand libraries, as well as to all schools, colleges, universities, and bookstores in the country.[37] The American propaganda office had art posters produced and distributed that answer symbolism with symbolism:[38] they show smoke and flames from the literary funeral pyre suffocating the desecrator of culture, Hitler. A committee for the

---

35 Mann's assumption had to be corrected when the existence of the extermination camps became generally known; see the annotations for the address of January 14, 1945.

36 Herbert George Wells (1866–1946), author of *The Time Machine* (1895) and numerous other science-fiction novels. Mann met him in 1924 at a dinner organized in his honor by the PEN Club in London.

37 The Council on Books in Wartime (1942–1946) was an organization of publishers and literary professionals focusing on the promotion of books and reading to further the war effort.

38 The United States Office of War Information was created in June 1942 and remained in operation until September 1945.

"Restoration of Burned and Banned Books in Europe,"[39] sponsored by some of the most prominent names in the country, commissioned a list of the works that should be the first to be returned to the library shelves of a liberated Europe or reissued. Radio plays and speeches by the most famous radio commentators went out over the networks and commemorated the barbaric merriment that was offered to the old cultural people of the Germans ten years ago. Raymond Gram Swing and Elmer Davis spoke on the topic, as did Sinclair Lewis, Ève Curie, and many others.[40] I won't even mention the expositions by publishing houses, the discussions and ceremonies in many schools. It is enough that here in this country the tenth anniversary of the German book burnings became a day of remembrance, a demonstration of a magnificent devotion to the idea of culture and to the expression "You will not kill the mind."[41] And we Europeans had to ask ourselves once more whether the values of occidental morality are not better preserved on this side of the ocean, whether they do not enjoy more generous protection, than they do over there on your side.

The philistines and cultural hangmen who claim to be idealistically defending the noble fortress of Europe against the alleged materialism of this country are the very same philistines and marauding swindle-revolutionaries from whose bloody hands the United States and its allies seek to liberate the old continent. Decrepit Wagnerians act as though they were in any position to look down their noses in contempt at the land of Walt Whitman.[42] And yet it is far more likely to be the latter,

---

39 Mann's source is unknown. The original German reads: "Wiederherstellung verbrannter und verbannter Bücher in Europa."

40 Gram Swing (1887–1967) was a journalist and radio commentator for CBS. Elmer Davis (1890–1958) was a journalist for the *New York Times* and a radio commentator for CBS before he was appointed the first director of the Office of War Information in 1942. 1930 Nobel Prize winner Sinclair Lewis (1885–1951) was the author of the novel *It Can't Happen Here* (1935), which deals with American fascism. Lewis was married to author and journalist Dorothy Thompson. Ève Denise Curie Labouisse (1904–2007), the daughter of Nobel Prize winner Marie Curie (1903), was a journalist for the *New York Herald Tribune* and a war correspondent.

41 This appears to be an allusion to a 1921 song by John Henry Mackay (1864–1933) "Ihr könnt das Wort verbieten": "Ihr könnt das Wort verbieten / ihr tötet nicht den Geist" ("You can forbid the word / you'll never forbid the spirit").

42 For example, the English-born Germanophile, Houston Stewart Chamberlain (1855–1927), was a spokesman for the Bayreuth Circle and the *völkisch* ideology that paved the way for National Socialism and expressed contempt for the United States as the embodiment of cultureless commerce. In "Von deutscher Republik" ("On the German Republic", 1922), Mann portrayed Walt Whitman (1819–1892), the poet of *Leaves of Grass* (1855), as the bard of American democracy.

and not the late-romantic, histrionic dramatist of Germanness,[43] in whose name the world of tomorrow will lay down its oath.

June 27, 1943

German Listeners!

We Europeans, even when we are just about to receive the citizenship documents of the New World, want to be proud of our old Europe.[44] It is a continent worthy of admiration! How much easier, more comfortable its peoples could have had it if they had calmly agreed to Hitler's nefarious "New Order," had consigned themselves to slavery, had collaborated with Nazi Germany, as it is called. They did not do so.

Years filled with the most brutal terror, filled with torture and executions, did not succeed in breaking their will to resistance. On the contrary, they only made it stronger, and Hitler's "unified Europe, which stands together in defense of its most sacred possessions against the invasion of the foreigners" is the most wretched of all Nazi lies. The foreigners against whom the most sacred of all possessions must be defended are the Nazis themselves and no one else. Only a thin, corrupt upper class, a gang of traitors who hold nothing sacred but money and advantage, stand together with them. The peoples refuse to do so, and, needless to say, the more apparent the allied victory becomes, the more their defiance of the intolerable gains in confidence.

Seven million people have been deported to perform forced labor, almost a million have been executed or murdered, and the hell of the concentration camps grips tens of thousands. All this cannot demoralize them—the unequal, heroic struggle goes on.

Do you Germans know that, of your troops and those of Italy in the occupied countries, easily one hundred and fifty thousand have perished? Do you know that across Europe at least two hundred fifty quislings—that is the collective term, of course, for the natives who serve the Nazis—have been murdered? In some regions, sabotage accounts for a thirty percent reduction of Axis war production. That is the work of the underground organizations everywhere that anonymously, without heroics, stake their lives on helping prisoners escape, on destroying war materials, and on nurturing the spirit of resistance in the people by distributing illegal print materials—newspapers with print runs that, at times, have reached the hundreds of thousands.

43 Mann is alluding to neo-Romantic and nationalist opera composer Richard Wagner.

44 Thomas and Katia Mann had initiated the lengthy process of naturalization at the American consulate in Toronto, Canada, on May 3 during their first transcontinental lecture tour in the spring of 1938. They took the oath of citizenship in Los Angeles on June 23, 1944. It was the second time Mann changed his citizenship after becoming a citizen of Czechoslovakia in 1936.

I say to you: Honor unto the peoples of Europe! And I will add something that may sound strange to some of you who are listening to me at the moment: Honor and compassion unto the German people, too! The proposition that no distinction can be made between the German people and Nazism,[45] that German and National Socialist are one and the same, is asserted from time to time in the Allied countries, and not without intellectual merit;[46] but it is untenable and cannot prevail. Too many facts speak against it: Germany has resisted and continues to resist, as effectively as the others. What is now taking place underground in the enslaved nations is more or less a repetition of what has been taking place in Germany for the past ten years, and to some extent makes use of the experiences of the illegal opposition in Germany.

Who can say how many in the Himmler state have paid for their idealism, their unbending belief in justice and freedom with torture and death? When the war broke out, there were two hundred thousand political prisoners in Germany, and in the German press, the publicized imposition of death sentences and prison sentences for high treason, sabotage, etc. continues without interruption—although, of course, these only represent the cases where the culprits were caught and only the cases that they want to admit. That is the Germany that stands united behind the Führer!

This summer, the world was deeply moved by the events at the University of Munich, news of which reached our ears through Swiss and Swedish papers,[47] at first vaguely, and then with ever more stirring detail.[48] We now know of Hans Scholl, the survivor of Stalingrad, and his

---

45 Whether "German" could be equated with "National Socialist" was the problematic point in the discussions about the "German problem" that emerged during the war. The most outspoken purveyor of the German-as-Nazi view was Robert Gilbert Vansittart, a British diplomat in the Foreign Office. Vansittart delivered lectures on German history during the "Blitz" on the BBC in the fall of 1940, which were published the following year and sold well under the title *Black Record. Germans Past and Present.* Mann read Vansittart's brochure on June 1 and 2, 1941, and Vansittart's thesis became a focus of his thinking about Germany.

46 Vansittart was a multilingual aesthete and a connoisseur of Austrian literature who had enjoyed the admiration of author Hugo von Hofmannsthal (1874–1929) and Erika Mann, who provided a flattering portrait of him for the fashion magazine *Vogue* in 1942.

47 The impetus for this address was an anonymous article in the *Nation*, "The Nazi Student Trial" (May 29, 1943, 779). It was the first time Mann learned of the existence of the "White Rose" and the dramatic events at the University of Munich.

48 In the early summer of 1942, after the bombing of Cologne and other cities, a resistance group called the "Weiße Rose" (White Rose) formed at the University of Munich. It produced four leaflets denouncing the Nazi government as a regime of lies, stating that the war could not be won, and that hundreds of

sister, of Christoph Probst, of Professor Huber, and all the others;[49] of the students' Easter protest against the obscene oration by a Nazi fat cat in the auditorium maximum,[50] of their martyrdom, of the pamphlet that they distributed containing words that atoned for sins committed at German universities against the spirit of German freedom over a number of unfortunate years. Indeed, it was heartbreaking, this susceptibility of the German youth—worst of all the youth—to the National Socialist revolution of lies. Now their eyes are open, and they lay their young heads upon the chopping block for their insight and for Germany's honor—they lay down their heads after saying before a court, to the Nazi President's face: "Soon you will be standing where I now stand"; after attesting in the presence of death: "A new faith in freedom and honor is dawning!"

Brave, glorious young people! You shall not have died in vain, shall not be forgotten. The Nazis have erected monuments in Germany to filthy hooligans, lowly killers—the German revolution, the true revolution, will tear them down and in their place immortalize your names, for, when darkness still covered Germany and Europe, you knew and proclaimed: "A new belief in freedom and honor is dawning!"

July 27, 1943

German Listeners!
Italian fascism is dead.[51] Not even the dogs will accept a piece of bread from it—in that country, fascism was barely even tolerated, and when it

---

thousands of Jews had been murdered in Poland. In February 1943, two further leaflets were produced and the slogan "Down with Hitler" (Nieder mit Hitler) was found painted on a wall at the university library. On February 18, three members of the White Rose were caught by a police officer distributing the leaflets in the atrium of the university, sentenced to death by the People's Court and executed on February 22. In a second trial on April 19, three more students were sentenced to death; eleven other co-conspirators received prison sentences.

49 Kurt Huber (1893–1943) was a psychologist and musicologist specializing in folk music and had served as an adjunct professor at the University of Munich since 1940. The first three students executed were Hans Scholl who studied medicine; Sophie Scholl who studied biology and philosophy; and Christoph Probst (1919–1943) who studied medicine.

50 The immediate provocation for student protests was a speech on January 14, 1943, on the occasion of the university's 470th anniversary, by Gauleiter Paul Giesler (1895–1945) who declared that the university should not be a hiding place for affluent daughters, whose war duties included bearing children for the Führer.

51 On July 25, 1943, Mussolini was deposed and imprisoned; King Vittorio Emmanuele III (1869–1947) replaced him as prime minister with Pietro Badoglio (1871–1956). Badoglio was a leading fascist, temporary Chief of the General Staff, and a brutal colonial ruler in Italian East Africa.

became allied with Hitler,[52] when it waged its despicable war against France,[53] when it reduced the nation to a Nazi Foreign Section,[54] when rivers of Italian blood flowed in Russia, when the defeats came, when the empire went to the devil, the contempt of the youth, of the intelligentsia, of the entire nation no longer knew any limits. The invasion of Sicily, the bombing of Rome, those were the final straws for Italian fascism.[55] Il Duce and his gang are in custody, including Herr Scorza, the Squadristi chief with the ricin bottle, one of the worst tormentors and killers, who at the last minute suddenly waxed poetic and beseeched listeners over the radio to rescue glorious, sacred Italy, God's miracle—when really he only intended to save his own hide.[56]

How soon, Germans, will you, too, have to hear these same sounds! I can already hear Goebbels and his henchmen warbling about their eternal Germany with its music, its profundity, its sacred cultural sites, for which all of you, entirely regardless of whether or not you are party members, must stand together to deliver Germany from the most terrible crisis in its history. They will also seek to conceal the fact that there is only one true way to stand in solidarity in defense of one's country, and that is to free it from its desecrators and debasers. These scoundrels of state, who have known nothing but lies, violence, and crime, and who have led their countries to the brink of the abyss—when the bell tolls for them, they hope to entrench themselves behind the peoples' natural love of their fatherland, behind the attachment to traditions and sacred sites, which are

---

52 The three Axis powers—Germany, Italy, and Japan—negotiated a pact on September 27, 1940. Prior to this, on October 25, 1936, Hitler and Mussolini had already signed a "friendship treaty."

53 After the armistice in France of June 22, 1940, Italy occupied the southeastern region from Nice to Grenoble, which had belonged to the as-yet-unoccupied part of the country controlled by the Vichy regime.

54 What we have translated as "Nazi Foreign Section," Mann wrote as "Gau," originally a Germanic term from the Middle Ages meaning a region of a country. The Nazi Party officially began to use the term in 1926 to designate its regional associations. When the Nazis took over in 1933, the "Gaue" of Germany became the de facto administrative regions of the country, and when Germany began to annex other countries' territory a variation on the term was coined and put into use: the *Reichsgau*. In the *Reichsgau* the administrative spheres of party and state were formally combined.

55 The landing of the Allies in Sicily on July 10, 1943, and their advance onto the Italian mainland led to Mussolini's removal from power. The first bombing of Rome by the Allies took place on July 19, 1943.

56 The Squadristi were the Fascist Party's paramilitary squads, also known as the Blackshirts. Mann is referring to Carlo Scorza (1897–1988), the leader of the Blackshirts and, alongside Mussolini, the strong man of Italian fascism. He was notorious for his preferred method of torture, whereby the victim was force-fed castor oil through a funnel.

indeed worth defending, but with which the Nazis' baseness has not the slightest thing to do, and which have been dragged down deep into the excrement by Nazi rule.

Germans, the world hopes and prays that you will not prove to be even more stupid than the Italians, whose musical intelligence does not tolerate such obviously false siren songs, but responds with the cry "Alla porta!"[57] That is a political people that seizes the moment when a regime, one sullied beyond measure, an entirely unendurable regime, must be abandoned, thrown overboard, and will not continue to prop it up until all is lost. Germans, if you cannot bring yourselves to this politically intelligent decision, if you cannot at the last moment manage to rid yourselves of this rabble, who have subjected you and all humankind to such shameful acts, then all is lost, life and honor.

The hour of truth is about to strike. It is extremely unlikely that Italy will continue fighting earnestly at the side of Hitler's Germany against the free nations. The people have decided. Not only do they cry out in the city plazas: "Down with fascism!," but also: "Out with the Germans!" and "Peace!" If Italy falls, if it becomes an Allied area of operation, then within a short time, the Balkans will be lost to your rulers, Turkey will openly join the United Nations,[58] and before you know it, "Fortress Europe" will be nothing more than "Fortress Germany," whose old cities tremble under the Allied air fleets' hail of bombs.

Act! Realize in your minds what has already come to pass. Fascism has been eradicated in the land of its origin. The days of the strong-jawed master's sneer, of Marinetti's heroic nonsense,[59] of the strutting vainglory of d'Annunzio,[60] of the entire swindle of recidivism masked as youthful and forward-looking are over. And with that, National Socialist ideology, this mutant subspecies of all fascism, is left hanging in the air, isolated and incapable of survival, incapable of keeping the German people alive and of leading them into the future. Did you not once pride

---

57 In Italian, literally "at the door"; here, "there's the door."

58 Turkey had signed a treaty of friendship with the Nazi regime on June 18, 1941 and remained neutral during the war. It was one of the founding members of the United Nations shortly after the war.

59 The Italian writer Filippo Tommaso Marinetti (1876–1944), author of the *Futurist Manifesto* (1909), founded the Partito Politico Futurista (Futurist Political Party) in 1918, which joined Mussolini's fascist movement the following year. Mann already quoted and derided Marinetti in his speech to workers in Vienna in 1932, in which he characterizes Marinetti's positions as "grotesque absurdities."

60 The eccentric writer and politician Gabriele d'Annunzio (1863–1938) was a leading figure in literary Décadence and advocate of the Italian quest for great power. He was the dictator of Fiume, the disputed peninsula in the Adriatic, from 1919 to 1920. D'Annunzio is the subject of criticism and ridicule in Mann's *Reflections of a Nonpolitical Man* (1918).

yourselves on being a people who embraced life, who comprehended its driving forces? National Socialism is as dead as fascism. It deserves to be buried deep, to be deeply forgotten.

August 29, 1943

German Listeners!

"The ruin of the people": that is what those of us for whom Hitlerism was, from the beginning, something horrible and disgusting have called those into whose hands our unfortunate fatherland fell ten years ago through an evil fate. That they are the ruin of the people, morally and physically, they have themselves shown beyond any shadow of a doubt. Everyone knows that Hitler has lost his war, and not even a general of the Reichswehr, not even a Nazi fat cat deceives himself any longer. It is undeniable and a hard, irrevocable matter of fact that Germany cannot win a war against the world. The surprise "Blitz,"[61] which was the only thing Germany could count on, will always fail, the way it has already failed two times before, and a protracted war of attrition and defense is hopeless from the outset. The German people will be spared the abhorrent fate of having to play the slaveholder and taskmaster, like inferior dreamers imagined they would. It will have to realize its in-born drive to universalism in other, more appropriate ways than by means of world *conquest*: namely by doing service to the world, by incorporating the world in its thoughts and desires, and by fostering its spiritual enrichment. If the masters of Germany ever meant well with you in the slightest, if they ever were the people who *could* mean well with their own country and with the peoples of Europe, if they were not exclusively concerned with saving their own skins, with the preservation of their gluttony for power, then they would recognize that their forsaken gamble is lost and forsaken, then they would step down and allow the German people to make their peace with the world, open to them the path to a better future. They would listen to the words of President Roosevelt, who declared before the Canadian Parliament: "If Hitler and his generals knew our plans, they would realize that discretion is the better part of valor, and that they should rather surrender now than later."[62]—But no! Sooner should Germany fall to ruins, drink the cup of agony to the very bottom, than that these wretches admit their bankruptcy, and by abdicating, somehow allow Germany to

---

61 Mann is referring to the German blitzkrieg. See annotations for the address of April 1941.

62 In an address to the Canadian Parliament in Ottawa on August 25, 1943, Roosevelt said, among other things: "Sometimes I wish that that great master of intuition, the Nazi leader, could have been present in spirit at the Quebec Conference. I am thoroughly glad that he was not there in person. If he and his generals had known our plans they would have realized that caution is still the better part of valor and that surrender would pay them better now than later."

be rehabilitated in the eyes of the world, which has made the country out to be the enemy of humankind. What the people of Germany and the whole of Europe are suffering is all but unbearable even *from afar*— how are you Germans supposed to endure it for days or even years to come? Only the high-stakes gamblers and thieves in the night who rule over you can bear it—they will never lose hope of avoiding judgment, if not through sheer force of weapons—which is no longer an option—then through politics. Not even through their own politics—since they are no longer in any position to pursue politics—rather their hope is nourished by the political differences of opinions held by others, by the socio-philosophical disagreements between East and West; their hopes are pinned on the collapse of the antifascist coalition. — Do you Germans really believe in that? Do you believe that Russia will ever, after all that has happened, make peace with the Hitler regime? Russia will only make peace with a Germany transformed by a true democratic revolution—and not Russia separately; rather, a free Germany will be in a position to conclude a peace with all. —

Differences between Russia and the West? They exist. But achieving a compromise between the two is one of the functions of this war: the accommodation of socialism and democracy, on which all the hope of the world rests. Germans, do not bank on discord between the allies! They stand united in their determination to put an end to international banditry and to safeguard humankind from the ignominy of fascist world domination. The authority with which they demand "unconditional surrender,"[63] *unbedingte Unterwerfung*, is grounded in just this unity.

It was a dreadful time when National Socialism could still assume the air of the sacrosanct executor of the will of history and of the World Spirit,[64] such that any act of resistance was to be considered a crime punishable by death. That time is over now. The air has been exposed for the insolent hypocrisy it always was. The historic mandate lies with the United Nations. It is on their authority and will that the new order of the peoples will be established, in accordance with the responsible exercise of freedom. To lay down arms before their authority does no dishonor to any people who have been led astray. To refuse to do so out of a false sense of honor can only mean prolonged, ever-increasing suffering and most woeful self-destruction.

63 The Western Allies agreed to pursue an unconditional surrender by the Axis Powers and ruled out any special agreement with Germany. This was the result of a secret conference between Roosevelt and Churchill in Casablanca (Morocco) from January 14 to 24, 1943.

64 In a letter on October 13, 1806, to fellow philosopher Friedrich Immanuel Niethammer (1766–1848), Georg Wilhelm Friedrich Hegel (1770–1831) uses the term "Weltseele" (later "Weltgeist" or world spirit) to describe the appearance of Napoleon Bonaparte as an embodiment of the will of the world seeking to impose itself absolutely by authority of the laws of nature.

September 29, 1943

German Listeners!
Is Germany lost beyond all salvation? No, it can be saved, still today, still tomorrow, from the utter destruction that threatens it: through a democratic revolution, through the resolute ousting of the regime of plunder and murder that is insufferable to the entire world, that lit the torch of this war, and the eradication of which would render Germany capable of peace, in the East and in the West. The manifesto of the German officers imprisoned in Russia has once again brought to light the fact that Germany is not fighting for its survival,[65] its honor, but that it is fighting only to postpone the demise of this reign of terror, a demise fundamentally settled, signed, and sealed, because it is a matter of absolute necessity.

Who will save Germany? The question likely burns with increasing distress in many a heart. The appeal by the students executed in Munich to the German people to throw off the yoke of infamy before it is too late was one indication of that.[66] Now news comes from Stockholm that the crews of the three largest units of the German fleet, 'Tirpitz,' 'Scharnhorst,' and 'Lützow,' arrived at the decision to sabotage their ships and thus made their deployment impossible. The report has not been confirmed; but even if it is certain that the perpetrators would be dealt with in a trial as short as that of the young heroes of Munich—one can easily put oneself in the state of mind of these German sailors, who have seen with their own eyes the failure of the submarine war, the devastation of Hamburg, Bremen, Kiel, Wilhelmshaven, the loss first of the French, then the Italian fleet,[67] and who take no pleasure in being commanded by Fleet Admiral Dönitz to embark on a suicide mission against the British navy.[68] *If* they really did what everyone says of them, then surely they intended at the same time to do their part in contributing to the containment of a war that it must seem rather absurd and criminal to continue, particularly to the eyes of a sailor.

---

65 Mann is referring to a four-page manifesto published by the National Committee for a Free Germany (Nationalkomitee Freies Deutschland, or NKFD), which was founded in July 1943 in Krasnogorsk under Soviet guidance and was made up of communist emigrants and officers taken as prisoners of war. The author Erich Weinert (1890–1953) was appointed president of the committee. The NKFD called for rebellion against the Hitler regime and for the formation of a strong democratic state power.

66 See the annotations for the address of June 1943.

67 After the armistice of September 3, 1943, Italy was obliged to surrender its navy (Regia Marina) and relocate it to Malta. A squadron from La Spezia seeking refuge in Sardinia was intercepted and sunk.

68 Karl Dönitz (1891–1980) was promoted to Commander-in-Chief of the Navy in 1943 and was Head of State for a few days after Hitler's suicide.

Which is not to say that the German armed forces on solid ground and in the air would have any reason to disagree. "Fortress Europe"[69] was never anything more than a propaganda bluff, for a fortress whose occupants with few exceptions fervently desire to be conquered hardly deserves such a name. In any case, calling a continent a fortress is nothing more than a disingenuous projection, and it has long been clear that the Nazis could defend large outer territories at best temporarily as a delay tactic, and only sought with any seriousness to maintain an inner ring around Fortress *Germany*. Their retreats fluctuated in character from strategic maneuver to catastrophic military failure. The retreat in Russia in particular, which every day cost thousands of dead and an unending hoard of munitions, hardly appears to have been an act of unforced initiative. The reductions at the front are rather drastic, and there will *never* be sufficient forces to stop the advances of the Red Army. After the loss of Smolensk,[70] which will evidently be followed by the loss of Kiev, the Dniester Line, and the former Polish border have been hailed as the ideal battlefront for the destruction of Bolshevism. Winning this position cost two million dead.

Sardinia in Italy's hands, Corsica conquered by the French,[71] southern Italy occupied by the British and the Americans: it is clear to everyone, that neither can Rome be held that way, nor is the Po Basin safe anymore, for all of Northern Italy smolders with sabotage and guerilla warfare, and the Allied Forces have what they need in Italy: airfields for sorties against southern Germany and the Balkans. The German plan of inner defense is nothing more than a plan of despair, and everyone knows that. No delay tactics at the land fronts no matter how stubborn they are can protect Germany from air attacks from the south and the west, in comparison to which everything they have suffered until now will be proven harmless.

What will become of Germany? One has no right to ask this question after all that has come to pass in Europe, and yet, because Germany was once your home, you do ask yourself, and your heart constricts. The Nazis know that they are lost. Their megalomaniacal Satanism demands that no one and nothing should ever perish *on a par* with them. It is to

69 Mann sarcastically invokes the Nazi propaganda slogan originally intended to make people believe that Europe, occupied and fortified by Germany, was impregnable.

70 Smolensk, a city southwest of Moscow, captured by the Wehrmacht in July 1941, was recaptured by the Red Army on September 25, 1943 in the Second Battle of Smolensk.

71 The Mediterranean island of Corsica, which belonged to France and was occupied by German and Italian forces, was liberated by resistance fighters (the *Maquis*) and Allied forces in September 1943, after Hitler had given the order to withdraw on September 12. Corsica thus became the first French territory to be liberated from Axis occupation.

be a downfall like no other, a catastrophe in a style never seen before, and they want to drag to hell with them anything that can be dragged down in blood and flames. The German people alone fight to realize the hellish magnificence of this brood's departure, they continue a war out of which nothing more, but also nothing other than utmost misery can grow. A verse, a cry from the heart from a drama that you have been banned from reading springs to mind:

"When will the hero come for this our country?"[72]

October 30, 1943

German Listeners!
The bestiality of the Nazis, their vandalism, their mindless and profligate barbarism, the scale of their atrocities near and far, of which you in Germany probably have only a faint conception—none of that prevents anyone in the world from sympathizing in terror with the horror and misery that is brought upon so many innocent people by the Anglo-American air raids on German industrial and port cities. The numbers—the official German numbers—are shocking. One million two hundred thousand native civilians have reportedly perished in these attacks, nearly seven million have lost house and home and are condemned to the existence of uprooted evacuees. Do not imagine that the civilized world lacks compassion for all of this misfortune! However, the manner in which the Nazi press gushes over this calamity; the way they exploit it in order to transfer from themselves and onto their opponents the curses that are German fascism's due, and which it well knows are its own doing, the curse of barbarism, the curse of the defilement of humankind; the way they act as though Nazi Germany had never so much as caused a ripple in the water, as though it were a victim who had been set upon by some criminal force of destructive rage—all of this is so fatuous and disgraceful that even the most civilized heart could lose its sense of compassion.

There is a weekly paper, the mouthpiece of the Gestapo, called *Das Schwarze Korps*—it has always distinguished itself through insolent mockery and petty gangster wit.[73] A few of the contributors, who somehow once acquired rudimentary writing skills, who know how to mimic a moral turn of phrase, and the displays of moral indignation and offended humanity that these literary whoremongers of violence now proffer, rank among the most shameless, most nonsensical, and most revolting

---

72 Quote from the end of Act I, Scene 1 of Schiller's liberation drama *Wilhelm Tell* (1804), which was banned by the Nazis in 1941.

73 *Das Schwarze Korps* (The Black Guards) was the official newspaper of the SS from March 1935 until March 1945, named for the black uniforms of the SS. The newspaper was published on Wednesdays and distributed free of charge to be read and circulated by SS members.

that National Socialism has ever foisted on its own people and the world. Anyone who might read these brilliant articles, having somehow lost their memory or lacking knowledge of everything that Nazi Germany has inflicted on other peoples since it embarked on its god-forsaken predatory war; anyone who knew nothing of the wanton debauchery of privilege and superiority in which the nation has wallowed for years, of its smugness in triumphant transgression; anyone who was not aware of Warsaw and Rotterdam and London and Coventry and the triumphant portrayals of satiated barbarism that the German press spread of these misdeeds—would break out in a cold sweat of terror when reading about the future of the Anglo-American powers, who evidently have no choice but to be morally suffocated by their nefarious acts of bloodshed. In fact, the poets behind these columns ask with grave concern about the fate of these races. What, they ask, is to become of them? Such crimes piled upon crimes against humanity must be avenged, they must be atoned for; the reckoning will have to be terrible ...

Can you believe it? The Gestapo's typing pool howls about the violation of humanity—a humanity that the system they serve has derided, pronounced null and void, trampled underfoot for eleven years. What were these people thinking? That the total war that they glorified,[74] that they declared to be the natural state of humankind, was a privilege granted to Germans only, and therefore that no others, even if their very lives were at stake, were entitled to resort to the same means? They counted on the civility of the others, that is, on the ostensible weakness and enervation of the democracies, thinking that they could stake their lives on it, exploit it to make themselves the masters and slaveholders of the world. Whoever was willing and able to wage war, they thought, the world belonged to them, and that meant them alone. For a while it appeared that they had speculated correctly. Is there anything more despicable than the howls of bloody murder with which they respond to the determination of free peoples to resort to the most extreme violence in order to put an end to extreme violence itself?

Vengeance and atonement. They have come. The delirium and intoxication of the German people is taking its revenge; the Germans must pay for the belief, fed to them by villainous teachers, in their entitlement to commit acts of violence, and unfortunately the payback has only just begun. Do you Germans have to be told that what you suffer today does not spring from the brutality and barbarism of foreigners, that it all comes

---

74 In a speech of February 18, 1943, in the Berlin Sportpalast, broadcast on the radio, Goebbels incited his carefully selected audience to answer his question: "Do you want total war?" with thunderous approval. Erich Ludendorff had popularized the term in his book *Der totale Krieg* (*Total War*, Munich, 1935). The term refers to war as a people's struggle for survival that affects all parts of society.

from National Socialism? National Socialism carried this suffering in itself from the beginning; nothing else could have come of it. That ought to have been apparent in 1932 and 33. That Germany did not see this when there was still time is its grave failing. It does not bear sole responsibility for this failing. Fascism was helped along from the outside—not out of a love for peace alone, but for sinister reasons too.[75] But it was always clear that one day the world would have to band together and rise up to eradicate this plague. The world, too, suffers badly enough for its complicity. But its victory is guaranteed—and not only for the sake of *its* own freedom, but for freedom itself, even Germany's freedom, it will win.

December 9, 1943

German Listeners!

It will hardly be necessary to inform you of the reality that the historic summit meeting in Tehran did not in fact bring about the anticipated call to the German People's Army,[76] to the German people themselves, that had been announced in your propaganda and talked about endlessly. The order to lay down arms would have been pointless at a time when your soldiers are still fighting in many places far from the borders of the Reich and when the resounding prophecy that some or other new and secret weapons will turn defeat into victory is once again numbing the German mind.[77] There can be no doubt that such weapons, if they exist, could at best only delay the final outcome of the war and, through the damage they might inflict, only increase the bitterness toward Germany, ultimately only worsening its situation. But all this is obviously part and parcel of the calamity and remains to be seen.

The absence of any direct address by the statesmen of Russia, Great Britain, and America to you Germans means that nobody wishes in the least

---

75 One of the "sinister reasons" why the Western powers let Hitler have his way was the fear of communism, against which fascism was supposed to form a bulwark.

76 Stalin, Roosevelt, and Churchill—"The Big Three"—met in Tehran from November 28 to December 1, 1943, to plan the final phase of the war against the Axis powers. They agreed to open the second front in France the following spring, which Stalin urgently desired. It was also agreed to move Poland's borders westwards to the Oder/Neisse line and to divide Germany into smaller territorial units. Final decisions were not made until after the war in Europe had ended, at the Potsdam Conference, July 17–August 2, 1945.

77 The Nazi's touted their so-called "miracle-weapons" (Wunderwaffen) as instruments of "vengeance" (Vergeltung) against the Allied forces. Two of the most famous miracle-weapons were in fact the "vengeance weapons"—the V-1 and V-2 missiles—long-range rockets that were used against Great Britain shortly after the Allied landings in Normandy in June 1944, and then against the territories conquered by the Allies in France and Belgium.

for a premature capitulation that would leave the German war machine more or less intact, a capitulation founded on ulterior motives that serve deceitful intentions and could only be offered in order to win a momentary reprieve, even if it lasted for decades: it means that they wish to end the war *through military action*, clearly, completely, and forever. No stab-in-the-back swindle,[78] no nationalist self-delusion in claiming to be "undefeated on the battlefield" should ever again be possible. The sole experience that can bring Germany to see reason, the experience of catastrophic, undeniable, and tangible defeat, the occupation and temporary disenfranchisement of the country, all of the provisions taken together that are necessary to make every further aggressiveness permanently impossible—you Germans must not and will not be spared this experience.

This will be a difficult experience—the details are unforeseeable today, even the general contours can hardly be predicted. It is a comfort that you in Germany—after everything that this scoundrel regime that scoundrels have imposed upon you has inflicted upon humankind in your name and with your hands—must long have been prepared for the utmost and will accept it as the natural consequence of insane national and international conduct. It must and will be assured that Germany can never again fall into such hands, that its faith and corruptibility can never again be so criminally misused.

It will fall to the responsible leaders of the world to make the decisions that will prevent this from happening. After everything that has happened—and entirely monstrous things have happened—it is not for us German emigrants, however deeply we may suffer over the fate of our homeland, to give the victors of tomorrow advice on how to deal with Germany after its collapse. Regardless of whether or not such advice would be listened to in the least, we cannot speak for the German people now, we must remain silent. You will understand this silence, not reproach us for not having found words in support of the better Germany, the one worthy of living on, in such an hour. Any wording that we could agree on today that speaks in favor of leniency regarding the future of Germany, the potential for life of a strong German democracy,[79] would only be

---

78 The "stab-in-the-back" scam (*Dolchstoß-Schwindel*) to which Mann refers was an attempt by the Supreme Army Command to whitewash the defeat in the First World War with the conspiracy theory that the German army had remained "undefeated in the field" and Germany had been brought down by its internal enemies (Social Democrats, Communists, Jews).

79 The Californian emigres' draft of a declaration of solidarity with the National Committee for a Free Germany (see annotations for the address of September 1943), from which Mann had withdrawn his signature, contained a call to "fight for a strong German democracy." Mann had the impression that this was an immoral attempt to protect Germany from the consequences of its misdeeds. He by no means shared the opinion that Germany should be spared.

seen as an affront to our host countries in their war, to the martyred and ravished states of Europe, as a merely patriotic and thereby immoral attempt to protect Germany from the consequences of its misdeeds.

We are Germans, and as such greatest modesty, greatest restraint, greatest precaution should be expected of us. We cannot enter into any compact that the forces of duplicity and violence would inevitably spoil if they are afforded even the slightest opportunity to regain strength. And still these forces are strong, they are still far from being defeated or admitting that they have been defeated. After a thousand atrocities, they announce even more and will doubtless commit them. They will commit the utmost even in demise, in your name, with your hands, and unavoidably, we will stand there, partially responsible, when we call out: "Germany is good!" in a moment when, before the eyes of the world, it proves itself devilish.

Let the military defeat take place, let the hour ripen that allows you to reckon with your corrupters so fundamentally, so mercilessly as is necessary for the future of Germany—then for us here on the outside the moment will have come to testify: Germany is free, Germany has truly purified itself, Germany must live on.

December 31, 1943

German Listeners!
Our country is incapable of breaking free from a counterfeit, uncomprehending, and ill-fated mimicry of Great Britain. The epithet of derision and disgust the world uses today to refer to you Germans: "Master Race," a name that is long since nothing but ridiculous, nothing but a mockery, was meant entirely earnestly on your part. You saw in the English a master race, and that is what you wanted to be; you suffered from the envious compulsion to copy Great Britain, to usurp for yourselves the role that you attributed to them; it was your dream to outdo Great Britain, to claim Great Britain's place for your own; not only *a* Master Race—you wanted to be *the* Master Race and wrest from Great Britain the naval supremacy on which its existence rests, whereas yours does no such thing and anything but.[80] This was the wellspring of the First World War.

Its origin was jealous buffoonery: the origin of the Second World War, which Germany now is also losing, was itself nothing more than a caricature of that buffoonery—just as, indeed, Nazidom is such a dreadful caricature of all the weaknesses and follies of Germanness that the

---

80 After the so-called Fleet Act of 1898, which made possible the development of a competitive German Imperial Navy, an arms race between Germany and Britain began. The expansion was intended to help Germany achieve a place in the sun by becoming a major colonial power, which threatened Britain's naval supremacy.

virtues of Germanness risk sinking into oblivion because of it. In Nazi-brains, the idea of the "master race" had lost every vestige of decency and deference before human rights, every feeling of responsibility and every healthy feeling for what the world can abide and what it can't. It had become a mere justification for theft and murder, the plundering, oppression, emasculation, and defilement of other nations—that is, a justification for an enterprise that from the outset could only be thwarted by the united powers of the world.

The Hitler system, this bloody and absurd travesty of power, is about to meet its demise. Is Germany to perish with it? So it appears. And why? Because Germany once again believes that it must copy Great Britain—Great Britain's apparently irrational resistance of 1940, when France had fallen and America was not yet ready, when Great Britain, bombed out and out of weaponry, stood entirely alone and appeared to be lost. Everyone expected Great Britain's surrender. And nonetheless, uplifted by a resolve hardened by tradition—that of a most chivalrous warrior disposition, Churchill's—Great Britain did not give in, did not capitulate, pressed on with the war, and they will win it. — And so, now Germany has to do the same, now, when the abyss is opening up before it as it once did before Great Britain. How could Germany ever fall behind Great Britain—in tenacity, in "stubbornness," as the British say, in hardheadedness and in the ability to endure suffering and defeat, in short: in heroic resolve? Both honor and rivalry with Great Britain dictate that Germany stay the course until the very end in a war that is self-evidently lost—whatever the end might entail.

That's what many Germans think. Do they not see the difference? It is the difference between the good and the bad cause. Great Britain was able to hold out, and under desperate circumstances too. It did not stand for itself alone, its honor and freedom, but rather the honor and freedom of humankind. Its defeats had a luster that even the victories of the bad cause do not have. It's true that Great Britain stood alone in that moment, but it could have faith that sooner or later the entire world would rise up against the defilers of the right to life of nations. Great Britain's cause was a cause of hope and confidence; because while it is true that the good cause does not always necessarily win on Earth, such a bad, so completely unacceptable cause like that of Nazi Germany cannot win.

Everything about the situation of Germany today is different, in fact, it is precisely the opposite of how things were for Great Britain at the time, which is why persisting in this mimicry is so nonsensical. Can Germany expect the world to rush to its aid in its misfortune? No, Germany can only look forward to a progressive decline in the number of hirelings who once gambled on its run of gangster good fortune.[81] Germany will not be able to regain lost ground, as Great Britain did, whose path led from initial defeats to victory. Germany's path leads from dazzling initial victories, which it owed to the advantage provided by armaments, to its inexorable descent into ruin. Germany's "stubbornness," its so-called heroic resolve, its perseverance, are ill-fated and forsaken, an utter counterfeit of the courage that attends a just cause. It is not only a crime against the entire world, which cannot and must not yield in this most sacrificial of struggles until the Nazi regime has been brought to heel; it is also a crime against Germany itself, against the German people and its cultural legacy, against the German cityscapes that are being reduced to rubble, against Germany's vitality, which belongs to all humankind, to the future, which can no longer be left to bleed to death pointlessly and senselessly.

Where are you, the Germans who understand that, today, German honor and courage do not demand that you "stay the course,"[82] but that you acquiesce to the will of humanity?

81 Mann is referring to Italy, which renounced its dependence on Hitler's Germany and agreed to an armistice with the Allies on September 3, 1943, in Cassibile, Sicily. See annotations for the addresses of July and September 1943.

82 "Durchhalten" is the favorite phrase of the protagonist of Mann's *Death in Venice* (1912), Gustav von Aschenbach, one that, in Mann's depiction, Aschenbach borrowed from Frederick the Great.

1944

January 30, 1944

German Listeners!
When you read certain statements that appear in Nazi propaganda, which continues its work mechanically and almost soundlessly, one wonders whether they are the product of pathological isolation, of an eerie detachment from the world and reality, whether they stem from the nonconformism of insanity, or whether they signify the impudent falsification of reason, the unconscionable perversion of the meaning of language, the deliberate turning of truth on its head. "Look at the world around you," Goebbels said, "and ask yourself whether life would still have any meaning for humankind if our enemies were to achieve their goal."[1]—Is that insolence or insanity? It is probably a combination of the two. But the combination is more repulsive than either alone would be. Just hearing the word "humankind" coming from this mouth—how does that make you feel? Where did he get it from? Is it even in his vocabulary? Does he lack any healthy awareness of the fact that anyone in a given position, a position necessarily informed by a set of doctrines and deeds, those of National Socialism for example, must refrain from invoking certain words and concepts, because they belong to another sphere, the counter-sphere, and those in certain positions are not entitled to use them? Does he think that one can simply steal and plunder and "expropriate" in the spiritual and moral realms like one does in the physical realm?[2] What gives him the right to talk about "humankind"? Did he ever believe in any such thing? Was it not he, his Führer, and their entire gang, all these hangmen philosophers and their henchmen, who mocked humankind, humanity itself, the very idea of the human being; decreed it away, maltreated, and murdered it wherever they possibly could? And he is humanely concerned about the meaning of life for all humankind, which would have to be forfeited if humankind were to rid itself of National Socialism! *That* is what he considers to be the raison d'etre of humankind—precisely *that*, against which the peoples of the world, longing for peace, have taken up arms in a late, desperate decision to save their humanity, their human dignity,

1   The source for this quote has not been identified.
2   The term "Enteignung" describes one aspect of the Nazi program of "Aryanization," which justified the practice of the expropriation of "non-aryan" possessions.

their freedom, from a descent into barbaric enslavement. East and West sacrifice and bleed because they have asked themselves the commonsensical, sound-minded question of whether life would still have a meaning if Nazi Germany achieved its goal, namely, global conquest. Goebbels knows this, which is why he seeks to turn the question on its head by engaging in the subterfuge of insane insolence or insolent insanity.

He also asked, word-for-word: "Is it conceivable that fate could have intended such a gruesome end for the peoples of the Occident as would be the defeat of Germany?"[3]—Yes, that is conceivable. It is in fact close to moving from mere concept to redemptive reality—simply because, to put it in the words of sound reason, the triumph of Nazi Germany would have been an all too gruesome end for the peoples of the Occident, an insufferable end. The Nazi way of propagandistic bonding with a fraternity of European peoples, who until now were, after all, inferior races, born to servitude; to act as though Hitler and Himmler's Germany stood up for these peoples, whom they invaded, plundered, enslaved, whom they endeavored to rob of their histories, their knowledge of themselves, their belief in themselves, and whom they sought in every conceivable way to reduce to their biology—this Nazi way of posing as European, as "Occidental," is an act of truly pathological audacity. When Mussolini fell,[4] the Italian people rejoiced. But what was this jubilance compared to the jubilation that will erupt when the German troops are finally forced to withdraw from a territory they once held occupied! When the Allies marched into Naples, there were scenes that could have shown Goebbels what the peoples of the Occident felt for him in their hearts.[5] "Thousands of people," an eyewitness reported at the time, "surged into the streets around us. We were dragged from our little car, they lifted us up onto their shoulders and hugged and kissed us."[6] It was impossible to disperse the masses of people. There was cheering, shouting, weeping, and sobbing. Above the clamor of the crowds, the words could be heard again

---

3   Mann's source is unknown. The original German reads: "Ist es vorstellbar, daß das Schicksal ein so grausames Ende, wie es die Niederlage Deutschlands wäre, für die Völker des Abendlandes beschlossen haben könnte?"

4   Mussolini was deposed on July 25, 1943; see annotations for the address of July 1943.

5   British and American forces arrived in Naples on October 1, 1943. Allied armies and bombers hammered military objectives in Naples, and once the Germans concluded that they could not hold the city, their forces destroyed what they could as they withdrew. The actions of the German demolition squads left the local population scrambling for survival, searching for water, gas, power, medical supplies, and shelter. As the Allies worked to rebuild Naples, the Germans continued their attacks on the city, planting time bombs and setting booby traps that destroyed vital infrastructure and caused further casualties.

6   The source for this report has not been identified.

and again: "Long live Great Britain, long live America! We are saved! Long live freedom!"—So it was in Naples, and so it will be in Rome, and so it will be even more so in the cities of France, Holland, and Belgium, as well as in Oslo, Copenhagen, Prague, Warsaw, Athens. When the misbegotten yoke of Nazism is lifted from the peoples of Europe, a delirium of joy will erupt, the likes of which the world has never before seen. Tears of joy and of redemption will flow all around, and from every mouth, in every language, these fervent cries will boom in German ears: "We are saved! Long live freedom!" In a chorus of jubilation, the word freedom will resound all throughout a Germany that, despite Kant, despite Schiller, has disdained it, whenever it did not refer to Germany's freedom to perpetrate violence, as the most empty of all words, and the mighty meaning of which for human life the Germans must now learn from the peoples of the Occident.

Must they really? Have they not learned what freedom means in these eleven years, and have they not experienced it personally and physically, that a people that has lost freedom suffocates and degenerates? No, in spite of all the horrors of defeat, there will be jubilation in Germany; even there, perhaps from the very bottom of their hearts, the cry of freedom will resound from millions of voices, and that will be something very new and grand in German history, a day of transition, and not to death, but rather to new life.

February 28, 1944

German Listeners!
The world is ashamed. They are reading a book that has just appeared in Boston and which is assured of a print run of hundreds of thousands of copies through its adoption by the "Book of the Month Club," the large American readers association.[7] It is by Konrad Heiden,[8] an

---

7   Mann is referring to Konrad Heiden's (1901–1966), *The Führer: Hitler's Rise to Power*, trans. Ralph Manheim (Boston: Houghton Mifflin, 1944). For a long time, this book was the main source of knowledge about Hitler in the Anglophone world. Founded in 1926 by Harry Scherman (1887–1969), the Book of the Month Club supplied books by mail to readers in the areas without local bookstores. *Stories of Three Decades* (1936) was the first Mann title to be distributed by the service. Three more followed: *Joseph in Egypt* (*Joseph in Ägypten*, 1938), *Doctor Faustus* (1947), and *The Holy Sinner* (*Der Erwählte*, 1951).

8   Heiden was a German-American journalist and historian. As a student at the University of Munich, he led a democratic student group. Beginning in 1920, Heiden began attending Hitler events and documented the rise of Hitler and his party in the *Frankfurter Zeitung* and the *Vossische Zeitung*. His first book, *Geschichte des Nationalsozialismus–Die Karriere einer Idee* (History of National Socialism–The Career of an Idea), was published in 1932 and was burned in Berlin the following year. Heiden fled to the Saarland, then Paris, and finally the

émigré German writer, who had previously written an instructive history of National Socialism and who has now published a book entitled *Der Führer: Hitler's Rise to Power*, making use of material that has only recently become available, once again presenting to the world his portrait of the most evil marauder in political history, life-sized and in full vividness. It is a document of the highest order. It will endure and will serve later historical researchers and moral philosophers in the study of the unfathomable that was possible on Earth in the second third of the twentieth century. Now the world is reading this book, in which it finds its own experience portrayed and analyzed, reads it in English, in Spanish, French, and German—and the red blush of shame rises on every cheek.

The world includes Germany in its shame, is ashamed for itself and for Germany, to the very soul, is ashamed—so the world wishes to believe—together with Germany as one. How was it possible that Germany and the world allowed this bloody nullity of a human being, this intellectual and moral inferiority, this lightless liar's soul, a coward at heart, this defiler of the word, of reason, of all things human and humane, this piteously miscarried individual, equipped with only some contaminated power of suggestion, to become historic and to erect a pedestal for himself founded on a shameless agglomeration of evil deeds, on which, at least to himself—and by now probably only to himself—he appears to possess greatness? This is the question that presents itself relentlessly while reading this book, which is no pleasure, but a penitence. Yes, it is a punishment and a torture to reread the history of this homicidal buffoon and second-rate mimic of greatness; to retrace how National Socialism, like a second-rate caliphate Islam, usurped possession of Germany only to drill it in crime, to reduce it to an instrument of its own boundless and idiotic crimes.

What a disgrace it is to commemorate the hecatombs of human lives that have fallen victim to and continue to fall victim to the forsaken hero of this book! He has been allowed to say: "I am prepared to pay for the achievement of my goals with the lives of two million Germans"—a goal that in the end comprised, after the desecration of Germany, the desecration of the entire world at the hands of National Socialism. Well, the figure of two million has long since been surpassed, even if you count only the German men who died on the battlefield. But the blood ledger of total war, which the world had to learn about from Germany, is an entirely different, a much more costly reckoning—and, of course, it is anything but an exclusively German ledger. Russia's losses, which are even higher, must be taken into account. The harvest that death has reaped and unceasingly

---

US via Lisbon with the support of Varian Fry (1907–1967) and the Emergency Rescue Committee. Heiden's study on Hitler was appreciated by, e.g., Mann and German-American historian and philosopher Hannah Arendt (1906–1975) in her 1966 book *Origins of Totalitarianism*.

continues to reap among the violated peoples of Europe must be taken into account, among Poles and Jews, Czechs, Greeks, Norwegians, Dutch, Yugoslavians, the mass murders, the suicides. We need to anticipate the terrible sacrifices that the Anglo-American peoples will still need to make in the final battle, they who themselves are condemned to wreak yet further death and destruction because they wanted peace for too long. And only then may we calculate what the repugnant windbag who is the subject of our book will have cost the world. Will it be twenty, twenty-five million human lives? Probably more,[9] many more, when all of the collateral forms of ruin brought about are accounted for. And to what end all these rivers of blood? So that an empty zero could bloat itself up blood red like the belly of a spider.

Humankind will never forgive itself for allowing what has come to pass and what is yet to come. And there will be an eternal shaking of heads about a people, the German people, who, when all delusions, all hopes, have long since vanished, continue to fight with the courage of a lion, with senseless tenacity, until Europe is reduced to a smoking field of ruins, inhabited by a scattering of half-animals roving like wolves—only to prolong the meager existence of a handful of confirmed miscreants and debauchers of power, whose rule is an unspeakable affliction to themselves and once and for all abhorrent to the world.

March 28, 1944

German Listeners!
In the free nations, total war, the bombardments of German cities from the air, and the misery for the civilian population that accompany them, pose a question of public conscience. Neither in Great Britain nor in America is there any lack of voices, loud and contrite, that condemn this cruel form of warfare—entirely uncensored—and that bitterly bemoan and denounce the fact that in so doing they were lowering themselves to the nefarious level of the enemy and demeaning the very humanity that they claim to be defending. These protests are honorable to the highest degree, and the sentiments from which they arise are familiar to every civilized human being. What has played out in Cologne, Hamburg, Berlin, and elsewhere *is* horrifying, and it is small comfort to tell oneself that extreme brutality can only be met with extreme brutality; that nemesis is at work here and that this is hardly a matter of deliberate *action* but much more a *manifestation* of vengeance. Certainly, the cultural clamor of the Nazis is despicable, their propaganda against the "Air Huns" stillborn, morally impotent. But this is about the very conscience of freedom, about the tragic nature of the fact that it must do what is alien and unnatural to

---

9   According to current estimates, the number of military and civilian victims of the Second World War stands at 75 million.

it, must do what according to its own moral law it ought not do and yet is forced to do, in response to the proclamation of violence on Earth. The dilemma is difficult, disquieting, and burdensome.

And then, suddenly, it is no longer a dilemma at all. A single word, a report from Naziland, renders it void, resolves the question, silences all doubt, provides clarity of thought that there is a final and diabolically brazen, an incorrigible and unbearable infamy of a lie that is irreconcilable with the essence of humanity, that cries out for nothing but the rain of brimstone,[10] that can only be rectified by the rain of brimstone, to which only one answer is possible: annihilation, bombs.

I pick up a newspaper and read: "In Seventeen Languages, the Nazi-controlled Press of the Continent Proclaims a 'New Socialist Europe'"![11]

Two thousand Air Huns a day above this swamp of lies—there is no other way. This unmitigated malevolence, this revolting, stomach-turning swindle, this filthy desecration of word and thought, this supersized sadistic murderousness toward the truth must be crushed, must be obliterated at all costs and by all means; the war against it is a desperate struggle of humankind, in which it dare not ask whether humankind itself suffers any harm in the struggle.

Socialism! Hitler and his band have been sustained and pushed into power by German and international finance capital.[12] They have lived and still hope to continue living off the bourgeois world's blind fear of socialism; for their only hope is that "Munich" is not dead,[13] that their secret friends in the Allied countries will continue to work on their behalf,[14] that the West-East two-front war will somehow disintegrate after all, and that the Nazis will be accepted as allies *against* socialism. The socialism of the fascist Volks-swindlers—what a shameless farce! It began in

---

10 According to Genesis 19:24, God "rained down burning sulfur on Sodom and Gomorrah" as punishment.

11 The source for this headline has not been identified.

12 Mann based his subsequent statements about the role of business bosses and capitalism in National Socialism on an article of September 1942 by Albert Norden (1904–1982), "The Third Reich of the Rich," in the newspaper *The German American*. Norden, the son of a rabbi, joined the Communist Party of Germany in 1920 and fled to France in 1933 and to the US in 1940. Norden returned to Germany in 1946 and became a citizen of the German Democratic Republic, where he held several high-ranking positions.

13 Here Mann is saying that the last hope of the National Socialists is that the spirit of the Munich Agreement of September 1938, in which France and Great Britain demonstrated a readiness for appeasement, might still be alive.

14 Mann suspected the Cliveden Set in England of sympathizing with Hitler's Germany; see the annotations for the addresses of July 1941 and March 28, 1943. Nazi Germany also provided financial support to several US groups, including members of Congress.

Italy, where the aristocracy and the bourgeoisie sold out to fascism and the people were driven into war and misery. In Germany, the working class was disenfranchised and robbed of the assets of its trade unions. The middle class was driven to the dogs by the Third Reich. But who is thriving and prospering over there are the plutocrats and the trust barons. They speak of state capitalism. There is no such thing. There is the capitalism of the political fat cats in addition to that of the money magnates from before the "Revolution." As the main shareholder of the Eher publishing house,[15] Hitler alone has surpassed most American multimillionaires in terms of gluttonous riches. Since the founding of his corporation, and now even more so since this enterprise has gone international by force of arms, Reichsmarshall Göring has put on so much capitalist fat that he is presumed to be the wealthiest individual in the world today.[16] The labor exploiter Ley oversees sixty-five joint-stock corporations.[17] Gauleiter Sauckel has built up his own trust of arms factories and munitions factories,[18] for which no balance sheet has ever been released. Has not the basic instinct of all Nazism always been envy, greed, and the drive to plunder, the wanton compulsion to wallow in power and money? To steal concepts and ideas is hardly the final craving of this debauched riffraff. The word "socialism" is just one piece of booty obtained by robber-homicide among many others. They have subjugated Europe, they intended to subjugate the world, so that the misery of the downtrodden peoples would serve to increase the profits of German big business. Monopoly and exploitation on a colossal scale—they call that socialism. Wherever the conquered nations are willing to demean themselves by collaborating, by doing business with these "revolutionaries," a corrupt elite is always present: reactionary grand bourgeois, aristocratic

---

15 Eher Verlag was founded in Munich in 1887 and was acquired by the NSDAP in 1920. Under the leadership of Max Amann (1891–1957), a confidant and promoter of Hitler, Eher Verlag was expanded into the party's central publishing house. Its most important publications included: *Der völkische Beobachter* (Völkisch Observer, 1920–1945), *Mein Kampf* (1925), and several collections of Goebbels's speeches and articles.

16 See the annotations for the addresses of June and July 1941.

17 Robert Ley had a long history in the NSDAP. He was a Gauleiter in the Rhineland before becoming Reich Organization Leader of the NSDAP and Leader of the *Deutsche Arbeitsfront* (DAF; German Labor Front). He is also known for attacking independent trade unions and his efforts as head of the *Kraft durch Freude* program (*KdF*; Strength Through Joy). See also the annotations for the address of January 15, 1943.

18 Fritz Sauckel (1894–1946) began as a Gauleiter in Thuringia and was appointed "General Plenipotentiary for Labor Deployment" in 1942. In this function, he was responsible for the organization of millions of forced laborers. At the Nuremberg Trials in 1946, he was sentenced to hang.

drones, and, at best, addicted writers who get their morphine from SS officers. Meanwhile, the local populations give vent to their desperation in assassination attempts directed more often at the collaborators rather than at the "socialist" occupation forces themselves.

German Listeners, Europe will be socialist as soon as it is free. *Social humanism* was the order of the day, it was the vision of the best at that very moment when fascism raised its ugly, leering scowl over the world. Social humanism, which is truly new, youthful, and revolutionary, will give Europe its external and internal form, as soon as the head of the serpent of lies has been crushed underfoot.

May 1, 1944

German Listeners!
The talk of the imminent "enslavement of the German people" that is employed in Nazi propaganda and in which Germany's false friends on the outside join in lamenting, is quite suited to become the new catchphrase of nationalist vengeance and to assume the role that the "stab in the back" and "shameful peace" played after 1918, lending voice to the fundamentally false notion of the "restoration of German honor" that led Germany into this war and into renewed defeat.[19]

The threat of the degradation of German people to the condition of slavery is a lie. The enslavement of any people cannot be the goal of the coalition of nations that the brain-damaged Nazi regime somehow succeeded in forging into a united foe. The war objective of the Allied Forces is to secure peace, it is a global system of collective security, which includes a free and democratic Europe. And, in this Europe, in turn, a free and democratic Germany should one day assume its dutiful and esteemed place.

I say "one day," and it is clear to me, as it must be clear to you, that the day cannot be tomorrow and not the day after tomorrow. Herr Goebbels, not blind to what lies ahead, declares today: "Humanity is unthinkable without Germany!"[20] It is indeed thinkable, and thinkable with pleasure, without *him*; and the worst of it is that Germany believed that *it* was thinkable without humanity, without recognition of human rights; that it wanted to enslave humanity and did in fact enslave Europe. Everything depends on its ceasing to think in the unholy categories of dominion and enslavement, and on not seeing its own enslavement in the liberation of Europe, in the restoration of dignity and national well-being

---

19 On the "stab-in-the-back" myth, see the annotations for the address of December 1943. The Treaty of Versailles, signed on June 28, 1919, was generally perceived as a "shameful peace" in Germany, including by Mann, as contemporary testimonies indicate.

20 The source for this quote has not been identified.

of the peoples it has subjugated, and in Germany's duty-bound cooperation in this restoration.

The Nazis have spoken a great deal to you Germans about "Europe," and claim still today to defend European culture along with European soil—they, the slave drivers and hangmen of the peoples of Europe. But after the war, Europe, its persecuted peoples, the rebuilding of the continent, and its protection against renewed attack will be the main concerns, not primarily Germany, its freedom and restoration. If a Germany that has come to its senses emerges from this war, a Germany that recognizes and deeply regrets the savage misdeeds against the property and blood of other peoples that it has been compelled to commit by its wicked rulers, then it will realize that the restoration of Europe takes priority over the welfare of Germany, and, above all, it will, on its own incentive, out of its own sense of justice, want to contribute to making amends for these misdeeds, to the extent that they can be redressed at all, even if this delays Germany's own recovery. This is not "enslavement," but rather liberation from the clutches of a disastrous delusion of superiority that the Germans have been talked into by false teachers. It is the clear-eyed return to sobriety from a ruinous intoxication of privilege and the right to do wrong. German culture is neither the highest nor the only form of culture, but instead one among many, and admiration has always been its deepest impulse; it is at present dying of vainglory. Germany is not the axis around which everything else revolves; it is only a small part of this vast Earth, and there are bigger questions on the agenda than the quandaries of the German spirit. The German is not a devil, as some claim, but also no archangel, blond-locked, in a silver suit of Aryan armor, but rather a human being like everyone else;[21] and must once again learn how to live as a human being and a brother to their fellow human beings. This and nothing more is what is meant by the word that we Germans have foolishly treated with contempt for too long, the word "democracy."[22]

May 29, 1944

German Listeners!
At the beginning of the war, when the British were bombing Germany with 'leaflets,' little propaganda brochures, the story was told of a British pilot who returned from a sortie to report that circumstances had left him no time to untie the string it was bound with and distribute his 'leaflets'

---

21 The wording is reminiscent of a striking passage in Act 3 of Wagner's opera *Parsifal*, in which Gurnemanz reports the death of Titurel: "he died—a human being, like any other" ("er starb—ein Mensch, wie alle").

22 Mann here counts himself among those Germans who "foolishly despised the word 'democracy' [...] for too long." The most important evidence for his former positions can be found in his *Betrachtungen eines Unpolitischen* (Reflections of a Nonpolitical Man, 1918).

individually; he had to quickly drop the entire packet at once. "For heaven's sake!," his superior is said to have replied. "Did it not occur to you that you could have injured somebody?" — This anecdote has elicited plenty of laughter. It may have been invented, but it is characteristic of the state of mind with which the civilized peoples—after six years of appeasement, six years of backing down, of yielding to attempts to pacify Hitler—entered into this war. Reluctantly, as unprepared psychologically as they were materially, still without any real inkling what this was actually all about: the German war, total war; they entered into it nonetheless. And then they learned. Slowly, at the same pace with which they upgraded their physical armaments, Great Britain and America prepared themselves psychologically for war—not because they, in accordance with Nazi-German philosophy, considered war the normal—and simultaneously ideal—condition of humankind, but rather because they recognized after much hesitation and resistance that perfidious violence that disdains the rule of law—with which there can be no coexistence, no peace, no agreement—can really only be confronted with violence, if one does not want it to exert absolute rule over the defiled Earth.

The free peoples know and feel deeply that stooping to the means of their opponent—this descent into violence—takes its toll on their collective psyche. It is the devilry inherent to evil that leaves those of goodwill only the choice between making themselves guilty by submitting to evil, or making themselves guilty by fighting back against it. Finding accomplices in guilt is what the guilty covet most. The German people are experts on this phenomenon. They know precisely that their scoundrel regime has done everything to make them complicit in its crimes—and that it has succeeded in the most terrible way.

No scoundrel wants to go to hell alone, he always wants to drag as many with him as possible. That others should be guilty with him, that is his pleasure. And it is this pleasure alone that speaks in the editorial that the German propaganda-devil recently produced and in which he denounced as barbaric murder the unavoidable cruelties of the aerial warfare necessary for the liberation of Europe.[23] In thinly veiled words he incites the German population to exact lynch law against the fallen Anglo-American pilots. Will they accept his invitation? I doubt it. The German population basically understands that Germany is only receiving what it has dealt, and it recalls the saying that those who sow wind, will

---

23 The equation of Goebbels with the devil has illuminating significance in the history of Mann's works. The "canny little man" had a deformed right foot from a congenital disorder; a clubfoot is one of the devil's traditional attributes. See Chapter 13 of Mann's 1947 novel *Doktor Faustus*, written shortly before this radio address, which features an eloquent but dubious lecturer at the University of Halle named "Schleppfuß" (literally: Schlepfoot).

reap the storm.[24] It may well be that you Germans never would have thought the Anglo-American peoples morally capable of doing what they are doing now. But this is only a reflection of what Nazi Germany has done to other peoples and still proceeds to do to them. You have no inkling—or at most only a terrible *inkling*—that this is so. In his memo to the Allied and neutral governments in January 1942, the Russian Minister of Foreign Affairs, Molotov,[25] said: "There is no limit to the cruelty and bloodthirstiness of the German fascist army in its invasion of our territory. Hitler's army is not waging a typical war, but rather a gangster war with the goal of exterminating a peaceful people ... The Hitler regime, which treacherously attacked the Soviet Union,[26] respects neither the statutes of the rights of nations nor the demands of human morality. It wages war first and foremost against unarmed populations, against women, children, and the elderly ..."[27]

Even Goebbels now speaks of women and children. He does so in the gentle, intimate *Völkische Beobachter*.[28] Paul Joseph Goebbels also speaks about the rights of nations. Pardon his self-indulgence. He expounds on the law for the entire German army, stating: "There is no article of war that absolves a soldier of guilt who is guilty of reprehensible acts simply because he was ordered by his superior to commit them." This same individual is somehow capable of writing the sentence: "It has always been our wish that war should be waged within the limits of chivalry, but our adversaries appear to be incapable of it."[29] Earth, heaven, and hell all lift their voices in derisive laughter, but the canny little man hears nothing.

He knows what he wants when he incites the German population to individual acts of vengeance against prisoners of war. More murder, that is what he wants, even more culprits, so that he and his ilk will not have

---

24 An allusion to Hosea 8:7, which reads, "For they have sown the wind, and they shall reap the whirlwind: it hath no stalk: the bud shall yield no meal: if so be it yield, the strangers shall swallow it up."

25 Vyacheslav Molotov (1890–1986) was the Soviet Foreign Minister from 1939 to 1949 and again from 1953 to 1956. A Bolshevik from the very beginning, Molotov enjoyed Stalin's trust.

26 Molotov writes "treacherously" because the attack on the Soviet Union on June 22, 1941, annulled the German-Soviet non-aggression pact of August 23, 1939, the Ribbentrop-Molotov Pact.

27 In 1942, Molotov issued a memorandum to "all ambassadors and ministers of countries with which the Soviet Union maintains diplomatic relations." Mann truncates and modifies the English translation of the paper, published by The American Council of Soviet Relations. See Vyacheslav M. Molotov, *The Molotov Paper on Nazi Atrocities* (New York: The American Council on Soviet Relations, 1942).

28 The *Völkische Beobachter* was the official organ of the NSDAP, founded in Munich in 1920; from 1923, it operated as a daily newspaper.

29 The source for this quote has not been identified.

been the only ones. For the ice-cold liar, the German women and children who have perished are as insignificant as the Polish, Czech, Dutch, British ones. His high-pitched wailing is nothing but the expression of satisfaction that others are becoming guilty by resisting evil. Scripture teaches us not to do this.[30] But scripture does not teach us how to escape guilt and infamy when we permit evil to reign without resisting it.

Guilt requires atonement. God willing, the free peoples will atone for the guilt that they, too, had to take upon themselves, by establishing a peace that will protect all against the moral terror of war for many generations.

---

30 The underlying precept not to repay evil with evil is expressed in various places in the Bible, most succinctly in Romans 12:17: "Do not repay anyone evil for evil. Be careful to do what is right in the eyes of everyone."

1945

January 1, 1945

German Listeners!
I spoke to you—or attempted to speak to you—back when Hitler's armies rolled victoriously across Europe and advanced to the Egyptian border, and I characterized his victories as false, deceptive, hopeless. I was silent when the tables turned, when the Nazis lost Rome, Paris, Brussels, the Balkans, when Fortress Europe became Fortress Germany, and the end of the war, the end of Hitler and his ilk seemed near. It is only logical that I am once again recording my short addresses, now, when Hitler or Himmler once again appear to be on a winning streak, the Wehrmacht forces have pulled themselves together for a furious counterattack and thereby once again secured a new timeline,[1] yet another stay of execution for the Nazi Regime. Will you believe me when I assure you that these victories, insofar as one can call them that, are just as empty, meaningless, and hopeless as those earlier ones? There is no Nazi victory. Everything that looks like one is bloody nonsense, is a priori null and void. These people live under the incomprehensible delusion that, since dominion over the Earth has eluded them once and for all, they could wear out the Allies through protracted resistance and force them into a negotiated peace, peace *with them*. A peace between Russia, America, and Great Britain and Hitler and Himmler! A peace, in which the Nazi regime would continue to exist! Do you believe that? Do you Germans, in particular those in the still small part of the country that is occupied, believe that?[2] For you, the hermetic seal separating Germany from the rest of

---

1   On December 16, 1944, *Operation Herbstnebel* (Operation Autumn Mist), intended to halt the Allied advance to the Rhine, began in Luxembourg and Belgium, and continued for three weeks, resulting in a massive loss of life among civilians and US troops. The "Battle of the Bulge," as it became known in English, was the largest and bloodiest US battle fought in the Second World War, also resulting in the second-largest surrender of US troops. Mann and the American public followed this costly winter battle with great interest.

2   This area around Aachen was liberated on October 21, 1944, marking it as the first major city on German soil to be free from National Socialist rule. The material superiority of the Allies proved enormous as they encircled the city, and the capitulation of such a geopolitically significant location was a shock for Hitler's Germany.

the world and its thoughts and feelings has been slightly torn open; some outside air is forcing its way in: you hear the voice of the world and no longer entirely share the bleak ignorantism of your brothers in Hitler's Reich. What do you believe? Or, I should rather ask: What is it that you fear? Can it be that you fear or even for a moment cling to the idea that, at the end of this war nefariously willed into being by Hitler, however near or far off that end may be, the Nazi regime will still be standing? No, nobody in their right mind can think that. The world needs peace, needs it as a matter of life and death, ergo it has *no need* for National Socialism, which has no other meaning or purpose than war. Whatever it may cost in time and sacrifice—the Earth must be liberated from National Socialism, humankind must be delivered from it. The Allied soldiers who now fight to that end do not project the bearing of dark fanaticism that Germany was trained in by its masters, the bloody comedians. Do not allow it to deceive you! Have no fear, or harbor no false hopes, if they appear unfazed to you! They have no need for the scowl of frightful superiority with which Hitler-Germany seeks to condition us all to a state of terror. They cannot stop wanting what must be, and rest assured that despite miscalculations, mistakes, setbacks, and disappointments, they will see it through. In contrast, that pose of ultimate heroism struck for mere appearance by Nazi Germany is nothing more than a mask—the face of terror borne by criminals who have long since been condemned to retributive justice, who have nothing to lose, nothing to hope for from capitulation, who will never surrender, can never win the peace, and therefore tell the people, who bleed for them, who sink further and further into misery and barbarism for them *alone*, that there can be no peace with a world whose declared and inviolable aim is, in fact, peace and the constructive cooperation of nations. Never before have the interests of a nation and its rulers been separated by as broad a gulf as the one that gapes between you Germans and your rulers today. Here, the people whose cause would be peace and reconstruction—there, the power-hungry wretches who are shackled to war, who have no hope beyond war and for that reason strangle with a slow rope anyone who wants to rescue Germany, who wants to return to it the right to the idea of peace and reconstruction after immeasurable devastation. You Germans living in occupied territory today already possess the right to this objective. In the young year 1945, let us continue to pursue it together.

January 14, 1945

German Listeners!
If only this war were over! If only what must happen and what will happen had already happened, however that might look at first! If the cruel people who have brought Germany where it is could only be eliminated, and if we could begin to think about beginning life anew, about clearing

away the ruins—both internal and external—about gradual reconstruction, about a sensible reconciliation with other nations and a dignified coexistence with them! —Is it this that you want? Am I expressing what you long for? I believe so. You have had more than enough of death, destruction, chaos, however fervently your most private impulses may have desired these things at times. You want order and life, a new order of life, as bleak and difficult as it might be for years to come. That demonstrates courage. It is in fact much more courageous than the spellbound fanaticism with which your youth in arms still believes it should defend the "sacred"—alas, the German soil that has long been so utterly desecrated and defiled by lies and criminal acts. But *one thing* is essential for a new beginning. There is *one* precondition for reconciliation with the world, the fulfillment of which is the basis for any moral rapprochement with other nations, and without the fulfillment of which you Germans will never understand what is happening to you. This precondition is the clear recognition of the inexpiable nature of what a Germany schooled in bestiality by nefarious taskmasters has inflicted on humankind; it is the complete and uncompromising recognition of abominable crimes, of which you actually still today know only the least, in part because they sealed you off, forcibly drove you into a state of ignorance and apathy, in part because you kept any knowledge of this horror far from your consciences out of an instinct for self-preservation. But this horror must penetrate your conscience if you wish to understand and live on, and a massive labor of investigation, which you must not dismiss as propaganda, will be necessary if you are to come to know what happened. What a shameful philosophy of the filthiest arrogance made it possible for your rulers to do—what they have done by your sons' hands, by your hands— is difficult to believe, but it is true. Do you, who are listening to me now, know of Majdanek near Lublin in Poland, Hitler's extermination camp?[3] It was not a concentration camp, but a gigantic murder facility. There is a large stone building with a factory chimney, the largest crematorium in the world. When the Russians came, your people wanted to destroy it in a hurry, but, for the most part, it still *stands*, a monument, *the* monument of the Third Reich. More than half a million European people—men, women, and children—were poisoned with chlorine in gas chambers

---

3   On Himmler's orders, construction on the Lublin/Majdanek concentration camp began in October 1941; the work was completed by Russian prisoners of war and forced laborers of various origins. The mass murder of Jews, Roma, Poles, and Russians in its seven gas chambers began in October 1942. The November 3, 1943 massacre at Majdanek was part of the largest Nazi massacre of the Holocaust. On July 22, 1944, the Red Army advanced as far as Lublin, so that the German operators abandoned the camp in a hurry, leaving the murder facilities and some documentation still intact. The Russian liberation of Majdanek on July 22–24, 1944 was the first liberation of a Nazi concentration camp.

there and then burned, 1,400 daily. Day and night the factory of death was in operation, its ovens constantly fuming. Work on an expansion had already begun ... Swiss Refugee Aid knows more.[4] Their agents saw the camps at Auschwitz and Birkenau.[5] They saw what no feeling person who has not seen it with their own eyes is prepared to believe: the human bones, barrels of lime, chlorine gas lines, and the incinerator, on top of that the piles of clothes and shoes that they took from the victims, many small shoes, shoes of children, if you, German countryman, you, German woman, care to know. From April 15, 1942 until April 15, 1944, in these two German institutions alone, 1,715,000 Jews were murdered. The source for this figure? Why, your compatriots kept records, with a German sense of order! The registry of deaths was discovered; on top of that, hundreds of thousands of passports and personal identity documents from no fewer than twenty-two European nationalities. These imbeciles also kept records of the bone meal, the fertilizer that this plant produced. For the remains of the incinerated persons were ground up and pulverized, packaged and sent to Germany to fertilize the German soil—the sacred soil that after all this the German armies still believe they had to defend, or might even be justified in defending, against desecration at the hands of the enemy.

I have given only a few examples of what you are about to learn for yourselves. The hostage shootings, the murder of prisoners, the Gestapo torture chambers found in occupied Europe, the bloodbaths among the Russian civilian population, the diabolical Nazi policy of depopulation in all countries so that the Master Race would always be numerically superior, the premeditated, deliberate child mortality induced in France, Belgium, Holland, Greece, and especially in Poland: it is not even possible to enumerate in only a few minutes everything that Nazi Germany has done to people, to humanity. Germans, you should know about this. Horror, shame, and remorse are the first necessities. And hatred of only *one* entity is necessary: that of the villains who have made the German name an abomination before God and the entire world.

---

4   The Swiss Central Office for Refugee Aid (*Office central d'aide aux réfugiés*), now Swiss Refugee Council, was founded in 1936 to support victims of the Nazi regime exiled to Switzerland.

5   The camp in Auschwitz, near Krakow, was built in May 1940, and was expanded and developed on a large scale; including the extension Birkenau, known as "Auschwitz II." Auschwitz was a concentration and forced labor camp, as well as an extermination camp with gas chambers, a crematorium, and execution sites. The SS camp administration began to evacuate the camp on January 18, 1945 after attempting to destroy the murder facilities; around 60,000 survivors, the majority of them Jews, were sent on so-called death marches to various camps on Reich territory. The Red Army liberated Auschwitz on January 27, 1945.

January 16, 1945

German Listeners!

Twelve years of Hitler. The 30th of January 1933.[6] Well alright, even that is a day of remembrance. It should be commemorated: certainly not with joy and not with pride, much less with a sense of defiance that has been sustained artificially, and likewise not with gallant despair or with self-contempt. Rather, it should be commemorated with self-possessed understanding of the terrible mistake that was part complicity, part fate, on top of that with hope, with certainty, that it will now soon be over, that the days of this most horrible and shameful episode of German history are numbered, that it will be like waking from a terrible nightmare that one wishes had been nothing more than a dream.

Unfortunately, it was a reality. Europe lies in ruins and with it, Germany. The devastation that National Socialism has brought about, both physical and moral, is unprecedented. The blood and treasure lost to its rapacity and murderousness, its fiendish politics of depopulation, is immeasurable; perhaps even more gruesome than that, the psychological havoc that it has wreaked with its terror, the desecration and depravity, the defilement and corruption of the human being caused by the compulsion to dishonesty and duplicity, the coercion of conscience. After committing a thousand iniquities in Germany itself, it unleashed the war that inhered in National Socialism itself, with which it was synonymous from day one. Is this the guilt of the German people who saw their savior in a bloody monster? We do not want to speak of guilt. It is no sufficient name for the fatal chain of consequences in a tale of misfortune, and *if* it is guilt, then it is intertwined with a great deal of guilt on the world's part. But responsibility is something different from guilt. We are all responsible for what became of the German essence and what Germany as a whole has perpetrated historically.[7] It is too much to expect of other nations that they distinguish neatly between Nazism and the German people. If it exists: Germany, if that people exists as a historical gestalt, as a collective personality with a character and a fate, then National Socialism is nothing more than the form that a people, the German people, gave to itself twelve years ago in order to undertake the most reckless attempt at world subjugation and enslavement known to history,[8] undertaken by employing the most comprehensive, horrible and insidious means—an attempt that

---

6   Mann regarded the day on which Hitler became Reich Chancellor, not merely Germany's defeat in the First World War, to be the beginning of the German catastrophe.

7   In other words, the representatives of the "other Germany," too, are responsible, Mann himself included.

8   Historians have not reached a consensus about whether Hitler strove for world domination. Mann was certain of it. A little-known keynote address

came within a hair's breadth of succeeding. This is how the world must see things, even if broad masses of the peace-loving German people cannot perceive it that way. Germany's opponents, who are all suffering severely—even the vast and prosperous country from which I speak sacrifices and suffers severely—these opponents have been confronted since the first day of the war with the entirety of German intelligence, ingenuity, bravery, love of obedience, military prowess, in short, by the entire power of the German people, which as such stands behind the regime and fights its battles—not by Hitler and Himmler, who would be absolutely nothing if German manpower and blind vassal loyalty were not still today fighting and dying for these scoundrels with the ill-fated courage of lions.[9]

Not for them, you say, but for Germany's sacred soil? Friends, German soil has long since been so desecrated and defiled by a government that Germany ought never to have allowed to be imposed upon it—by lies, injustice, crime—that by now its defense has become meaningless, has become stubborn defiance and not praiseworthy valor. Any valor that persists in defending what has been proven evil is in truth fear of the end and the new beginning, a cowardice that is particularly unbecoming for this people of "Die and Become."[10] A young poet in Germany had the courage, in the midst of war, under the Nazis, to write this verse:

Our common word, so long inured to lying,
Is never more fit for sacred song.[11]

As with the German word, so it is with the desecrated German sword. It has long been unfit for the defense of a Germany that is ever sacred to us. Throw it away and have done with it, so that a new beginning, a new life becomes possible!

---

by Hitler to the National Socialist German Student League at the University of Erlangen of November 13, 1930 supports that position.

9 By decree of the Führer on September 25, 1944, the male civilian population was called to arms to avert the threat of military defeat; the target of a 6 million strong national army was not even close to being met. Likewise in the fall of 1944, Himmler launched "Operation Werewolf," dedicated to infiltrating enemy lines to carry out targeted attacks. The first mayor of liberated Aachen to be sworn in by the Americans, Franz Oppenhoff (1902–1945), was one of the most prominent victims of a Werewolf operation.

10 "Die and Become" ("Stirb und werde") is a line from Goethe's 1817 poem "Selige Sehnsucht" (Blissful Longing) from his collection *West-östlicher Divan* (West-Eastern Divan).

11 Josef Leitgeb (1897–1952) was an Austrian poet, member of the Brenner circle around Ludwig von Ficker (1880–1967), and translator of *The Little Prince* (1950) by Antoine de Saint-Exupéry (1900–1944). The verses quoted by Mann are from the sonnet cycle *Herbst* (Autumn, 1937) and read in the original: "Ach, unser Wort, so lang' gewohnt zu lügen, / Es taugt nicht mehr zum heiligen Gesang!"

January, 31 1945

German Listeners!

The wretched specimen that still calls itself Germany's Führer, that is still allowed to threaten with an ignominious death anyone who opposes the insane continuation of this war lost time and again—Hitler, that is—celebrated the twelfth birthday of his dominion, the blackest day on the calendar in German history, with a radio address that you inhabitants of an occupied territory will not likely have listened to.[12] What do you care what heights he might reach with his familiar trashy rhetoric, heroically glorifying the fast-fading run of his disastrous existence and positioning himself as "God's champion," as the chosen "defender of Germany against a world full of treacherous haters,"[13] as the "standard-bearer of Europe against the Eastern hordes with no thought in their minds but destruction"![14] Once again, he seeks to anesthetize himself and the German people, with the same feeble-minded and of course infinitely insolent drivel.

"He" invokes the name of Germany, of the country that he blighted, robbed of its spirit and intellect, ruined from the ground up and in every sense; that country he brought to the lowest point in its history and made an abomination before God and the world. "Europe," he says—and he means the whole globe that he has trampled underfoot, tormented, defiled, emasculated, massacred, from which he extorted twenty-six-and-a-half billion dollars in so-called occupation costs and uncompensated goods, and whose "protector against Eastern and Western soullessness" he now claims to be.

Can any German still listen to this person's rancid ramblings about the "plutocratic-Bolshevist-Jewish world conspiracy" against him, the defender of the greatest virtues of the Occident without the uttermost

---

12 Hitler's address to the German people of January 30, 1945, held at the Reich Chancellery, was his last. In it, the dictator defends the war as the German nation's struggle for survival against the hordes of the East and stylizes himself as one chosen by providence: "The Almighty has created our Volk. By defending its existence, we defend His creation." Referring to the assassination attempt of July 20, 1944, Hitler explains: "That the Almighty protected me on that day is something I regard as a confirmation of the mission I was assigned." See Domarus IV, 3004–3008.

13 Mann, a Wagner connoisseur, is alluding to Hitler's well-known obsession with Wagner and self-stylization as a Wagnerian hero-type such as Lohengrin defending humanity against a scapegoated group like the Nibelungen in Wagner's *Ring des Nibelungen* (Ring of the Nibelung).

14 In Wagner's *Lohengrin*, the "enemies of the Reich" (*Reiches Feinde*) also come from the East. The threat from the East was an integral component of the Nazi worldview.

revulsion?[15] He has lied to the German people and poisoned their minds with every word he has ever barked and howled into their ears.

Now he wants to rescue himself from the inevitable doom he was born to, rescue himself and his crime-ridden regime. And again he lies to his people who have already given their all for a corrupt cause. So that they hold out longer and ever longer, bleed and sacrifice themselves in a hopeless battle, he swears to them that nothing that they have suffered until now could even come close to comparing with the horrific agony to be expected as a consequence of having admitted defeat. He acts as though Germany will suffer the same fate as those countries into which the Gestapo followed his troops.[16] He acts as though Germany's opponents were the Nazis and as though they will behave like Nazis in their treatment of those they have defeated.

Germany's opponents and vanquishers are, however, not SS-butchers and beasts, but rather human beings—you inhabitants of the occupied territories in the West already know this. Precisely because they are human beings who, in fundamental distinction from National Socialism, still feel bound to some honor code of justice and ethics, they were for a time at a disadvantage against an enemy that knew nothing of such inhibitions. General Eisenhower said to you,[17] the people of Aachen and the surrounding areas: "We come as victors, but not as oppressors." You know that this is true. You have more experiences that contradict the fear-mongering speeches filled with lies about the destruction of Germany, about the annihilation of the German people than do your brothers in the Nazi Reich.

More miserable than it is right now Germany can never be. There is no deeper misery than Nazi rule. There is no condition, no life conceivable that would be more terrible than the dehumanizing horror of a war that one continues in misguided defiance of its already-sealed fate.

Anything will be better than this. A difficult, desperate existence awaits Germany—how could it be any different?—a life that, for quite some time, will need to be dedicated not first and foremost to Germany's

15   Nazi propaganda characterizes both Bolshevism and the Western democracies as equally dangerous manifestations of the Jewish world conspiracy, so that the Soviet Union and the Western Allies can be portrayed as making common cause.

16   In his address, Hitler appealed "to the entire German Volk [...] to arm themselves with an even greater, hardened spirit of resistance [...]. I expect every German therefore to fulfill his duty to the utmost, and to take on every sacrifice that will be and must be demanded of him." See Domarus IV, 3008.

17   Dwight D. Eisenhower (1890–1969) was the Supreme Commander of the Allied forces that landed in Normandy on June 6, 1944 and brought the war in Europe to a victorious conclusion on May 8, 1945. Eisenhower later became the 34th President of the United States (1953–1961).

own national well-being, but rather to the attempt at making amends for the outrageous atrocities that Hitler's Germany inflicted upon other nations. A terrible hatred has proliferated everywhere and must be eroded away gradually, ameliorated gradually. But peace, the protection of the law, a slowly reawakening pleasure in life, freedom from the burden of the arrogant delusion that you are a chosen people that must subjugate the world, reconciliation and collaboration with the nations of the collective cultural milieu—won't that be better than the present hell? Is that not what you Germans long for in the deepest part of your souls?

February 16, 1945

German Listeners!
The declaration of the three statesmen who met in Yalta conveyed nothing the least bit surprising.[18] It announced so little in the way of new measures against the defeated Hitler-Germany, so little that the German public will not already long have been prepared for, that Nazi propaganda had to lay its lies on thick in order to make this announcement out to be a song of hatred, a Jewish murder plot, or however the hysterical rhetoric may read.

The disarmament of the country and the dissolution of the General Staff, along with the occupation by the troops of the victorious powers for a considerable time; the discontinuation or surveillance of the sector of German industry that could serve in the production of munitions; atonement and provisional reparations for the most reprehensible Nazi crimes committed in this war; the complete obliteration of the National Socialist Party along with all of its laws and institutions, its entire influence on public life—those are the obvious measures that one was given to expect. And they find elaboration and clarification in the following words: "It is not our purpose to destroy the people of Germany. But only when Nazism and militarism have been extirpated will there be hope for a decent life for Germans, and a place for them in the comity of Nations."[19]

With good reason Goebbels's propaganda has withheld this conditionally conciliatory and forward-looking passage from you Germans. It pretends that with one manifesto, which contains only what is clearly necessary, reasonable, and inevitable, the enemy has "dropped its mask"—one

---

18 The second conference of the victorious powers (after Tehran and followed by Potsdam) took place in Yalta in Crimea from February 4–11, 1945. Stalin, Roosevelt, and Churchill (De Gaulle was absent) reached further agreements about ensuring peace after the war. The negotiations revolved around three main topics: arrangements for dealing with Germany after its defeat, the entry of the Soviet Union into the war against Japan, and the foundation of the United Nations with the participation of the Soviet Union.

19 Franklin D. Roosevelt, Joint Statement with Churchill and Stalin on the Yalta Conference on February 11, 1945.

wonders, what mask?—and that behind it, the "diabolical scowl of the Jew" is exposed—as if the presence of the Jew were required to arrive at the conviction that the eradication of Nazism, is a necessity if life on Earth is to once again become tolerable. It is clear enough: whatever the communiqué from Yalta might have proclaimed, if it included the destruction of Nazi dominion over Germany, then it was the "shameless revelation of a hellish murder plot" and an "attack on humankind and humanity." This is how it is being presented to you Germans, so that you will do the utmost, more than the utmost, for a regime that led you into this ruination, in the belief that you are doing it for yourselves.

Never have these scoundrels thought of you, of Germany, but only ever of themselves, of the power in which they wallowed and which they, unrestrained by any fear of God, exercised for twelve years in their defilement of human life. Never has a people had rulers who were crueler, who insisted more mercilessly that the country and the people perish with them. Should they cease to be, then supposedly there will no longer be any Germany at all. They are the ones who are destroying Germany. They, alone.

Had the German people been capable—even if belatedly, perhaps after the invasion of France[20]—of breaking free from the trap into which they fell in 1933, of freeing themselves from their rulers' desperate gamble and making peace—the Reich would likely have retained roughly the same borders as in 1918, just as France remained intact after Napoleon's downfall. He was a tyrant and a parvenu, to be sure. But he had an interest in his country, in its future and continued existence. When he was defeated, defeated forever, he vacated the throne, abdicated, submitted to arrest, and therewith bequeathed the diplomat, the despised Talleyrand, with the opportunity in Vienna to obtain anything for France that he could.[21]

Not so with our "heroes." By forcing the misfortunate people to continue the war that they nefariously began beyond its irretrievable loss to the point of insanity, to the point of utmost ruin, they will cause Germany, exhausted and shattered, to fall to pieces that will perhaps never again find their way back together. Never have there been more wicked traitors to their country than these nationalists. A curse will shriek after them unlike any that has ever beset those who lead astray the minds and unscrupulously abuse the powers of a great people.

---

20 Mann is referring to the Allied Invasion of Normandy on June 6, 1944, also known as D-Day. By the end of August 1944, the Allies had liberated all of Northern France and set the stage for the invasion of Germany.

21 Charles Maurice de Talleyrand-Périgord (1754–1838) was the French chief negotiator at the Congress of Vienna in 1814/15, which regulated the balance of power in post-Napoleonic Europe.

March 4, 1945

German Listeners!
Even by mortal standards, historical epochs are quite short, at least in Europe, things have never remained the same for broad stretches of time, as in ancient Egypt or China. The entire French monarchy lasted, crudely estimated, five hundred years, an uncommonly long period, the likes of which has never occurred in Germany. There, a hundred years is already a long time for one historical epoch.

Who would have thought that the German Empire of 1871 would only be granted a lifespan of forty-seven years? If we were to add the interlude of the Weimar Republic, during which the former Prussian-German Empire continued to exist, we arrive at sixty-two years, and that is all. But even if you decide to take a broader perspective and date the era of German history—which now, thanks to Hitler, is coming to its catastrophic conclusion—back to Friedrich II of Prussia and his wars of conquest,[22] we arrive at approximately two hundred years and not more, for what is a very generous historical overview.

That's why it was especially absurd that the custodians of National Socialism driveled on about the thousand, what am I saying, the thirty thousand years that their Reich was supposed to last, when it was all too apparent that it would be too long for Germany, if they remained for even ten years. They were permitted to wreak their havoc for twelve years. And the result is so appalling that one cannot comprehend why ever greater contingents of the German People's Army still stand up for these bankrupts and risk their hides for them with a fighting spirit as tenacious as it is hopeless.

When one hears in response: "The German soldier is not fighting for them, but for Germany, which is threatened with destruction," one can only reply: That is sheer nonsense! For Germany is not synonymous with the dark and sinister chapter that bears Hitler's name. It also is not synonymous even with the Bismarck era of the Prussian-German Empire. It is not even synonymous with the period of German history that spanned two centuries, which can be dubbed the era of Friedrich II.

Germany is not dying. It is in the process of taking on a new form and transitioning into a new state, and it is afraid of this change, and is still resisting it. There is a historical instinct to persevere that appears to be heroism, but is in fact only fear of the new, of a new situation that is still in the process of formation and transition, but which promises more happiness and genuine dignity, perhaps more in concert with the nation's

---

22 The three Silesian Wars fought against Austria (1740–1742; 1744–1745; 1756–1763), themselves theaters of the wider War of the Austrian Succession and the Seven Years' War, allowed Prussia to become a major European power.

innermost predispositions and needs than the erstwhile, the old state, from which it is so reluctantly breaking away.

No historical entity lasts forever. I am not even talking about National Socialism at this point. But why should the old Prussian-German centralist and the pseudo-democratic empire of Bismarck have been the final word in German history? Was this so exceptionally German? Did things look particularly happy and life so worth living in this form? Was it sufficient to bring about sheer joy for the world and for itself? All of this can be disputed. And what should be stressed is that the demise of the martial empire clustered around Prussia did not mean the end of Germany, the death of the German people.

The occupation of the country by the troops of the victors is imminent. The imperial government will cease to exist. But as far as we know, there are no plans to actually dissolve the empire against the will of the German people themselves. Germany's reconstruction is beginning anew. From the smallest subdivisions of self-government that are working together with the occupation powers for the time being, larger ones and ultimately a new system of states may be established. Germany as a federation of nine or ten states of roughly equal size, with the newly rebuilt cities Hamburg, Bremen, Berlin, Cologne, Frankfurt, Weimar, Dresden, Breslau, among others, as centers—is that so unthinkable? Would it be so unbefitting for a people whose innermost inclination has always been oriented toward the diversity and freedom of its members?

The hardship is grievous. But to respond by shouting: "It is all over for Germany!," shows a fatuous lack of faith. Germany can live on and be happy without the General Staff and the arms industry. It can even live more justly and more honorably without them. It can also live on and be happy without the parts of its territory in the East and the West that it lost in the catastrophe of the war.[23] Even without them, it remains a vast, glorious country, capable of any cultural achievement, one that can count on the competence of its people as well as on the support of the world, and one for which, once the worst is behind it, a new life, rich in achievements and esteem, may be in store.

March 20, 1945

German Listeners!
One could argue that Germany is being held to an unfair standard, if one refuses to marvel at its present desperate struggle, its refusal to accept defeat, its resistance down to the last man, the last bullet, the last drop

---

23   At the Yalta Conference of February 4–11, 1945, Roosevelt, Churchill, and Stalin agreed on the cession of the former German territories east of the Oder and Neisse rivers, including East Prussia, Silesia, and Pomerania, which were annexed to Poland and the Soviet Union after the war.

of blood, and if one refuses to recognize the heroism that is thereby demonstrated. History has always celebrated as noteworthy and heroic such resistance to the very last, and now all of the sudden, in the case of Germany, it is supposed to count for nothing, or as a criminal act.

This argumentation is false. The continuation of the war by Germany beyond defeat to the point of annihilation has nothing to do with heroism, but is, in fact, a crime—committed against the German people by its Führers. The people's suicidal struggle is not voluntary, but is being extorted from them through moral and physical terror—by rulers who cultivate the illusion that the people are bleeding to death for their own honor and self-preservation, while in reality they are giving their last, more than their last, for the survival of the scoundrels who drove them into this war, and who will not abdicate at any cost, not even the cost of the total ruin of Germany. On the contrary: they chain Germany's complete ruin—which is in no way in the interests of Europe or the world— to their own downfall and in doing so seek to force the victors to make peace with them—a peace that, self-evidently, would only be a reprieve for them of ten or even twenty years before the renewal of war.

No one has ever called it heroic when a band of robbers and murderers, surrounded by the police, fires in every direction down to the last bullet in order to sell their condemned hides at as high a price as possible. "Never surrender!" is their slogan, too, but there is nothing admirable about surrender when surrendering means the gallows. Such gangsters, however, at least get their own hands dirty and are respectable in comparison—compared, namely, with the Nazi wretches who, to save themselves, are sending an entire country to the chopping block, allowing the German cities to fall to ruin and deliver the people completely intentionally into a condition that, in the end, will be worse than after the Thirty Years' War—all in the despicable hope that the enemies would shy away from letting a territory of squalor, misery, and desperation develop, a seat of disease in every sense, right in the middle of Europe, and would prefer instead to make peace with them, the Nazis.

This is the extortionate dilemma that these degenerates present to the Allied powers. In particular it is the Western, the Anglo-American nations that they thereby seek to shock and to bait, for they christen as "Bolshevism" the desperate condition into which the Allies threaten to plunge Germany, and thereby seek to transform the two-front war that they have already lost, for which Germany has the Allies to thank, into a war against Russia only. On the Rhine, they make it known that they will lay down their weapons if their opponents negotiate with them, and will concentrate all of their remaining fighting power on the Eastern Front in order to protect the Europe they hold so dear from "Bolshevism." In short, they hope to be able to talk the democratic powers into betraying their socialist allies—and any grasp of the infamy of such a betrayal eludes them, it appears entirely natural to them.

Now their radio stations are waving before you armistice in the West, now their Ribbentrop is at work in Sweden,[24] their mass-murderer Himmler at the Vatican.[25] Now they are even deploying their wives, because *L'Humanité* in Paris wants to know that Mrs. Arch Marshall Göring and Mrs. Minister Ribbentrop have paid their respects in Switzerland, and that the former has visited the wife of the British Envoy in Bern.[26] They have never grasped, and still today do not grasp, that there can be no negotiation and no peace with them, with these hundredfold treaty-violating scoundrels and hangmen of Christianity, that they are considered outrageous the world over, and have nothing left but to disappear. If they wish to lay waste to Germany,[27] that is their and Germany's business; then the Allies have no choice but to put an end to them both. They will not allow themselves to be sweet-talked by Madame Göring nor by Madame Ribbentrop, and if Hitler should possess the audacity to marry, they will not conclude peace with Mrs. Führer either.[28] The idea of peace belongs to a world that is beyond the grasp of Nazi brains.

24 In the final stages of the war, Foreign Minister Ribbentrop reached out several times to gauge interest in peace talks, including to neutral Sweden, as can be seen in a telegram dated March 3, 1945, from the American ambassador in Stockholm Herschel Johnson (1894–1966) to the US State Department. According to this memo, Ribbentrop sent a confidant, Privy Councillor Fritz Hesse (1898–1980), "to convey following peace proposals to the Allies, a) to have its 1939 frontiers, and b) Britains and Americans to join Germany against Russia."

25 The Vatican was neutral during the Second World War, but maintained good relations with Nazi Germany, so that, like Sweden, the "Holy See" was a suitable mediator. However, Himmler's communications about peace ran through the Swedish diplomat Count Folke Bernadotte (1895–1948), who, as a representative of the Red Cross, negotiated the release of Danish Jews and Jews of other nationalities from the Theresienstadt concentration camp. Himmler used this contact in the last weeks of April to propose to Churchill and Truman that Germany would surrender to the Western powers and join them in continuing the war against the Soviet Union.

26 *L'Humanite* (1904–present) was a daily newspaper headquartered in Paris. Originally founded as a socialist paper, it was banned from 1939–1945.

27 The purpose of Hitler's "Nero Decree" of March 19, 1945 was to "leave only scorched earth" and to destroy the infrastructure of the abandoned territories, in order to prevent the victorious powers from using them. Named after Emperor Nero (37–68 CE), who is said to have given the order to burn down the city of Rome.

28 Mann is referring to photographer and Hitler's secret lover Eva Braun (1912–1945), whom Hitler married the day before they committed suicide together.

April 5, 1945

German Listeners!
How was it possible that National Socialism could call itself "the German freedom movement,"[29] when, to all human understanding, such an abomination could not possibly have anything to do with freedom? It was made possible by a distortion of the concept of freedom to which German thought has always tended and which, like everything else that is false and sinister about that thought, was driven to the extreme by the Nazis.

Freedom, understood politically, is foremost a moral and domestic-political concept. A people that is not internally free and does not hold itself responsible does not deserve external freedom; it cannot have a say in freedom, and if it employs this resounding term, it employs it falsely. The German concept of freedom was always only directed outwards; it meant the right to be German, only German, and nothing else, nothing beyond that; it was a concept of protest, one of self-centered defense against everything that sought to condition and restrict ethnic egotism, tame it and coerce it into the service of the community, of humankind. A stubborn individualism toward the external, in relation to the world, to Europe, to civilization; to a disconcerting degree, it was internally compatible with a lack of freedom, a state of legal immaturity, torpid subservience. It was a militant serf mentality, and National Socialism, if anything, even stretched this disproportion between external and internal desire for freedom into a barbaric exercise of freedom.

Harnessed in the iron armor of the state, which stifled freedom and justice, Nazi Germany made the frantic attempt to subjugate the world and make it the object of its exploitation. It trampled upon the natural rights of the nations of Europe, plundered them, reduced them to slaves, robbed them of their institutions of learning, sought to take away the memory of their history, their national cultures. Then it was driven back, defeated, overwhelmed. The country that allowed itself to be seduced to crimes unprecedented in the annals of humankind is being captured and occupied by foreign troops that, of course, do not behave at all the

---

29 National Socialism's claim to be a freedom movement has a history of which Mann was well aware. When the NSDAP was banned in 1924 in response to the attempted coup of November 9, 1923, those who were not charged regrouped under the leadership of Erich Ludendorff and Albrecht von Graefe (1868–1933) with a new name, "Nationalsozialistische Freiheitsbewegung" (National Socialist Freedom Movement). The NSFB won thirty-two seats in the Reichstag elections in May 1924. The following year, the NSFB was absorbed into the NSDAP, which had since been readmitted. By adopting this name, the NSFB, and thus the NSDAP, coopted the mantle of the anti-Napoleonic freedom movement of 1806 to 1813.

way Hitler's armies behaved in other countries, but nonetheless naturally demand obedience from the local population.

And no sooner had Germany's devastating attack on the freedom of the peoples collapsed in failure, no sooner was Germany itself liberated from the agents of its ruin, than Nazi propaganda claimed for itself the very word that they had ridiculed and spit on for twelve years, the word "freedom." Shamelessly German propaganda begins to harp on this term, which is an idea of humanity, and which it used and butchered as it did the terms "Europa," "Socialism," "revolution," and so many others. German propaganda is taking a gamble on the imperfect and immature German pathos of freedom that is directed only outwards, the militant serf mentality. In the name of freedom, it directs the people to do what the raped peoples of Europe rightly did: to resist, to wage underground warfare, to avenge their violated freedom through acts of terror. The rabble-rousers are well aware that such behavior is utterly futile in the case of Germany, lacking any spark of reason and justice, but they hope that the people will not notice. The people should run amok for them, they should behave fanatically, and defend their freedom—that is, the misdeeds that they committed in the countries all around them under the leadership of scoundrels—like voracious wolves. The German, the Nazi, freedom movement is to be known as "the Werewolf"[30]—the name itself a practiced gamble of grifter-psychology on the instincts of the national psyche, which they have always insolently and coldly exploited: the inclination toward the primal, the pre-rational and pre-Christian, the obscurity of legend and fairy tale. Already, the propaganda boasts of isolated senseless and futile acts of bloodshed that the free German Werewolf has allegedly committed.

I do not believe that they will be able to run amok for very long, do not believe that the German people, who have been punished harshly enough and cruelly disillusioned, will have much interest in the romantic murder kitsch expected of them still today. They know that nobody would have infringed on their freedom if they had only spared the freedom of others. They know that nobody will think of infringing on their freedom once they have become a free people.

April 19, 1945

German Listeners!
A great man has died, an artist of state and a hero, a friend to the people and a leader of the people, who lifted his nation to a new level of its social development,[31] and guided it to the maturity necessary to dedicate its power to the service of the community of peoples, to the collaborative

---

30 Mann is referring to "Operation Werewolf." See annotation for the address of January 16, 1945.

31 This is an allusion to Roosevelt's "New Deal," introduced immediately upon his inauguration and continued in his second administration. These included

promotion of peace, to which his life and his struggle were dedicated: Franklin Delano Roosevelt.

Clever as the snakes and as unimpeachable as the doves,[32] fine and strong, sophisticated and yet simple like genius itself, illuminated by intuitive knowledge of the necessities of time, and the will of the world spirit[33]—including the knowledge that they are the happiest, who serve that will most courageously and most obediently, most tenaciously and gracefully. Precisely the man of that "faith," which Goethe says "forever elevates itself, sometimes pressing boldly forward, now patient and nestling, so that goodness might work, grow, serve ...,"[34]—this is how I saw him, how I knew him, how I admired him, how I loved him, and I was proud to become a *civis Romanus*,[35] an American citizen,[36] under the aegis of this Caesar.[37]

In the figure of the fascist dictator, the world had seen the man of will and of action, the modern master of the masses, whose entire cunning and energy were dedicated to the service of evil. But here was the born and self-aware counteragent of that abysmally evil and abysmally stupid and obliviously mindless diabolism that Europe gave rise to. The fact that, in response, democracy *also* proved itself capable of producing the doer— the man of action, of strength, tenacity, and wisdom, the caretaker of humankind, the great *political advocate of the good*—that was its salvation, the salvation of the human being and their freedom.

---

state pensions, job creation through state-subsidized public work projects, and stricter regulation of banking.

32 According to Matthew 10:16: "I am sending you out like sheep among wolves. Therefore be as shrewd as snakes and as innocent as doves" (New International Version). The latter characterization is difficult to reconcile with Roosevelt's political practices and owes much to Mann's admiration of the president.

33 "Weltgeist" refers to Hegel's philosophical concept of a collective spirit or consciousness that shapes historical development. See the annotation for "World Spirit" in the address for August 29, 1943.

34 The quote is from Johann Wolfgang von Goethe's poem reflecting on the character of his recently deceased friend Friedrich Schiller, "Epilog zu Schillers Glocke" (1805): "[...] sich stets erhöhter / bald kühn hervordrängt, bald geduldig schmiegt, / damit das Gute wirke, wachse, fromme, [...]" Johann Wolfgang von Goethe, "Epilog zu Schillers Glocke," in *Goethe's Werke*, vol. 13 (Stuttgart and Tübingen: J. G. Cotta'schen Buchhandlung, 1829), 159–64, here 163.

35 "Civis Romanus sum" (I am a Roman citizen) is a Latin phrase used in Cicero's (106–43 BCE) *In Verrem* (70 BCE).

36 Thomas and Katia Mann pledged allegiance to the American Constitution on June 23, 1944 in Los Angeles.

37 Mann viewed both Roosevelt and Caesar (100–44 BC) in a similar and favorable light, admiring their popular appeal despite their elitist backgrounds.

No one was immune to the magic of his personality. The tragedy that he had to leave his work unfinished has left no heart unmoved.[38] A greater loss, everyone feels, could not have befallen humankind in its hour of destiny, and so the mourning for him is felt the world over. It is not surprising that his friends and allies are shaken, that Churchill, the old warrior, is not ashamed of his tears; that Stalin, who must know well what an irreplaceable mediator between him and the British, between revolution and Toryism,[39] has been lost, celebrates his memory. But what do you Germans make of the fact that the Prime Minister of Japan[40] referred to the deceased as a great leader and expressed his country's sympathy to the American people for their loss?

Do you not agree that this is astounding? It is astounding even to us—it must be utterly unfathomable to you. Japan is engaged in a life-and-death war with America, one it was seduced into by a group of ambitious feudal lords. But a great deal would have to have been different for the undoubtedly pernicious rule of this class to have brought about a moral disintegration and stupefaction, to have brought the country to the dogs, the way that National Socialism has succeeded in doing in our poor Germany. There, in the East, there still exists a sense of chivalry and human decency, a reverence for death and greatness. This is the difference: what was above in Japan, though intimidating and ominous, was still an "above." Twelve years ago in Germany, the lowest, the very last and lowest humanly possible, came to the top and defined the face of the country.

All of Germany's misery becomes evident when one sees how this once most educated nation in the world is responding to the death of this man, who was certainly not Germany's enemy, but in reality the most powerful enemy of those who brought about Germany's ruin.[41] Mindless insults—that was all that the German press could come up with. And then came the raggedy scarecrow Hitler himself and declared in an order of the day that "providence had removed from the Earth the greatest war criminal of all time."[42]

---

38   i.e. the victorious end of the Second World War and the foundation of the United Nations on October 24, 1945 in San Francisco.

39   The members and supporters of the Conservative Party in the United Kingdom are colloquially referred to as "Tories." Churchill was a Tory.

40   Danshaku (Baron) Suzuki Kantarō (1868–1948), formerly an admiral, was Prime Minister of Japan in the last months of the war until the surrender on September 2, 1945.

41   The phrase "All of Germany's misery" parallels a line in Goethe's *Faust* from the scene "Kerker" (A Dungeon; line 4406), spoken by Faust: "I'm gripped by all of mankind's misery."

42   In his address to the "Soldiers of the German Eastern Front" on April 16, 1945, Hitler implores the German soldiers to persevere in and not to let up in the fight against the "deadly Jewish-Bolshevik enemy," because in the "moment, in

Disgrace enough, you genocidal moron, that *He* had to go and you still live! What gives you the right to continue to exist? Where *He*— became pure spirit, all that is left of you is a spook. Hide out a while longer in the mountain cave that your worshippers dug for you![43] Your days are numbered; they were numbered as soon as this opponent rose up against you, and even in death he will be your terror.

May 10, 1945

German Listeners!
How bitter it is when the defeat, the deepest humiliation of one's country results in the jubilation of the entire world! How terribly apparent now is the abyss that has opened between Germany, the land of our forebears and great masters, and the civilized world!

The bells of victory and bells of peace are ringing out, there are glasses clinking, there are hugs and congratulations all around. The German, however, who was once denied his very Germanness by the least qualified of all,[44] who had to avoid his own country, which had become abominable to him, and create a new life in happier places—he hangs his head amid the worldwide joy; his heart clenches inside him at the thought of what it means for Germany, what dark days, what years of the inability to self-reflect and the humiliation of atonement it will still have to endure after all it has already suffered.

And nonetheless, the hour is great—not only for the world of the victors, but for Germany too—the hour in which the dragon has been subdued, the desolate and sick monstrosity called National Socialism gasps its last breath, and Germany is at the very least liberated from the curse of being known as the land of Hitler. If Germany had been able to liberate itself, earlier, when there was still time to do so, or even late, just at the last moment; if Germany itself had been able to celebrate its liberation, its return to humanity, to the sound of bells and Beethoven's music, instead of the end of Hitlerism being at the same time the total collapse of Germany—truly, that would have been better, would have been the most desirable turn possible. It simply could not be. The liberation had to come from outside; and above all, I believe, you Germans should recognize this as an achievement, not explain it to yourselves as the mere result of mechanical superiority in human and material resources, and not claim: "Ten against one, that's not fair." Defeating Germany, the only

---

which Providence has removed the greatest war criminal of all time from this earth, the turning point of this war is being decided." See Domarus IV, 3040.

43 Mann wrongly assumed that Hitler and his men were posted in the mountains, presumably near Berchtesgaden.

44 This happened when he was expatriated in 1936, along with thirty-eight other "national pests" (*Volkschädlinge*).

participant that prepared for the war with utmost thoroughness, was a monumental task even in a war with two fronts. The Wehrmacht stood before Moscow and at the Egyptian border. The European continent was under German control. There was seemingly no possibility whatsoever, no advantageous terrain, no point of attack, for the defeat of this unassailably entrenched force. The Russian march from Stalingrad to Berlin, the landing of the Anglo-Americans in France on June 6, 1944, which was unprecedented in military history, and their march to the Elbe, were military-technological feats of bravura to which the German art of war hardly has anything worthy of comparison. According to all the rules of the art of war, Germany has been truly defeated, if only at a tremendous cost, and Germany's unrivaled military superiority has been proven a myth. For German thinking, for Germany's relationship to the world, this is crucial. It will benefit our sense of modesty, will help to eradicate the delusion of the Germans as Übermenschen. We will no longer speak of the "military idiots" over there.

May the lowering of the party flag, which was an object of disgust and horror to the whole world, also signify the inner renunciation of the delusions of grandeur, the self-exaltation over other peoples, the provincial-superior and unworldly arrogance, the most vulgar, most insufferable expression of which was National Socialism. May the removal of the swastika flag signify the real, radical, and irrevocable severance of all German thinking and feeling from the stealth of Nazism's second-rate philosophy, its renunciation forever. One must hope that the member of the German surrender committee, Count Schwerin-Krosigk,[45] not only wished to appeal to the victors when he declared that rights and justice must henceforth be the supreme law of German national life, and respect for treaties must be the foundation of international relations. That was an oblique and all too lenient disavowal of the moral barbarism in which Germany lived for over twelve years. One would have wished for one that was more direct, more explicit; but at least it echoes the curse that I believe the German people bear in their hearts today against those who brought about their ruin.

I say: in spite of it all, this is a great hour—Germany's return to humanity. It is difficult and sad, because Germany was not able to bring it about on its own. Tremendous damage, difficult to undo, has been done

---

45 From May 2 to 23, 1945, Johann Ludwig Graf Schwerin von Krosigk (1887–1977) was a leading member of the short-lived Flensburg government under Grand Admiral Karl Dönitz, whom Hitler had appointed as his successor as Reich President. Schwerin-Krosigk served as Finance Minister in the Papen and Schleicher governments in 1932 and was retained in this function by Hitler. Schwerin-Krosigk was sentenced to ten years in prison in the Nuremberg War Crimes Trials in 1949; he was released after being granted amnesty in 1951.

to the German name, and all might is now squandered.[46] But might is not everything, it is not even the main thing, and German dignity was never a question of mere might. It was once German, and it could be again, to win respect, admiration, not through might, but through human and humane contributions, through the free spirit.

December 30, 1945

German Listeners!
The BBC has requested that I once again speak to you and repeat to you over the radio the reasons given in my open letter why I cannot think of a return to Germany.[47] I have been very hesitant to comply with the request out of a feeling that the barely relevant topic, about which so much has already been said, in no way justifies the resumption of my German broadcasts. Even the irrational attacks that, here and there, have been directed against my remarks will not lead me to change my mind. It is too obvious that these attacks have been drafted in the interest of self-aggrandizement, of glorification, of one's own heroism for them to have any profound impact on me. I have spoken honestly and faithfully and cannot prevent malice or stupidity from abusing my words, mangling them, and making them out to be documents of egoism, of self-pity, disloyalty, and unscrupulous advantage. I am too firmly convinced that it would be the greatest folly of my life, as well as the last, if I did what a number of those at home declare to be my duty, and that is, that I should leave America, where I have after all sworn my oath,[48] toss its citizenship down at its feet, shatter the hard-won way of life of my old age, leave my children and grandchildren, give up my work, and hurry back to a devastated Germany. To what end? To allow myself to be pummeled, which is to say, in order to, firstly get a taste of a festive return home as one who had been right all along, which is not a pleasant position to be in. Then to impose myself as the standard-bearer of a new German intellectual

---

46 The concluding sentences of the address are identical to the conclusion of Mann's essay, "Die deutschen KZ" (The German Concentration Camps) of May 12, 1945.

47 In an open letter dated August 4, 1945, Moravian-Austrian author Walter von Molo (1880–1958), Mann's former colleague in the literary division of the Prussian Academy of the Arts, called upon the exiled writer to return as a "good doctor" and help heal the defeated nation's wounds. Mann responded to Molo in an open letter of September 7, entitled "Why I Won't Go Back to Germany" (Warum ich nicht nach Deutschland zurückkehre) in which he criticized the so-called inner emigration and its compromises with the Nazi regime, triggering a broad wave of criticism of Mann, the "American." The title of Mann's letter is somewhat misleading since he only refuses to return to Germany for the time being, but by no means rules it out at a future date.

48 See annotations for the addresses of October 15, 1942 and June 27, 1943.

movement that is still entirely mystifying to me, namely to even zealously embark on a path to politics and then in short order to be demoralized, worn down, found suspect everywhere, both by Germandom and by the occupation, as one to whom the universal lament of fools applies: "But I meant well," and finally to find a fool's regrettable end? What treachery, what secret lust for ruination hides behind this charming suggestion, I cannot fathom.

Rejecting this suggestion, that is the nature of my egoism. I will defend this form of egoism before God, and posterity will call it reasonable. Egoism, it seems to me, could be expressed just as well by remaining in Germany as by fleeing. I had nothing in common with the monumental indifference of a Richard Strauss, as he proclaimed in a conversation with an American journalist to the world's amusement.[49] The devil's excrement that calls itself National Socialism taught me hatred. For the first time in my life, real, deep, inextinguishable, deadly hatred, a hatred that I mystically imagine was not without influence on all that has happened. From the first day onward, I have labored with my entire soul to bring about the downfall of this mischief that desecrates humanity. Not only with my radio broadcasts to Germany, which were a single, impassioned appeal to the German people to rid themselves of it. And what do you think was one of the things I was trying to achieve? At the very least what is being asked of me today, now that it is too late. My return home.

How I hoped for it, for many years as a guest in Switzerland,[50] how I dreamed of it, how eagerly I embraced any sign that Germany had grown weary of its humiliation. How different everything would have been if Germany had possessed the wherewithal to liberate itself. If between 1933 and 1939, the redemptive revolution had broken out over there, do you think I would have waited for the train after next? Instead of taking the very next one to return home? It was not to be, it could not be. It was not possible. Every German says so, and so one has to believe it. One has to believe that a dignified people of 70 million and of high standing can under certain circumstances, do nothing other than endure for six years

---

49   German composer Richard Strauss (1864–1949) was a co-signatory of the Munich Wagner protest—which sealed Mann's decision to go into exile—and served the regime as president of the Reich Chamber of Music (*Reichsmusikkammer*) until 1935, when he was forced to resign because of his attachment to his Jewish librettist and author Stefan Zweig (1881–1942). The American journalist in question is Klaus Mann (1906–1949), the son of Thomas Mann and a staff writer for the US Army newspaper *Stars and Stripes*. Klaus Mann interviewed Strauss in Garmisch on May 15, 1945 and published the interview on May 29 with the title "Strauss Still Unabashed About Ties With Nazis." See Klaus Mann's letter to his father of May 16, 1945.

50   Thomas Mann first resided in Switzerland from February 1933 to September 1938.

a regime of bloody scoundrels that is repugnant to them in the deepest part of their souls, that it would then wage a war that it realized was sheer insanity and for another six years give its utmost, all of its ingenuity, valor, intelligence, love of obedience, military punctuality, in short, dedicate all its strength, to help this regime to victory and thereby to its eternal perpetuation.

This is how it had to be, and entreaties such as my own were completely superfluous. Those who were blind did not listen, said the author Frank Thiess, a member of the inner emigration,[51] and those who knew were always a few lengths ahead of what was being said, at least at the very end. That's how it was in Germany, according to Frank Thiess. In subjugated Europe and in the wide world, many a tormented heart was comforted by my superfluous chatter, and for that reason I do not regret it. Yet, as much as these addresses amounted to love's labor for Germany foolishly lost, they are suddenly supposed to obligate me to go back there. You have made yourself out to be the intellectual Führer of the people, now live among this people and not only share their suffering, but alleviate it. Stand up to the foreigners who subject them to it. *And where is Germany?* Where can it be found, if even only geographically?[52] How do you return home to your fatherland that no longer exists as a single entity? A country torn into occupation zones that hardly know each other anymore? Should I go to the Russians, to the French, to the British, or to my new compatriots, the Americans, and let their bayonets protect me from a National Socialism that is no less than dead and buried, but continues to make every effort to corrupt our soldiers? In the face of such audacity, should I also find the suffering somehow uncannily uplifting, should I protest against Germany's suffering, rebuke the occupational forces for the mistakes they make in the treatment or administration of the country? No, precisely that is something I cannot do. As a German, I could speak to Germans to warn them of the approaching Nemesis.[53] But precisely as a German who feels deeply that everything that can be called German is

---

51 The author Frank Thiess (1890–1977) polemicized against exile authors, including Thomas Mann, and was an advocate for inner emigration. Thiess used the term "inner emigration" in berating Mann's *Deutsche Hörer!* broadcasts for criticizing the collective guilt of the Germans, arguing that Mann had no right to do so from the relative safety of Switzerland and the US, overlooking the fact that Mann had agitated against the National Socialists in Germany since the early 1920s.

52 Mann is referencing the 95th epigram of Goethe and Schiller's parodistic *Xenien* distiches of 1796, entitled "Das Deutsche Reich" (The German Empire): "Germany? But where does it lie? / I don't know how to find the land, / Where the academic starts, there the political ends."

53 Nemesis was the Greek goddess of vengeance who rewarded noble and punished evil acts.

complicit in the terrible national guilt, I cannot allow myself to offer criticism of the victors' policies that would always only be interpreted in terms of an egocentric patriotism and of callousness toward what other peoples have suffered at the hands of Germany over many years. Anyone who has long shrunk back in terror at the mountains of hatred that have risen like towers around Germany, anyone who has long spent sleepless nights imagining how terrible the retaliation against Germany would have to be for the inhuman actions of the Nazis, any such person can only look on in commiseration at what is being done to Germans by Russians, Poles, and Czechs and see in it nothing but the mechanical and inevitable reaction to misdeeds committed by a people as a whole, which unfortunately is not about individual justice, not about the guilt or innocence of the individual.[54] Better to advocate for European aid here on the outside, for the rescue of German children from death by starvation,[55] than to take on the role of goodwill agitator over there, never knowing whether doing so might not unwittingly serve the ends of National Socialism. For I am no nationalist. You may forgive me for this or not. But I suffered under the misery as the nations trampled underfoot by Germany, just as I saw Germans and Germany suffer calamity, and as for my decision to stay away, the time that my country has accorded me to do so not only brought about a resigned habituation, but it has also taught me to sincerely embrace what fate has decreed.[56]

I had awaited my return home, but just now a letter came before my eyes in print that I had addressed to a Hungarian friend already at the start of 1941, and in which it reads: Exile has become something quite different than it was in earlier times. It is not a state of waiting in which one is always thinking of returning home, but rather already portends a disintegration of nations and the unification of the world.[57] Everything national has long since become provincial. Prison air, so they scold me, those who, because they never spoke out against the looming calamity,

---

54 Mann is referring to the expulsion of the Germans from the areas east of the Oder-Neisse line and from the former Sudetenland (the German term for the northern, southern, and western areas of former Czechoslovakia).

55 According to a letter to Agnes Meyer (1887–1970), Mann signed an appeal for aid for German children "based on the idea that one supports the democratic forces in Germany when one addresses the misery."

56 The Nietzsche expert Mann is alluding to one of Friedrich Nietzsche's principal concepts, "*amor fati*" (love of fate), to describe his stance toward his own exile. In Book Four of *Die Fröhliche Wissenschaft* (*The Gay Science*, 1882), Nietzsche explains that *amor fati* is an affirmation of one's fate in a revolt against nihilism toward creating a life of beautiful flourishing.

57 Mann's letter of February 18, 1941, to his "Hungarian friend", classical philologist and mythologist Karl Kerényi (1897–1973), includes much of the same language in his analysis of the modern experience of exile.

preferred to remain at home in 1933. That, however, is a misapprehension. Being abroad has done me good. I took my German heritage with me. But I was also truly never exempted from any of the German misery in these years, even if I was not present when my home in Munich collapsed in ruins. May no one begrudge me *my cosmopolitan Germanness*, which was already organic to my very soul when I was still at home, nor my prominent position in German culture, one that I will seek to uphold with all rectitude for a few more years of my life.

Index

Adenauer, Konrad, lii
Adorno, Theodor W., lii
aesthetics, 11, 81
Alexander the Great, 5
Allied Forces, xviii, xlvii–xlviii 69, 71, 88, 90–91, 95, 98, 104, 110, 115–116, 122, 124, 127
Allies, the xix, xlvii–xlviii, li, lvi, 69, 78, 87–88, 93, 98, 108, 113, 127, 128
    advantages of, 115
    Italian armistice with, 102
    radio broadcasts of, xix, xxxv
    successes of, xlvii, 91, 95, 104, 124
America, *See* United States of America
Ancient Greece, 10
Anglo-American, 43, 56, 78, 97, 112, 127, 134
    air raids, 96
    people, 3, 85, 107, 113
Anglo-Soviet Agreement, 22
anticommunism, lii
antifascism, lii, *See* fascism
Anti-Nazi-Archive, 85
antisemitism, xxii, xxv, xli, 20, 23, 62, 123–124
    Jewish world conspiracy, xxxix, 121–122
ARCADIA Conference, lvi
Arendt, Hannah, 106
Astor, Lady Nancy, 80
Atlantic Charter, 28, 44, 48, 51
Atlantic Ocean, liii, 3, 20, 27–28, 30, 51
Atlantic Summit, 27
Attlee, Clement, 8
Auden, Wystan Hugh, xxxi, xxxiii
Außerordentliche Befriedung (emergency pacification), 41
Austria, xl, 52, 62, 125
    Vienna, 66–67, 91, 124

Austrian, 79, 135
    authors, 84
    literature, 88
    poet, 120
Austro-Hungarian dual monarchy, 50
auto-da-fé, 85
Axis Powers, 11, 44, 46, 90, 93, 98
    ambitions of, 22
    occupation, 95
    sabotage of, 87

Bach, Johann Sebastian, 7, 24
Baden, Max von, 50
Badoglio, Pietro, 89
Baldini, Antonio, 60
Balkans, the, 60, 91, 95, 115
Baltic Sea, 84
Battle of Britain, 3, 15
Battle of Thermopylae, 16
Bayreuth Circle, 86
Beer Hall Putsch, xxii, 4
Beethoven, Ludwig van, xliii, 7, 24, 32, 133
    Fidelio (1805), 7
    Symphony No. 3 (*Eroica*, 1805), xvi
    Symphony No. 9 (*Ode to Joy*, 1824), 7
Belgium, xxiii, xlvii, 1, 2, 15, 98, 105, 115
    Brussels, xxiii, 115
    child mortality in, 118
    evacuation of, 50
Bernadotte, Folke, 128
Bertram, Ernst, xxii, xxviii
Bethlehem, 6
Bible, the, 114
    biblical language, xliii
    Book of Genesis, 108
    Book of Hosea, 113
    Book of Matthew, 131
    Book of Romans, 114

Decalogue, 83
New Testament, 55
Old Testament, xxxvii, 55
Bismarck, Otto von, 125, 126
blitzkrieg, 2, 15, 92
Bock, General Field Marshal Fedor von, 35
Boes, Tobias, xliii
Bolshevik Revolution, the, 48
Bolshevism, 21–22, 33, 48, 68, 78, 80, 113, 121–122, 127, 132
  destruction of, 95
  opposition of, 11
Bonaparte, Napoleon, xlv, 5, 29–30, 36, 76, 93, 124
  comparison with Hitler, 29, 124
  downfall of, 29, 124
Bonaparte, Napoleon III, liv
book burnings, 84–86
  Committee for the Restoration of Burned and Banned Books in Europe, 86
  Council of Books in Wartime, 85
  Society of Friends of the Burned Books, 85
Borgese, Guiseppe Antonio, xxxi
bourgeoisie, 28, 32, 108–109
Brasillach, Robert, 60
Brauchitsch, General Field Marshal Walther von, 35
Braun, Eva, 128
Brecht, Bertolt, xliv, 26, 53
Brenner Circle, 120
Brinitzer, Carl, xxxiv, 12
British
  authors, 82
  occupation of southern Italy, 95
  Royal Navy, 71, 94
British Broadcasting Corporation (BBC), xiv, xxix–xxxiii, xxxiv–xxxvii, xxxix, xl, xlvii, l–li, lv, lxii, 4, 12, 37, 44, 88, 135
  German Service, xxx–xxxi, xxxiii–xxxiv
  Monitoring Service, xl–xli
British Hong Kong, 47
British Malaya, 47
Bromfield, Louis, 82
Brun-Warendorp-Haus, 46
Buddenbrook House, 46

Bulgaria, 13
Bülow, Bernhard von, 6
Bund Deutscher Mädel (BDM; League of German Girls), 33
  Mating Days, 33
Burckhardt, Jacob, 54
  Weltgeschichtliche Betrachtungen (World-Historical Considerations, 1905), 54
burlesque, 55

Caesar, Gaius Julius, 5, 36, 74, 131
Canada, xiv, 3
  Newfoundland, 28
  Ottawa, 92
  Parliament, 92
  Toronto, 87
capitalism, 48, 68, 108–109
Carossa, Hans, 60
  Ungleiche Welten (Different Worlds, 1951), 60
Caucasus Mountains, 31, 56, 71
Cecchi, Emilio, 60
Chamberlain, Houston Stewart, 86
Chamberlain, Neville, xxxi, 4, 8
Charlemagne, 5
China, 8, 22, 44, 80, 125
Christianity, 6, 7, 9, 33, 38, 64, 128, 130
  Christmas, xii, 6–9, 34, 64
  conversion to, 21
  Easter, 89
  persecution of, 21
Churchill, Winston, xxxi, xxxviii, lvi, 8, 20, 27–28, 48, 71, 93, 98, 101, 123, 126, 128, 132
  speeches, 20
Cicero, Marcus Tullius
  In Verrem (70 BCE), 131
citizenship, xxx, l, 4, 65, 87, 135, *See* American, citizenship, *See* Czechoslovakia
Columbia Broadcasting System (CBS), xxxix, lii, 86
communism, lii, 7, 30, 74, 84, 94, 99, 108
  fear of, 98
communist, 7, 30, 74, 80, 94, 99
Communist Party of Germany, 108

concentration camp, xxiii, xl, xlix, 14, 52, 63, 117, 128
   Buchenwald, xlix
   Dachau, xxiii
   liberation of, 117
   Mauthausen, xl, xli, 52
      mass murder, 52
   Theresienstadt, 128
Cooper, Alfred Duff, 1st Viscount Norwich, xxxi
Council on Books in Wartime, 85
Curie, Eve, 86
Curie, Marie, 86
cynicism, 14, 17, 74
Czech, lv, 2, 28, 53, 114
   authors, 84, 135
   history, 59
Czechoslovakia xxx, l, 4, 62, 87, 107, 138
   Bohemia, 2, 53, 59
      kings of, 53
   citizenship, xxx, 4
   Czech language, 59
   destruction of, 28
   Hradčany, 53
   Lidiče, 53–54
   Moravia, 2, 53, 59, 135
   occupation of, 59
   Prague, 28, 52–54, 82, 105
   protectorate, l, lv
   Sudetenland, 4, 138

d'Annunzio, Gabriele, 91
Das Schwarze Korps (newspaper), 96
Davis, Elmer, 86
De Gaulle, Charles André Joseph Marie, 123
death marches, 118
death sentence, 53, 72, 74, 88
dehumanization, 25, 52
democracy, vii, xiii, xviii, xxii, xxvii, xlvii, li, 43–44, 78, 93, 111, 131
   accusations against, 46
   American, xi, xxi, 20, 86
   Anglo-American, 43, 56
   antidemocracy, x–xi, xviii, xxii, 43, 111
   defense of, xviii, xxii, xlvii, 4, 17, 131
   German, xlvii, li, 99, 111,
   progress of, 27, 47–48
   weakness of, xiii, 97
Denmark, 2, 10
   Copenhagen, 105
   Danish Protectorate, 2
   German war with, 46
Der völkische Beobachter (newspaper), 109
Deutsche Arbeitsfront (DAF, German Labor Front), 23, 109
Deutsche Studentenschaft (German Student Union), 84
Deutsches historisches Museum (German Historical Museum), 79
Dewey, Thomas, 58
Dietrich, Marlene, xxix
dignity, xii–xiii, xvii, 9, 17–18, 42, 66, 71, 74, 76, 103, 110, 125
   German, 32, 51, 135
   French, 29
Diocletian, Roman Emperor, 21
Dionysus (Greek god), 57
Döblin, Alfred, xl
Dönitz, Karl, 94, 134
Dürer, Albrecht, 6, 7, 24, 67
Dutch, *See* Netherlands, the

Earth, 9–10, 14, 21–22, 27, 38, 40–41, 43–44, 58–59, 62, 66, 69, 84, 101, 106, 108, 111–113, 115–116, 124, 132
East Africa
   Italian Colonization of, 89
East, the, xlviii, 6, 14, 35, 77–78, 89, 94, 108, 121, 126
   social philosophy of, 93, 132
Eckart, Dietrich, 23
   "Sturm" (1919), 23
Egypt, xx, 125
   border of, 115, 134
Eher Verlag, 109
Eisenhower, General Dwight D., 122
Eisler, Hanns, 53
Elbe River, 134
emigration, x, 24, 94, 99, *See* exile
Emmanuele, King Vittorio III, 89

English Channel, 41, 45, 71, 78
Entartung (degeneracy), 54, 59
Ermächtigungsgesetz (Enabling Act, 1933), 13–14
Erskine, Jozzerman, xxxii, xxxvi, 19
ethics, 122
eugenics, xl–xli, xlvii, lvi, 8, 14, 28, 40, 47, 54, 59–60, 65, 68, 76, 101
  Aryans, 36, 111
  Lebensborn e.V. (Fount of Life), 33
  Master Race, 37, 100, 118
  Nazi politics of, 28, 30
  Übermenschen, 134
Eurasia, xiii
Europäische Schriftsteller Vereinigung (European Writers' Association), 60
European Poets' Meeting, 60
Europe, xiv, xviii, xl–xli, xlv, xlvii–xlviii, l, lix, 2–6, 8, 22, 28–29, 32, 34, 37–38, 40, 42–43, 59–62, 71, 78, 87, 89, 95, 98, 100, 105, 107–112, 115, 118, 121–122, 127, 129–131, 134, 137
  conceptions of, lix, 43, 59, 60–61, 67, 68, 110–111, 130
  culture of, 67–68, 85–86, 111,
  devastation of, 49, 60, 65, 100, 107, 119, 121, 129
  enslaved people of, 78
  flight from, 85
  Fortress Europe, 91, 95, 115
  history of, 87, 124–125
  liberated, 86, 110, 112, 122
  Nazi occupation of, xviii, xli, 40, 48, 59–60, 62, 64, 68, 70–71, 75, 89, 95, 109–110, 115, 118, 121, 134, 137
  New Order, the, 29, 59
  Northern, 6
  oppressed people of, 26
  peoples of, xlviii, l, 4, 22, 26, 43, 52, 56, 59, 61–62, 64, 66–67, 69, 78, 86–88, 92–93, 104–105, 107, 111, 117–118, 130
  spirit of, 29
  unification of, 59, 87

exile, xviii, xx, xxii–xxviii, xxxii, xxxviii, xl–xlii, l, lii, liv, 3, 52–53, 62–63, 136–138
extermination camp, 85, 117–118
  Auschwitz-Birkenau, xlviii, xlix, 118
  Majdanek, 117

fascism, iv, vii–viii, xviii, xx, xxiv, xl, xlii, xlvi, 12, 44, 48, 60, 66, 91, 93, 108, 110, 113, 131
  American, 86
  bourgeois, 28
  death of, 92
  eradication of, 91
  European, 8
  French, 28
  German, xiii, xxiv, 96, 98, 109, 113
    intolerance of, 89
  Italian, 12, 89–91, 109
    death of, 89
  Norwegian, 22
  opposition to, xiv, xviii, xxii, xxviii, xxxi–xxxii, xxxix, lii, liv, 58, 82, 91
  Spanish, 44
fear, xii–xiii, xxiv, 27, 33, 35, 43, 51, 55, 61, 74, 116, 122, 124
  of change, 120, 125
  of communism, 98
  of continued Nazi regime, 17, 116
  of socialism, 108
Feuchtwanger, Lion, vii, xl, 82
Ficker, Ludwig von, 120
Fiedler, Kuno, xxx
film media, 47, 53, 82
Finland
  military deaths, 60
First World War, xviii–xix, 18, 30, 78, 99–100
  Fourteen Point Peace Plan, 50
  German defeat in, 119
Fischer, Gottfried Bermann, xxiv
Fleet Act (1898), 100
France xxiii, xxx, 1–2, 5, 10, 18, 28–29, 36, 41, 60, 63, 67, 70, 95, 98, 105, 108, 124, 134
  Alsace-Lorraine, 50

armistice in, 90
child mortality in, 118
collapse of, 47, 101
Dieppe, 71
French Navy, 69
Grenoble, 90
Nice, 90
Paris, xxiii, xli, 5, 28, 53, 60, 63, 85, 105, 115, 128
occupation of, 15, 28, 30, 67
subjugation of, 14–15, 30, 41, 47
Toulon, 69
Vichy regime, 63, 68–69, 90
Franco, Francisco, 44
Frank, Bruno, 82
Frank, Hans, 41
freedom, xii–xiv, xxi, xxxix, xlii, lvi, 1, 3–5, 7–9, 11, 15–19, 23, 25–27, 32, 34–35, 41–44, 48–49, 51, 56–57, 59, 61, 64–66, 76, 83, 89–91, 93, 96–98, 100–101, 104–105, 107, 110–112, 114, 123–124, 126, 129–131, 135
American, 1, 4, 64–66
British, 3, 10
belief in, 88–89desire for, 13, 42, 48
exercise of, 93, 129
from cruelty, 21
German, 35, 57, 89, 98, 105, 111, 129–130
longing for, 58
of religion, 43
of speech, 20, 43
of thought, 66, 85
spirit of, 28, 89
voice of, 26
Freemasonry, 32
French, 29, 30, 38, 41, 63, 69, 71, 82, 95, 106, 124–125, 137
authors, liv, 24, 84
conquer of Corsica, 95
fleet
loss of, 69, 94
language, 5, 82, 106
North Africa, 69
people, 30, 35, 63, 69
deception of, 30
press, 128
resistance, 29
Revolution, 38
French Indochina, 47
Friedrich II (King of Prussia), 5, 36, 102, 125
Fry, Varian, 106
Führer, xiii, lvi, lxi, 4, 7, 11–12, 14, 18, 23, 27, 31–33, 36, 41–43, 49, 53, 68, 73, 77, 81, 88–89, 103, 120–121, 127–128, 137, *See* Hitler, Adolf
Funk, Walther, 8

General Electric, 67
General Motors, 67
Genghis Khan, 70
genocide, xii, xli, xlix, 27, 37, 42, 52, 58, 107, *See* Holocaust, the
in France, 30
of disabled people, 33
of Jewish people, xlv, xlix, 37, 52, 117
of Poles, 33, 41
of Serbs, 33
George, St, 21
German
authors, xi, xviii–xlv, 1, 39, 62, 65, 106
bravery, 89, 120
character, xliii, 12, 24, 119
culture, xxvi, xlvii, 54, 102, 111, 139
emigrants, 24, 99, *See* emigration
ethnic community, 73
government, *See* Nazi regime
history, xlii, xlvi, 59, 88, 105, 119, 121, 125–126
honor, xliv, 32, 40, 51, 74, 88–89, 94, 102, 110
Imperial Navy, 15, 68, 94, 100
ingenuity, 120
intellectual history, 16, 24
intelligence, xxxii, 120
intelligentsia, 25
language, 11, 64, 120
losses, 79, 80, 95
love of obedience, 120
military, *See* Wehrmacht
national identity, 17, 32, 52, 55, 87, 133, 139

Index • 145

virtues of, 101
weakness of, 100
nationalism, 24–25, 47, 59, 68, 85
  end of, 76
  logic of, 30
occupation, 3, 13, 22, 30, 52, 62, 67, 77, 99, 126, 136
oppressors, 4, 9, 30
people, xv, xviii, xxv–xxvi, xxxii, xxxv–xxxvii, xliv, li, liii, liv–lvi, 3–6, 8, 11–12, 19, 21–22, 24–25, 27, 38, 41–43, 49, 51, 65, 70, 73, 77, 79, 92–94, 96–99, 107, 110, 112, 119, 121–122, 124, 126, 127, 130, 134, 136
  belief in their Führer, 27
  compassion for, 88
  crime against, 102
  destruction of, 27
  distinction from Nazis, 88, 119
  expectations of, 50, 100
  extermination of, 49
  guilt of, xiii, xlv, xlix, 34, 38, 41, 119, 137–138
  hope for, 91
  Huns, 78, 107, 108
  immaturity of, 51
  lacking pride, 31
  opinion toward, 76
  oppressed, 26
  power of, 120, 124
  support for, 49
  unpolitical, 25
  press, xxxii, xxxvi, 1, 13, 19, 72, 88, 96–97, 113, 132
  public, lv, 19, 72, 123
  soil, li, 115, 117–118, 120
  state, 79
  workers, 76
  youth, 67, 89
German Freedom Library, 85
German troops, *See* Wehrmacht
German-American Loyalty Hour, 64
German-Americans, x, 3, 64–65, 105–106
Germanism, 84
Germany, ii, iv, vii, x–xvi, xviii, xix, xx–xxxi, xxxvi, xxxix–xlix, l–lvi, lviii, lxi, 1–7, 9, 11–13, 17–21, 23, 25, 27, 30–34, 36–41, 43–51, 53, 56–57, 59–60, 62–68, 70–71, 73–74, 76, 78–79, 80, 84–85, 89–95, 98–102, 104–106, 108–113, 116, 118–130, 132–138
  Aachen, xlviii, 120, 122
    liberation of, 115
  Allied occupation of, xlviii, 48, 126, 137
  annihilation of, 19, 57, 65, 70, 122, 127
  arms race with Great Britain, 100
  Berchtesgaden, 35, 133
  Berlin, xxii, xxiv, xxvi, xxviii, xliv, 10, 32, 38, 42, 60, 71, 105, 107, 126, 134
    Bebelplatz, 84
    Sportpalast, 10, 29, 38, 71, 97
    State Opera, 84
  Berlin Arsenal, 79
  Berliner Tageblatt (newspaper), 84
  Berlin Olympics, xxvi
  bombings of, xix, 45, 88, 107, 111
  Bonn, xxvi, xxix, liv
  Bremen, 94, 126
  Breslau, 126
  Cologne, xix, 45, 107, 126
    bombing of, 88
  colonialism, 6, 100
  crimes of, xlii, xlv, xlviii, xlix, 8, 13–14, 97, 102, 106, 112, 117, 120, 127, 129
  culture of, xviii, xxvi–xxvi, xlvi–xlvii, 24, 54, 90, 111, 139
  declarations of war, 20
  defeat of, xlvi, 133
  denazification of, xliii, 123
  disarmament of, 123
  Dresden, 75, 126
  Düsseldorf, xix, 45
  exceptionalism, xxix, xlvii, 44, 59
  Federal Republic of Germany (FRG), lii
  flight from, xvi, xxv, xlv, 63, 105, 108
  Fortress Germany, 91, 95, 115

Frankfurt, li–lii, 126
Frankfurter Zeitung (newspaper), 105
future of, 26, 46, 49, 95, 99–101
German consulates, 19
German Democratic Republic (GDR), li, 108
German Empire, xxi, 23, 125
government of
    Reichskommissar, 22
    Reichstag, xxii, 6, 14, 37, 129
Hamburg, xix, xxvi, xxxiv, li, 45, 94, 107, 126
Innerlichkeit, xlvi
Kiel, 94
leaders of, 21
legacy of, xlix, 23, 25–26, 74, 107
Lübeck, xix, 45–46
    attack on, 45
    bombing of, xix, 46
militarism of, xliv, 123
Ministry of Propaganda and Public Enlightenment, xxxv
Munich, xxiii–xxiv, xxviii, xxx, xli, xliii–xliv, lvi, 4, 33, 52, 57, 88–89, 94, 105, 108–109, 113, 136, 139
Nazi Party of, *See* Nazism
negotiations with, 17
Nuremberg, xvii, xli, 74, 80
    Apollotheater, 81
Nuremberg racial laws, xli
People's Army, 98, 125
place in the sun, xiii, 6, 8, 100
plans for conquest, 30, 51, 56–57, 92, 104, 125
political prisoners in, 88
pre-Nazism, 24
reconstruction of, xxxv, xlviii, 39, 116, 126
reparations of, 111
ruin of, 76
Social Democratic Party of, xxiii, 32, 99
suffering of, 45
surrender of, xlii
traditions of, 46, 90
transport to, 52
true character of, xliv
victory of
    German public response to, 48
Volksgemeinschaft, xxv, 73
war against, 45
Weimar, xviii, xxi–xxii, xlix, li, 60, 65, 75, 125–126
Weimar Republic, xviii, xxii, xxiv, 75, 125
    justice system, 74
Wilhelmshaven, 94
Geschichtsphilosophie Movement, 54
Gestapo, 14, 48, 53, 57, 60, 62, 72, 74, 96–97, 122
    torture chambers, 118
    victims of, 85
Giesler, Gauleiter Paul, 89
God, xxi, xxxii, xlix, lvi, 6, 8, 32, 36, 40, 57, 60, 75, 81, 83–84, 108, 114, 118, 121, 124, 136
Goebbels, Joseph, xxiii, xxviii, xxix, xxxi, xxxv, xli, liii, 23, 32, 38, 60, 62, 65, 72, 76–77, 84, 90, 103–104, 109–110, 112–113, 123
    as the devil, 112
    propaganda, 27
    speeches, 75–76, 97
    statement from, 49
    suicide of, 23
Goethe, Johann Wolfgang von, xxi, xxxviii, xliii, xliv, li, 1, 7, 24, 29, 32, 65, 120, 131–132, 137
    Faust (1808), 55, 132
    Des Epimenides Erwachen (Epimenides' Awakening, 1814), xliv, 29
    Iphigenie auf Tauris (Iphigenia in Tauris, 1787), 7
    West-östlichen Divan (West-Eastern Diwan, 1819), 120
    "Selige Sehnsucht" (Blissful Longing, 1817), 120
Gogol, Nikolai, 67, 78
    Gogol Museum, 67
Göring, Emma Johanna "Emmy", 128
Göring, Hermann Wilhelm, 20, 44, 48, 67, 74, 78, 109
    suicide of, 23
Graefe, Albrecht von, 129

Great Britain, iii, xxiv, xxix–xxxii, lix, 1–4, 8, 10–11, 13–14, 18–20, 22, 28, 30, 36, 44, 51, 56, 68, 71, 75, 78, 80, 98, 100–102, 105, 107–108, 112, 115
   appeasement of Germany, xxx, 4, 80, 108, 112
   arms race with Germany, 100
   Beveridge Report (1942), 56
   Birmingham, 3
   bombing of, xix, xxxii, 44, 101
   British Commonwealth, 43
   British Intelligence Service, 37
   Coventry, xix, 3, 44–45, 97
   German mimicry of, 100–101
   London, xiv, xix, xxiv, xxxii–xxxiv, xxxvi, xliv, lv, 3, 15, 53, 60, 62, 78, 82, 85, 97
      bombing of, 48
   naval supremacy of, 100
   Oxford, xxix
   Royal Air Force, xix, 45
   Scotland, 78
   war with Germany, 21, 27
Greece, 15–16, 34, 107
   Athens, 15, 50, 105
   child mortality in, 118
   Mount Olympus, 15
   starvation in, 60
Grosser, Johann F. G., l–li
Guam, 47
guerilla warfare, 95
guilt, xiii, xlv, xlix, 34, 38, 41, 112–114, 119, 137–138
Gundolf, Friedrich, 62

Haffner, Sebastian, xlv
   Germany: Jekyll and Hyde (1940), xlv
Hanseatic League, 46
happiness, ix, viii, 8, 43, 125
   longing for, 58
Hauptmann, Gerhart, xxvii–xxix
Haushofer, Karl, 57
   Bausteine zur Geopolitik (Foundations of Geopolitics, 1928), 57
Hegel, Georg Wilhelm Friedrich, 93, 131

Heiden, Konrad, 105–106
   Der Führer: Hitler's Rise to Power (1944), 106
Helbling, Carl, 84
Herder, Johann Gottfried, 33, 54
Heroes Day of Remembrance, 42
Hess, Rudolf, 78
   suicide of, 78
Heydrich, Reinhard Tristan, 52–54
Himmler, Heinrich, 23, 28, 33, 48, 53–54, 88, 104, 115, 117, 120, 128
   success of, 115
   suicide of, 23
Hitlerjugend (Hitler Youth), 33, 67, 84
Hitler Putsch, *See* Beer Hall Putsch
Hitler, Adolf, xiii–xvi, xviii–xix, xxii–xxiv, xxvi–xxvii, xxix–xxx, xxxvii–xxxix, xlvii, li–liv, lvi, 4, 10–18, 20, 24, 26–27, 29–30, 32, 35–40, 42–45, 49, 56–58, 60–61, 65–73, 77–78, 80, 87, 90, 92–93, 95, 98, 101, 104–106, 108–109, 112–116, 119–123, 125, 128, 130, 132–134
   ambitions of, 22
   assassination attempts on, xv, xlv, 53, 121
   bunker of, 23
   comparison with Napoleon, 29
   concept of peace, 17–18, 22, 48
   declarations of war
      Great Britain, xxx, 13
      Russia, 21
      United States, xlii, 20, 35
   downfall of, 29, 55, 92, 115
   desecrator of culture, 85
   enemy of humankind, 22
   enemy of peace, 19
   evilness of, 52
   lies of, 35, 43
   Mein Kampf (1925), 109
   Nero Decree, 128
   regime of, 46–47, 85, 91, 102, 116
      rebellion against, 17, 26, 49, 89, 94
   revolution of, 18
   rise of, 18

speeches of, 4, 10, 12, 14, 29, 54, 70, 81, 120
   on culture, 81
success of, 55, 115
suicide of, 94
triumph of, 18, 29, 31, 55, 57
war of, 12, 26, 73, 76–77
Hitlerism, *See* Nazism
Hofmannsthal, Hugo von, 88
Holland, *See* Netherlands, the
Holocaust, the, xl–xli, xlv, xlviii, xlix, 33, 52, 61, 63, 117, *See* genocide
   Night of the Long Knives, xxiv
   use of poison gas, 37, 52, 117–118
   Warsaw ghetto, 40, 62
Homer
   Iliad, the, 10
Homosexuality
   criminalization of, 74
honor, xxi, xxviii, xxix, xliv, 15, 28, 32, 40, 51, 61, 69, 74, 83, 85, 89, 91, 93–94, 101, 122, 127
"Horst-Wessel-Lied" (The Horst Wessel Song, 1929), 7, 77
hostages, 29, 30
   murder of, 30 53, 118
Hottentots, 63
Huber, Kurt, 89
Hugo, Victor, liv, 52
human rights, 38, 101, 110
humanism, x, xii, xvi, xxi–xxii, xxvii, xxxiii, xxxv, liii, 6, 8, 11, 13, 16–18, 20–21, 23, 25, 42, 48, 54, 58, 67, 68, 81–83, 96–97, 102–103, 107, 110, 118, 121, 124, 130, 133–134 136
   question of humankind, 23
humanity, xxvii, xliii, 6, 8, 11, 13, 16–18, 20–21, 23, 25–26, 33, 39, 42, 45, 48, 53–54, 58, 67–68, 81–83, 96–97, 102–103, 107–108, 110, 118, 121, 124, 130, 133–134, 136
humiliation, xlvi, 30, 58, 61, 68, 133, 136
Hundred Years' War, the, 36
Hungary
   military deaths, 60
Huns, *See* German

I. G. Farben, 67
"I Had a Comrade" (song), 77
imperialism, 47, 58, 68, 126
individualism, 129
inner emigration, xxix, l, 135, 137
insanity, xv, 2, 7, 10, 40, 54, 59, 78, 99, 104, 121
inspiration, xliv, liv, 1, 53, 67–68
intelligentsia, 90
International Free World Association, 58
international law, xii, 21
Iran, xii
   Tehran, 98, 123
Isherwood, Christopher, xxxi
Islam, 106
Italian, xxxi, 3, 12, 15, 34, 69, 71, 89–91, 104
   fascism, 90
   fleet 94
Italian-Americans, 3
Italy, xlii, 11–12, 36, 60, 90–91, 95, 102, 109
   Axis power, 46
   Corsica, 95
   Military
      deaths, 87
   Naples, 104–105
   naval surrender, 94
   occupation of French territory, 90
   Rome, 95, 105, 115, 128
      bombing of, 90
   Sardinia, 94–95
   Sicily, 90
      Cassibile, 102

Japan, xlii, 11, 36, 47, 78, 90, 123, 132
   Axis power, 46
   conquests of, 47
   victory of, 47
Japanese
   Empire, 47
Jesus Christ, 6, 7
Jewish people, xx, xxv, xl–xli, xlv, xlix, 6, 28, 30, 32–33, 37, 40, 61–63, 84, 99, 107, 118, 128
   attitudes towards Germans, 61
   authors, 84, 136

mass murder of, 52, 89, 117–118,
    See Holocaust, the
Joan of Arc, 36
Johnson, Herschel Vespasian, 128
Judaism, 84
justice, 7, 18, 22–25, 32, 34–35, 43,
    46, 49, 58, 74, 111, 116, 122,
    129–130, 134, 138
    belief in, 88
    longing for, 58
    sense of, 53, 74
    social order of, 48

Kant, Immanuel, 54, 105
Kerényi, Karl, 138
Kiev, 95
Kleist, Heinrich von, 76
    "Was gilt es in diesem Kriege?"
    (What is at Stake in this War?,
    1809), 76
Knappertsbusch, Hans, xxiv
Knopf, Alfred A. xix–xx, xxix–xxx,
    xxxv–xxxvi, xlix, lv, lxiv
Korrodi, Eduard, xxv
Kraft durch Freude (KdF, Strength
    Through Joy), 109
Krosigk, Johann Ludwig Graf
    Schwerin von, 134

L'Humanite (newspaper), 128
Labouisse, Ève Denise Curie, 86
Lang, Fritz, 53
    Hangmen Also Die (1943), 53
Lányi, Jenö, 3
League of Nations, lvi, 50
Leitgeb, Josef, 120
    Herbst (Autumn, 1937), 120
Lend-Lease Act (1941), xxxii, 8, 11,
    13–14, 20, 28
Leonidas I, 16
Lewis, Sinclair, 86
    It Can't Happen Here (1935), 86
Ley, Robert, 23, 74, 109
    suicide of, 23, 74
liberation, xlii–xliii, xlviii–xlix, 12, 39,
    96, 110–112, 117, 133
Libya
    Tripoli, 72
lies, 11–12, 14, 18, 23, 29, 68, 77,
    83, 103, 106, 108, 110, 114, 122

Life Magazine, 1, 2
Lindbergh, Charles, 20
Liszt, Franz, 55
    Les Préludes, 55
literature, xxv, xxvii, xlv, 82, 84–85, 88
    science-fiction, 85
Lithuania, 84
Loon, Hendrik Willem van, xxxviii, 82
Los Angeles Times (newspaper), xxxix
Lowe-Porter, Helen T., xxix–xxx, lviii
Luce, Henry R., 2, 58
    "The American Century" (1940),
    58
Ludendorff, Erich, 50, 75, 97, 129
    Der totale Krieg (Total War, 1935),
    97
Ludwig, Emil, 39
Luftwaffe, *See* Wehrmacht
    head of, *See* Göring, Hermann
Luxembourg, 1, 115

Mackay, John Henry, 86
    "Ihr könnt das Wort verbieten"
    (1921), 86
Maisky, Ivan Mikhailovich, 78
Malta, 94
Mann, Elisabeth Borgese, xxxi
Mann, Erika, xxi, xxiv, xxxi–xxxiii,
    xxxvii, xlviii, li, lx, 88
Mann, Golo, li
Mann, Heinrich, 84
Mann, Katia, xxiii, xxx, xxxvii, xli, lx,
    87, 131
Mann, Klaus, xxi, xxiv, xxxi, li, 84, 136
Mann, Monika, 3
Mann, Thomas
    ambition of, xxvii
    attitude toward Germany, xlii
    censorship of, xxxiv–xxxvi
    controversy, li
    Czechoslovakian citizenship, xxx
    diaries of, xxvii, xxxiii
    exile of, xxv, xxviii, 138
    media saviness of, xxxv
    motivation for art, 31
    potential return to Germany, 135
    self-characterization of, xxii
    taunting of Germany, liii
    United States citizenship, 64, 135

Mann, Thomas, works of
  "An Appeal to Reason" (1930), xxiii, 32
  Betrachtungen eines Unpolitischen (Reflections of a Nonpolitical Man, 1918), xviii, xx, xxii, xxvi–xxv, 91, 111
  "Bruder Hitler" ("That Man is my Brother," 1938), 58
  Buddenbrooks (1901), xviii, xxii, lviii, 65, 84
  "Das Gesetz" (The Tables of the Law, 1944), xxi, 81–83
  Der Erwählte (The Holy Sinner, 1951), 105
  Der Zauberberg (The Magic Mountain, 1924), xviii, xxii, xxviii
  Die Geschichten Jaakobs (The Tales of Jacob, 1933), lii
  Die vertauschten Köpfe (The Transposed Heads, 1940), xxxix
  Doktor Faustus (1947), xv, xvii, xxi, xlv–xlvii, xlvi, xlix–lii, 105 112
  Ein Briefwechsel (A Correspondance, 1937), l
  "Germany and the Germans" (1963), xlv, xlvii, 24
  Joseph, der Ernährer (Joseph the Provider, 1943), xx
  Joseph in Ägypten (Joseph in Egypt, 1936), xxiv, xxxix, 105
  Leiden an Deutschland: Tagebuchblätter aus den Jahren 1933 und 1934 (1946), xl
  Lotte in Weimar (Lotte in Weimar: The Beloved Returns, 1939), xxi, xxxviii–xxxix
  Order of the Day: Essays and Speeches of Two Decades (1942), xix, xx–xxvi, xxix–xxx, liii–liv
  reception of, l
  Stories of Three Decades (1936), 105
  "The Coming Victory of Democracy" (1938), xxvii
  "The Problem of Freedom" (1939), liii
  The War and Democracy, xxxviii
  This Peace, together with the Address of November 9, 1938, in New York (1938), xxx
  This War (1939), xxix–xxxiv
  Tod in Venedig (Death in Venice, 1912), xxii, 102
  "Von deutscher Republik" (On the German Republic, 1922), xviii, xxii, 58, 86
  Voyage with Don Quixote (1934), xxv
Mann, Viktor, xxviii
Marek, George R., 83
Marinetti, Filippo Tommaso, 91
  Futurist Manifesto (1909), 91
martyrdom, xxviii, 7, 30, 56, 67, 89, 100
Marxism, *See* communism
mass murder, *See* genocide
  of Jewish people, *See* Holocaust, the
master race, *See* eugenics
Maurois, André, 82
Mediterranean, the, xii
Medusa (mythological figure), 13, 56
Mexico, xii, 60
  Mexico City, 82
Meyer, Agnes, xxxii, xxxvii, xxxix, xlv, xlvii–xlviii, liii–liv, 138
Michelangelo di Lodovico Buonarroti Simoni, xxi, 67
Midas (mythological figure), 57, 59, 61
Middle Ages, xlvi, 24, 55, 90
Middle East, the, xii
misery, xii, 3, 5, 7–9, 12, 31–34, 38, 40, 59, 61, 96, 107, 109, 116, 122, 127, 132, 138, 139
Molo, Walter von, l, li, 135
Molotov, Vyacheslav, 11, 113
Molotov-Ribbentrop Pact, 11
Montenegro, 50
moral law, 82, 83, 108
Morocco
  Casablanca, 69, 93
Moses, xxi, 81, 83
Mount Horeb, 83
Mount Sinai, 83
Munich Agreement, 4

Mussolini, Benito, 12, 90–91, 104
  imprisonment of, 89
  removal from power of, 90
Myrmidons, 10
mysticism, 25

Namibia, 63
Napoleonic Wars, 77, 124
  Congress of Vienna, 124
Nation, The (newspaper), xxix, xxxix, xliii, liii, 39, 88
National Broadcasting Company (NBC), xiv, xxxiv, lv, lxii, 12
National Committee for a Free Germany, 94, 99
Nationalsozialistische Freiheitsbewegung (NSFB, National Socialist Freedom Movement), 129
National Socialism, vii, x–xviii, xxi–xxxvii, xl–lv, 1–8, 14, 20, 23, 26–28, 30–32, 37–41, 44, 46, 48–60, 63, 65–76, 78, 80–81, 84–89, 91, 93, 95, 97–98, 101, 103–115, 118–119, 121–138
  anti-intellectualism of, 28, 41
  atrocities of, 85
  concept of peace, 28
  critics of, 84
  cultural policy of, 54
  death of, 92
  devastation of, 119
  distinction from German people, 88
  effects on the German people, 73
  empire of, x
  historians of, 5
  Hitlerism, 13, 25, 30, 57, 92, 133
  ideology of, 91
  lead up to, 86
  militarism of, 73
  misuse of socialism, 108–109
  press, 96
  promised benefits of, 73
  purpose of, 116
  rise of, xxii, 51
  roots of, xlvii, 24
  sympathizers, 80
  threats of, 75
  Wunderwaffen, 98
National Socialist German Student League, 120
National Socialists, 26
  bestialism of, 38, 96
  crimes of, 52
  mentality of, xlvii
  self-pity of, 53
National Socialist regime, x, xii–xv, xxv–xxxiv, xl–xliv, xlvii–xlviii, li, 1, 18, 23–24, 31, 37, 40, 46, 66, 69–70, 84, 87, 91, 96–97, 101–102, 104, 108–110, 115–117, 120, 122, 135
  as enemy of humankind, 27
  corruption, 74
  cultural destruction of, 67, 104
  defeat of, 49, 77, 115
  failure of, 77
  future of, 115
  invasion, 48
  recognition of own demise, 95
  seizure of power, 10, 90
  silencing of opposition, 48
  tyranny of, xliii, 51
  victims of, 118
National-Zeitung (Newspaper), liv
nationalism, xix, l, 47, 85, 87, 99, 110, 124, 138
Nationalkomitee Freies Deutschland (National Committee for a Free Germany), 94
Nazi, *See* National Socialism
Nemesis (Greek goddess), 107, 137
Netherlands, the, xxxviii, xl–xli, 10, 15, 37, 52, 60, 63, 71, 107, 114
  Amsterdam, xxiii, 37
  government, xli, 52
  Holland, xxiii, xli, l, lv, 1–2, 52, 105, 118
  Rotterdam, xix, 1, 45, 97
    bombing of, 45
Neumann, Sigmund, lii–liii
New Order, 8–9, 13, 19, 27–30, 37, 47–48, 51, 56, 59, 68–69, 87, 93, 117
New World, 1, 87
New York Herald Tribune (newspaper), liii, 86

New York Times (newspaper), xxvii, xxxix, 86
Niebuhr, Reinhold, xliii, liii–liv
Niethammer, Friedrich Immanuel, 93
Nietzsche, Friedrich, 59, 138
    amor fati, 138
    Jenseits von Gut und Böse (Beyond Good and Evil, 1886), 59
    Die Fröhliche Wissenschaft (The Gay Science, 1882), 138
Nobel Prize
    for Chemistry, 86
    for Literature, xviii, 32, 65, 82, 86
    for Physics, 86
Norden, Albert, 108
Norway, 2, 3, 10, 71
    citizens of, 3, 69, 107
    flight from, 82
    occupation of, 22
    Oslo, 105
Nuremberg War Crimes Trials, xvii, 23, 41, 67, 78, 82, 109, 134

Oakland Tribune, The (newspaper), 21
obedience, xii, lix, 7, 9, 34, 120, 130, 137
Oder-Neisse Line, 138
open letter, xxiv, l, 135
Oppenhoff, Franz, 120
Ovid, 57
    Metamorphoses (8 CE), 57

pacifism, xxii, xxvii, 58
paganism, 6
Pallas Athena (mythological figure), 13, 50
Partito Politico Futurista (Futurist Political Party), 91
Pat, Jacob, 61
patriotism, 58–59, 61, 77, 138
Patton, General George, xlix
Paulus, Friedrich von, 77
Pazifische Presse, xl
peace, xxii, xxvii, xxxviii, xlvii–xlviii, lvi–lvii, 2–4, 8–9, 12–14, 17–20, 22, 24, 26, 28, 34–35, 38, 42, 44, 48–50, 56, 58–59, 61, 69–70, 74–76, 78, 93, 98, 103, 107, 110, 112, 114–116, 123–124, 127–128, 131, 133
    between Germans and the world, 92
    established in official documents, 48, 51
    Germany with the world, 94
    lack of in Nazi Regime, 31
    need for, 116
    negotiations of, 115
    plan for, 50
peace treaty
    negotiations, 78
PEN Club, 60, 85
Pfitzner, Hans, xxii, xxiv
Philippines, the, 47
Platen, August von, xxv
plutocracy, 48, 80, 109, 121
Poland, xxix–xxx, xli, 2, 11, 37, 40–41, 50, 59, 61–63, 89, 95, 98, 114, 126
    child mortality in, 118
    Krakow, 41, 118
    Lublin, 117
    massacres in, 45
    Minsk, 62
    occupation of, 2
    subjugation of, 14
    Warsaw, xli, 40, 61–63, 97, 105
    Warthegau, 59
Polgar, Alfred, 82
police, xii, 14, 41, 89, 127
Polish, 28, 33, 107, 138
Portugal
    Lisbon, 106
post-war world, 80
Potsdam Conference, 98
power, xiii, xviii, xxiii, xxxv–xxxvi, xlvi, li, liv, lv, 3–4, 10, 12–13, 18, 23, 25, 28, 31–32, 36, 39–40, 51–52, 54, 61–62, 76, 92, 101, 104, 106–109, 120, 124–125, 127, 130
    colonial, 100
    consolidation of, 80
    evil, 54
    hunger for, 116
    politics, 25
    seizure of, 78
Praxiteles (Greek sculptor), 67, 68

Pringsheim, Alfred, xli
Pringsheim, Hedwig, xli
Pringsheim, Peter, xli
prisoners of war, 40, 41, 94, 113
Probst, Christoph, 89
propaganda, xiii, xviii, xix, xxiii, xxvi–xxvii, xxx, xxxi–xxxii, xxxvi, xlv–xlvi, lii–liii, lviii, 19, 27, 40, 43, 47, 64–65, 70, 80, 85, 95, 98, 103–104, 107, 110–112, 117, 122–123, 130
Prussian Academy of the Arts, 135
purification, xliii, 39
Pushkin, Alexander, 78
Putin, Vladimir, xii

Quisling, Vidkun, 22

race myth, *See* eugenics
racial supremacy, *See* eugenics
racism, x, xlvi, 24
raison d'etre, 35, 103
Rathenau, Walther, xxii
Red Cross, the, 128
Red Menace, the, *See* Bolshevism
refugee, xii, 3, 37, 85
Reich Chancellery, 54, 121
Reich President, 14, 134
Reichsgau, 90
Reichsrat, 14
Reichs-Rundfunk-Gesellschaft, xxx
Reichssicherheitshauptamt, 53
Rembrandt Harmenszoon van Rijn, 67–68
resistance, xiii–xiv, xliii, xliv, lii, 4, 13–15, 28, 39, 41, 44, 59, 68, 87, 101, 112, 122, 126–127
  crime, 93
  Czech, 53
  French, 29
  illegal distribution of print materials, 87
  Maquis, 95
  spiritual, 26
  The White Rose, xliii–xlv, 88
    execution of members, 89
  to allied forces, 115
  underground organizations, 87

revolution, xv, xlii, 18, 27, 38–39, 43–44, 46–48, 58, 61, 66, 68, 130, 136
  democratic, 93, 94
  faith in, 48
  German, 89
  National Socialist, 56, 89
  Russian, 56
  social, 47
  success of, 47
Rhine river, 115, 127
Ribbentrop, Anna Elisabeth Henkell, 128
Ribbentrop, Joachim von, 11, 23, 45, 113, 128
  execution of, 23, 45
Robin Moor (ship), 20–21
Rochelle, Pierre Drieu La, 60
Röhm, Ernst, xxiv
Roma
  mass murder of, 117
Romains, Jules, 82
Romania, 50
  military deaths, 60
romanticism, 84, 87
Romanticism, xlvi, 24
Rommel, Field Marshall Erwin, 71–72
Roosevelt, Eleanor, xxxviii
Roosevelt, Franklin Delano, xvi, xx, xxxii, xxxvii–xxxix, lii, lvi, 2, 4, 8, 11, 17–18, 20–21, 27–28, 30, 33, 42–43, 48, 56, 58, 66, 68, 93, 98, 123, 126, 130–131
  death of, xxxix, 130
  Fireside chats, xiv, 17, 30
  Four Freedoms, 43
  reelection of, 4, 20
  speeches of, 17, 92
Russia, *See* Union of Soviet Socialist Republics (USSR)
Russian, viii, 22, 28, 35, 39–40, 55–56, 66, 77–79, 113, 134
  authors, 84
  civilian deaths, 118
  people, 56, 77–78, 117, 137–138
    mass murder of, 117
  prisoners of war, 117

Saint-Exupéry, Antoine de, 120

The Little Prince (1943), 120
San Francisco Symphony, xvi
Satanism, 95
Sauckel, Ernst Friedrich Christoph, 109
Scandinavia, 6
Schiller, Friedrich, xliii, 7, 27, 32, 54, 96, 105, 131, 137
    Don Carlos (1787), 7
    Geschichte des dreißigjährigen Kriegs (A History of the Thirty Years' War, 1792), 27
    Wilhelm Tell (William Tell, 1804), 7, 96
Schirach, Baldur von, 67–68
Schlageter, Albert Leo, 30
    execution of, 30
    national hero and martyr, 30
Scholl, Hans, xliii, xliv, 29, 88–89
    "Weiße Rose Flyer" (White Rose Flyer, 1942), 29
Scholl, Sophie, xliii, xliv, 29, 89
    "Weiße Rose Flyer", 29
Schuster, Max, 82
Schutzstaffel (SS), 3, 23, 48, 52, 63, 96, 110, 118, 122
science, 81, 85
    dignity of, 74
Scorza, Carlo, 90
Second World War, xiv, xviii, xx, liv, 15, 22, 48, 73, 78–79, 100, 115, 128, 132
    Ätherkrieg, xviii
    Allied Invasion of Normandy, 98, 122, 124
    anticipated German defeat, 75, 87–88
    Attack on Pearl Harbor, xxxi, xlii, 20, 28, 36
    Balkan Campaign, 34
    Battle of France, 71
    Battle of Stalingrad, xlvii, 66, 77
    Battle of the Bulge, xlvii, 115
    Bombing of Coventry, 44
    combatant deaths, 106–107
    continuation of, 31
    D-Day, xlvii
    declaration of war, 44
    Eastern Front, xlviii, 127, 132
    glorification of, 97
    North African Campaign, 71–72
    Operation *Herbstnebel* (Autumn Mist), 115
    Operation Werewolf, 120, 130
    Retreat from Dunkirk, 71, 72
    Russian Campaign, 28, 35, 55, 77
    the Blitz, xxxii, xliv, lxii, 88, 92
    V.E. Day, 122, 133
    War in the Pacific, xlii, 47, 123, 132
    weapon advancements, 98
self-determination, 28, 50
Serbia, 15, 33, 50
Seven Years' War, 125
Shakespeare, William
    Love's Labour's Lost (1598), 1
Sicherheitsdienst (Security Service), 53
Siemens-Schuckert, 67
Sikorski, Wladislaw, 62
"Silent Night" (song), 7
Silesian Wars, 125
Simon & Schuster (publishing house), 82
Simon, Richard, 82
slavery, xiii, liii, 4, 17, 27, 35, 47, 68, 104, 110–111, 119
socialism, 23, 40, 44, 57–59, 61, 69, 73–74, 78, 93, 98, 103, 108–110, 116, 128, 130
socialists
    persecution of, 74, 128
South Africa, 63
Spain
    Guernica, 44
    Spanish Civil War, 44
spiritualism, xiii, xxxv, xlii, 6, 8, 14, 25, 92
    castration of, 28
Squadristi, 90
Stalin, Joseph, xxxviii, 79, 98, 113, 123, 126, 132
    speeches, 78
Stars and Stripes (newspaper), 136
Strauss, Richard, xxiv, xxvii–xxix, 136
Streicher, Julius, 23
    Der Stürmer (newspaper), 23
student protests, 29, 89, 94
Stülpnagel, Otto Edwin von, 29–30

resignation, 30
Sturmabteilung (SA), xxiii–xxiv, 7, 14, 32, 84
　slogans of, 23
Suzuki, Danshaku Kantarō, 132
swastika, xiv, 15, 17, 134
Sweden, l, lv, 128
　Stockholm, xix, 82, 94, 128
Swedish, 71, 82, 128
　press, 46, 88
Swing, Raymond Gram, xxxix, 86
Swiss, 39
　authors, 39
　press, liv, 80, 88
Swiss Central Office for Refugee Aid, 118
Switzerland, xviii, xxii–xxiii, xxviii, l, lii, lv, 63, 128, 136–137
　Basel, liv, 63
　Bern, 128
　exiles in, 118
　Zürich, xxiv, xxix

Talleyrand-Périgord, Charles-Maurice de, 124
Tchaikovsky Museum, 67
terror, xv, xvii, 4, 8–9, 21, 26, 29, 33, 48, 53, 74, 87, 94, 96–97, 114, 116, 119, 127, 130, 133, 138
the East, xli, xlviii, 6, 14, 63, 94, 121, 132
The German American (newspaper), 108
The New Yorker (magazine), 82
The Ten Commandments: Ten Short Novels of Hitler's War Against the Moral Code (1944), 81–82
Thiess, Frank, li, 137
Third Reich, *See* Nazi regime
Thirty Years' War, 127
Thompson, Dorothy, lii, 86
Timor, 47
Tolstoy, Lev Nikolayevich, 67, 78
trade unions, 109
Tripartite Pact (1940), 11, 13, 36
Truman, Harry S., 58, 128
Turkey, 50, 91

Übermenschen, *See* eugenics
U-boats, 3

Uhland, Ludwig, 77
Ukraine, xii, 67, 71
Undset, Sigrid, 82
Union of Soviet Socialist Republics (USSR), 8, 11, 15, 20–22, 30, 33, 35–36, 39, 43–45, 48, 66, 71, 78–80, 93–94, 98, 106, 113, 115, 122–123, 126–128
　ally to Americans, 22
　death in, 31, 49
　evacuation of, 50
　Italian military deaths in, 90
　Krasnogorsk, 94
　Moscow, 22, 67, 95, 134
　　Nazi conquer of, 31
　Operation Barbarossa, 30, 47, 77, 95
　opposer of Germany, 21
　Red Army, xlviii, 55, 79, 95, 117–118
　　advances of, 95
　Rostov-on-Don, 55–56
　Smolensk, 95
　　Second Battle of, 95
　Stalingrad, 66, 71, 77, 88, 134
　　occupation of, 77
　war in, 21, 26
United Nations, lvi, 66–67, 76, 91, 93, 123, 132
United States of America, x, xiv–xvi, xviii, xx–xxii, xxvii, xxix, xxxi, xxxiii, xxxv, xli–xlii, xlix, lii, liv–lv, lix, 1–4, 8, 11, 13–14, 17–22, 27–28, 35–36, 42–44, 51, 64–68, 78, 80–82, 85–86, 98, 101, 105–108, 112, 115, 128, 132, 135–137
　actions against German government, 19
　alliance with
　　Great Britain, 22
　　Russia, 22
　America First movement, 20
　American consulates, 19
　American isolationism, xiv, xvi, xxxiii, 2, 20
　assuming responsibility, 28
　attempted intimidation of, 21
　authors, 82, 84
　border, xii

Boston, Massachusetts, lii, 105
California
    Los Angeles, xiv, xxxiv, lv, lx, lxii, 12, 87, 131
    Pacific Palisades, xiv, xvi, lx
Chicago, Illinois, xxxi
citizenship, l, lii, 2, 64, 131
Congress, iii, xxxi, xlv, 8, 19–21, 36, 50, 66, 108
    Senate, 14
contemporary politics, x
contempt for, 86
German retaliation against, 19
government of, 19
Library of Congress, lxvi
military of, 115
Neutrality Act, xxxi, 36
New Deal, xx, 56, 130
New Jersey
    Atlantic City, liii
    Princeton, xx, xxiii–xxix, xxxiv
news media, 46, *See* American, press
New York, xiv, xxv, xxvii, xxxiv–xxxvi, liii, lv, lxvi, 82, 85, 86
    Public Library, 85
Office of War Information, 85–86
opposer of Germany, 21
people, xiv, xxvii, xxxv, 3, 19–20, 22, 43, 64–65, 115, 132, 137
press, xxvii, xlix, 10, 35, 46, 61, 108
voice of, 20
war against Germany, 20
Washington D.C., xxxii, xlv, lvi, 24, 28, 44
White House, xvi, xxxvii–xxxviii, 42, 68
University of Erlangen, 120
University of Halle, 112
University of Munich, 57, 88–89, 94, 105
University of Prague, 28
USS Kearny (ship), 30

Vansittart, Sir Robert, xliv, 24, 39, 88
    Black Record: Germans Past and Present (1941), xliv, 24, 88
Vansittartism, xliv

Vatican, the, 128
vengeance, 14, 26, 61, 97–98, 107, 110, 113, 137
Versailles, Treaty of (1919), xlvi, 110, 124
Viereck, George Sylvester, 19
violence, xii, xiv, 3, 7–8, 13–14, 16, 22, 44, 51, 59, 61, 65, 74, 84, 90, 96–97, 100, 105, 108, 112
    despair from, 30
Vogue (magazine), 88
Völkische Beobachter (newspaper), xxxii, 113
Volksempfänger, xiii–xxxiv, lxi
Volkssturm, xv
Voltaire, François-Marie Arouet, xxi
Vossische Zeitung (newspaper), 105

Wagner, Richard, xxiii–xxiv, xxxii, xliv, 37, 44, 87, 111, 121, 136
    Die Meistersinger von Nürnberg (The Master-Singers of Nuremberg, 1868), xxiii
    Parsifal (1882), 44, 111
    Ring des Nibelungen (Ring of the Nibelung, 1876), xxii–xxiii, 37, 121
    Siegfried (*Ring Des Nibelungen*), 37
Wagnerians, xxiv, 86
Wallace, Henry A., 58
Wannsee Conference, xli, 62
War
    end of, 47
    fear of defeat, 48
    opposition to, 49
    technology, 15, 21
    war machine, 15, 23, 26, 99
war crime, xvixvii–xlviii, 22–23, 47, 67, 82, 134
Wehrmacht, xlviii, l, 1–2, 13, 15, 41, 47, 60, 69, 71, 76, 79, 95, 104, 115, 132, 134
    Luftwaffe (German Air Force), xix, lxii, 3, 15, 20, 44–45, 107–108
    Kriegsmarine (German Navy), 94
    Lützow (ship), 94
    Scharnhorst (ship), 94
    Tirpitz (ship), 94

Weinert, Erich, 94
Wells, Herbert George, 85
   The Time Machine (1895), 85
Werfel, Franz, xl, 82
   The Song of Bernadette (1943), 82
Wessel, Horst Ludwig Georg Erich, 7, 77
West, Rebecca, 82
West, the, xii, xviii, lii–liii, 6, 14, 16, 40, 43, 66, 68, 82, 93–94, 104–105, 108, 120–122, 127–128
   morality of, 21, 86
   social philosophy, 93
Whitman, Walt, 86
   Leaves of Grass (1855), 86
Wilhelm II (Emperor of Germany), 6
Wilson, Woodrow, xxiii, 50

winter solstice, 6, 8
world conquest, 5, 16, 20, 25, 35, 51, 56, 92–93, 119
   German plans for, 21
   Jewish conspiracy, 80
World Spirit, 93, 131
Wullenweber, Jürgen, 46

Xerxes I (King of Kings of the Achaemenid Empire), 16

Yalta Conference, 123–124, 126
Yasnaya Polyana Museum, 67
Yugoslavia, 15, 107
   massacres in, 60

Zuckmayer, Carl, 82
Zweig, Stefan, 136

Printed in the United States
by Baker & Taylor Publisher Services